A Dark Day on the Blaskets

To Pat Maloney,
My Canadian long lost cousin
Apr. 2005

Brian McElroy

MÍCHEÁL Ó DUBHSHLÁINE

# A DARK DAY
## ON THE BLASKETS

The Drowning of
Dónal Ó Criomhthain and Eibhlín Nic Niocaill
on the Blasket Islands, 13 August 1909

A Brandon Paperback

First published in 2003 by Brandon
This edition published 2005 by Brandon
an imprint of Mount Eagle Publications
Dingle, Co. Kerry, Ireland

British Library Cataloguing in Publication Data is available
for this book.

ISBN 0 86322 337 0

2  4  6  8  10  9  7  5  3  1

Mount Eagle Publications receives support from
the Arts Council/An Chomhairle Ealaíon.

Front cover photograph by George Thomson, Landing a
*naomhóg* at Cé an Bhlascaoid, *c.* 1930, reproduced by
permission of Ionad an Bhlascaoid Mhóir, Dún Chaoin.
Cover design by id communications, Tralee
Typesetting by Red Barn Publishing, Skeagh, Skibbereen
Printed in the UK

# CONTENTS

# Buíochas

To those who generously gave of their time and their knowledge:
Denis Ryan Senior and Junior, Baile Átha Cliath agus Baile an
Fheirtéaraigh; Bab Feiritéar, Baile na hAbha, Dún Chaoin; An tAthair
Tomás Ó hIceadha, SP, Baile an Fheirtéaraigh; Walter McGrath, Cork;
Séamus Ware, Dublin; Páid Curran, An Daingean; Carolyn Hayes,
Dublin; T. P. Ó Conchúir, Gallaras; Ray and Barbara Stagles,
Wokingham, England; An Canónach Seán Mac Ginneá, An Daingean;
Séamus Mac Ginneá, An Daingean; Pádraig Ó Niallagáin, MA, An
Daingean; Séamus Foy, Washington, DC, USA; Pádraig Ua Maoileoin,
RIP; Seán Ó Lúing, RIP; Eilín Uí Lúing, OS, Cill Mhic an Domhnaigh;
Danny Mac an tSíthigh, Baile Eaglaise; Fr Mícheál Galvin, Rock Street,
Tralee; Deirdre Connolly and Orla Ní Chléirigh, Pearse Museum, St
Enda's Park, Rathfarnhan, Dublin; Seán Mac Mathúna, Iar Ardrúnaí,
Conradh na Gaeilge, Baile Átha Cliath; Maureen Moran, librarian,
County Galway Library Headquarters; Pádraig Ó Snodaigh, Baile Átha
Cliath; Clíodhna Cussen, Baile Átha Cliath; Noel Ó Cíobháin, Ceann
Trá; Breandán Ó Ciobháin, Ceann Trá; Deasún Mac Aindriú, RIP;
Pádraig Hamilton, An tSeantóir, Dún Chaoin, agus Droichead na
Bandan, Corcaigh; Caitlín Ní Mhurchú agus Áine Ní Mhainín,
Leabharlann an Daingin; Éamonn de Brún, Leabharlann an Chontae,
Trá Lí; Ambrose de Róiste, Bóthar na hOllscoile, An Ghaillimh;
Mícheál de Mórdha, Ruth Uí Ógáin agus Doncha Ó Conchúir, Ionad an
Bhlascaoid, Dún Chaoin; An Dr Conchúr Ó Brosnacháin, An Daingean;
Gearóid Ó Leidhin, Leabharlann Náisiúnta na hÉireann, Baile Átha
Cliath; An Fhoireann, Leabharlann Náisiúnta na hÉireann, Baile Átha
Cliath; An Fhoireann, Roinn Bhéaloideas Éireann, Baile Átha Cliath;
An Fhoireann, Cartlann na hÉireann, Baile Átha Cliath.

Do mhuintir an Oileáin, go háirithe: Seán Pheats
Tom Ó Cearnaigh, RIP; Seán Mhaidhc Léan Ó
Guithín, RIP; Muiris Mhaidhc Léan Ó Guithín; agus
Seán Mharas Mhuiris Ó Catháin, RIP
*Dob iad san na laethanta . . .*

# Illustrations

# Preface

IREAD WHAT Tomás Ó Criomhthain said in *An tOileánach* about a great local tragedy that befell the Blasket Island on Friday, 13 August 1909. The whole account takes less than a page of the raw, stark style that has made his work famous.

> Not many years afterwards a noble young woman from Ireland's principal city came to visit us on the island for her holidays and she wasn't there long before she picked my daughter as a companion; some become friends quicker than others that are around. They would spend part of each day together. They would spend a day on the hill and another day by the strand and when the weather was soft and warm they would go swimming.
>
> On such a day as they were like this the full tide was too strong and at the time they should have been drawing in to the land they were instead drifting out, till they became exhausted. It happened that there was one of my sons digging potatoes close to the house – it was at the beginning of harvest – a son that was lively and could swim as well. He was eighteen years old, and he saw the two women in the water and knew immediately who they were and that they wouldn't make it. He threw from him the spade and ran every shortcut by cliff and rock until he reached the strand. . .[1]

These words contain an enormous amount of quiet loneliness and sorrow. I needed to find out more. I found some answers among the Blasket people themselves, others among the people of the neighbouring mainland of Dún Chaoin and Ventry. Some I found in old faded newspapers and books of the time, others in old letters and manuscripts, official handwritten accounts and faded pictures. Other questions were without answers. I have tried to bring all the answers together and recreate the story of that eventful late summer and early autumn of 1909.

The result was first published in Irish as *Óigbhean Uasal ó Phríomhchathair Éireann,* by Conradh na Gaeilge in 1992. Since then I have tried to piece together the story to get to know Eibhlín Nic Niocaill, her family and friends and the people and events surrounding her death. The tragedy of Domhnall and Eibhlín has one redeeming feature to us looking back on the event: it led to much writing, both official and personal. These sources give us a window through which we can observe the life of the people of Corca Dhuibhne almost 100 years ago.

I am very grateful to Conradh na Gaeilge for permission to translate parts of *Óigbhean Uasal,* and in particular to Seán Mac Mathúna. I am also very grateful that Brandon Press has published *Dark Day* at this time of the fiftieth anniversary of the leaving of the last inhabitants of the Blaskets in November 1953.

A special thanks to my family, Donie, Sorcha, Sinéad and Breandán, and in a special way Nicole, my granddaughter, and above all, to Áine, my wife, for her patience and dedication.

# Introduction

The mass drew to a close. The priest dismissed his congregation with: "*Tá an t-aifreann thart, imigí fé shíocháin.*" "The mass is over, go in peace."

The people poured out of the little rough stone church in Dún Chaoin, Corca Dhuibhne, west Kerry, the men pulling on their caps as they crowded out of the most westerly church in the most westerly parish in Ireland, overlooking the the Blasket Islands, sturdy rocks in the wild Atlantic.

Usually neighbours gather to chat for a while outside, while some hurry home for the cup of tea, but on this morning people drifted in ones and twos into the adjoining medieval cemetery where beneath green mounds the bones of the former generations lie. The grass had been freshly cut by the County Council a few days before, and the earth smelt fresh and balmy. It was mid August – Sunday, 13 August, to be exact.

They waited there among the stone markers and the small raised graves and talked quietly. Old men, *lucht na gcaipíní,* the men with the caps, came in and stood shyly aside. The Blasket men could be easily recognised, falling into old age, dressed in navy suits, crowned by peaked caps. Some looked over the wide Bealach of the Atlantic to the Blasket, some three miles out in the ocean. It could be seen clearly, very close at hand, a sure sign that rain was in the air, though the sun shone down on the gathering here now. There was a feeling of familiarity among the people, especially here, the resting places of their friends and relatives under the simple unnamed stone markers. True, there

11

was a headstone for Seán Ó Dálaigh, the old master, who
had taught quite a few of them and their fathers and mothers before them. Then there was the King's headstone,
homemade with concrete and sea sand. There were other
resting places, unmarked but known to the old people, like
*Uaigh Bhacach na Seantórach,* the Grave of the Seantóir
Beggar. The poor beggar, whose name no one knew, had
passed away one winter's night in 1904 in the home of the
de Lóndra family in the Seantóir, famous for their hospitality. Then there was, in the middle of the old medieval
church ruins, the the grave of Seán an Chóta, or Seán Óg
Ó Caomhánaigh, who had died lonely in Stephen's Green,
Dublin, on a cold March morning in 1947 and was
brought home to lie in the place he loved best. There were
other resting places, marked only by a rough stone hewn
out of the cliffs in Com Dhíneol or down at Béal Átha and
carried to this spot on the *srathair fhada* on donkey back.
Others had no markers at all, remembered by none but
God himself.

The priest walked to one of the graves, the one with the
great memorial of Carlow limestone, with the *naomhóg*
and the four rowing fishermen inscribed on the flat,
smooth stone, carved by Séamus Ó Murchú of Cork, Stone
Mad Murphy himself. This was the grave of Tomás
Dhomhnaill Ó Criomhthain, An tOileánach (The
Islandman), so called from the book written in his twilight
years.

The local teacher, myself, stood up on a table tomb and
spoke nervously. I welcomed them, here on the eightieth
anniversary of the drowning of Domhnall Ó Criomhthain
and Eibhlín Nic Niocaill on the Blaskets. We were going to
unveil a small monument to Domhnall, in commemoration
of his brave act, his attempt to save another from drowning, an attempt in which he had lost his own life.

An old Blasket man doffed his cap, showing a grey mop.
He listened to the Irish as he pulled thoughtfully on his
pipe. As he did, perhaps his thoughts drifted back through

the years, and he was listening again to his father telling the story as they sat around the fire in their island home while the storm from the south-west howled and whipped outside and the waves could be heard crashing and lashing into the black cliffs below at the Tráigh Bhán . . . the story of *an Óigbhean Uasal*, the lady who had come to them across the waves from Ireland's principal city.

# CHAPTER 1

## *Fáilte Anoir*

## *Welcome, Traveller from the East*

Pinch o' pepper, pinch o' pepper,
Westward went the Dingle train.
Pinch o' pepper, pinch o' pepper,
Was the theme of its refrain.
Pinch o' pepper, pinch o' pepper,
Sure it seems but yesterday
Since I made the journey westwards
O'er the hills and far away.[1]

IT WAS A golden sunny evening in the old west coast town of Dingle in the county of Kerry in the fine summer month of July 1909. The town, set between the mountains and the sea, with its narrow scatter of streets, lay basking in the warm sunshine. Scattered little groups of men stood at the street corners or sat on the *Droichead Beag* (the small bridge) at the top of the town and at *Droichead Bhun an Bhaile* (bridge at the bottom of the town) at the other end discussing the weather and the crops. Even the ever-present sheepdogs were silent and lay sleeping in the dusty streets. It's not every day that the Dingle Peninsula is blessed by sunshine, but when it is, it's not the same life. Everyone slows down and relaxes. There is a lightness in everyone's step. Dingle becomes a Mediterranean village with doors remaining open till late, people talking to each other from house to house, and remembering that they are really the one people.

The arrival of the Dingle train was the main daily event in the town of Dingle in the year 1909, and some people went there just to be part of it. Others, of course, were going to meet friends or relatives coming in on the train from Tralee or places farther from home, even as far away as Ireland's principal city.

The first train from Tralee to Dingle ran on Monday, 21 March 1891. The great engineering feat of building the 3 foot gauge line the thirty miles to Dingle had opened up the, till then, almost inaccessible peninsula to visitors. Previously the only way to get to the thirty-one miles from Tralee to Dingle was by the "jingle", or mail coach, changing horses at Annascaul, a journey which took almost all day.

With the Dingle train, a traveller could journey between the two towns at a reasonable price, making amazing speed through the mountains and glens. Depending on circumstances, it took the train two to three hours to cover the journey. The train pulled up at thirteen stations for various lengths of time, depending on the thirst of the driver and crew.

It was a friendly, social train. The passengers sat lengthways in the carriage, facing each other. The travellers from Dublin were struck by the difference in the people, from Tralee on. They were full of easy personality; everyone spoke to everybody else, regardless of whether they knew each other or not. The sense of humour, the storytelling, the rich dialect laced with Irish brought people into another world that most thought had long passed away.

> Once you have rounded Ballintaggart, Dingle harbour strikes the vision; across the water is Burnham House, Lord Ventry's residence, and a mile from that the train lands in Dingle – the most Irish speaking town in the world. It is a small town peopled by a couple of thousand souls, but once it had a big trade

with Spain; and once it had walls to protect it from invaders; and once it had a Royal Charter; and once a sword and mace were carried before its leading man. Today the fishing industry is the most it can boast of, and to tell the truth, it is all the better off.[2]

The whistle was heard at Dingle station as the train approached from Baile an tSagairt. She finally puffed into the little station, doors clacked open, and the Dingle train spilled out her contents on the platform. It was twenty past six. Late as usual. Out stepped two young, well-dressed ladies, who wove their way through the crowd out to the entrance. Two young barefooted boys ran to help with their luggage.

With a loud whistle – the signal that the day's work had ended – the train steamed out of the station on its last short journey to the quay to unload the fishboxes for the night's catch. It would be collected and brought to Tralee on the morning train. Fresh Dingle Bay prawns for the Tralee people.

Everyone new is noticed in Dingle, especially fine handsome young women, dressed in the latest fashions and with their youth in full bloom. One of the young ladies was Eveleen Nicolls, or Eibhlín Nic Niocaill as she preferred to be known at that time. The other was Mrs Mary Nolan, or Máire de Buitléir as she was better known. They had arrived from Dublin to spend a holiday in Corca Dhuibhne, Máire for about a week, during which she intended to visit the Irish college, and Eibhlín to spend a full, long, two months. Máire, well known as a writer, had written on, among other subjects, Irish women's fashions. Although of Anglo-Irish stock and a cousin of Edward Carson, the famous Protestant unionist leader, she was an Irish language activist. She had married Tomás Nolan, a classical scholar whom she had met on the Aran Islands, some two years previously.[3]

Outside the station, the old town spread out before them. The sun was sinking over the mountains to the west, shimmering on the blue water of Dingle harbour. They must have been struck by the smell of the sea air, the strange west Kerry accents, the women folded in their shawls and the men in their navy blue ganseys and tweed caps, strong and hardy and tanned from the constant exposure to wind, sun and sea spray. Below the town lay the bay, with the woods beyond, and beyond that again the mountains. In Dingle itself stood the RIC station, the church clock tower, the three-storied poor house and Fearnakilla House, the high red sandstone residence of the Protestant minister.

Eveleen Constance Nicolls was born Dublin on 22 October 1884, which made her twenty-four years of age at the time of her arrival in Dingle. She was the only daughter of Archibald J. Nicolls, LLB, and his wife Mary. They belonged to the ever-increasing professional Catholic middle class, which was coming into its own in the city of Dublin and throughout provincial Ireland following generations of restrictions. She had an uncle in the Jesuits, Revd P. Head, an important appendix to any middle-class family. The Nicolls family started out at 36 Eccles Street in the early seventies, where Archibald also had his office. The professional Catholic class had been growing slowly but steadily in importance since the granting of Catholic Emancipation in 1829. The legal profession, like so many others, had been predominantly Protestant for over two hundred years, but Catholics were coming to their own and clawing back some of their lost power. Catholic lawyers and other of like professions had centred round Eccles Street. The big Georgian mansions of Mountjoy Square and Henrietta Street were already crumbling into tenements as the well-to-do moved out beyond the canals to the new suburbs of the old towns of Rathmines and Rathgar, and villages like Rathfarnham and Harold's Cross, which up to then were but rural hamlets surrounded by farmlands, with cows and horses in the green fields and country people selling their vegetables on Saturdays.

Around 1885, the year of Eibhlín's birth, her family changed homes and moved to 18 Garville Avenue, in the new suburb of Rathgar, as the ever-expanding Mater Hospital took over their old home. It is there in Rathgar they are found in the 1901 census. Archibald J. describes himself as a barrister-at-law, born the first year of the Great Famine, 1845. The son of a doctor, he was born in the County Longford and, interestingly, could speak both Irish and English.[4] It is most unlikely that he learned his Irish in Longford. He had studied law in Trinity College, Dublin, and was called to the Irish Bar in 1868. About 1885 he was appointed secretary to the Loan Fund Board of Ireland and remained in that post for the rest of his working life. This new post was a great advancement to his career. The appointment was by the Lord Lieutenant himself, and Archibald J. had his office in Dublin Castle, the centre and hated stronghold of English government in Ireland. He could therefore be described as a higher government official.

The Loan Fund of Ireland had been established by the government in 1836 to administer a system for the advancing of small loans, not exceeding £10, to industrious people for some progressive project, such as a farmer buying a horse, a fisherman a boat or a weaver a loom. The loan was to be repaid by very reasonable instalments. The Fund could be described as a forerunner to the Credit Unions of today.

Archibald J.'s wife, Mary, nine years younger, was born in 1853, and was a native of Limerick, probably Pallas in the east of the county. Their eldest son, Jasper, a medical student, was born in 1881. Next was Eveleen, whose name he enters on the 1901 census form as Eibhlín Nic Aonghuis Ní Niocail, who could speak both Irish and English. It was most unusual for anyone to fill in a name in Irish at that time, either on an official form or otherwise, especially a high government official such as Archibald J. Even people in the native-speaking part of the country were slow to use the Irish form of their names. Indeed, it would have been met with a sarcastic smile or a knowing shrug of mockery in most parts of the country for someone to profess an interest in the native language or culture. Eibhlín was sixteen at the time of the census. There were two more sons in the family, George, who was fourteen, and Edward, who was twelve, both going to school. By the time of the 1901 census, taken on Sunday, 2 April, the family had moved to 3 Kenilworth Road.

Both addresses were in parts of Dublin that could be described as upper class, in particular Kenilworth Road, where the majority of householders were Protestant, with occupations such as wine merchant, insurance agent, bank official, manufacturer and civil servant. Archibald J., by that time 66 years of age, had retired. In 1911 they had a domestic servant, twenty-seven-year-old Brigid Grogan, from County Meath. Meath was, at least up to the end of the previous century, a strong centre for Gaelic tradition, with long memories of the 1798 Rising.

Though there are four children included in the 1901 census, Archibald put down that they had originally had five children, and that four were still living. It is likely that one of their children died young. Eibhlín was the only girl.

Soon after Jasper had completed his medical studies he emigrated to Bolivia, where he seems to have spent his entire life. We know much more about George, or Seoirse as he was also called in later, more nationalist times. He was awarded a BA degree in 1908 and, following in his father's footsteps, became an attorney, taking up a position in the city of Galway. I have failed to find any account of the other son, Edward, and my only conclusion, at this time, is that he was a tragic figure.

The family names of Archibald, George, Jasper and Edward would strongly suggest that the family were of English Protestant origin who may have embraced the Catholic religion in recent times, perhaps when Archibald J. and Mary married. The surname is found widely throughout England, Scotland, Wales and Ireland in various forms.

We don't know where the two young women spent the first week of their holidays. There were two fashionable hotels in Dingle, Benner's and Lee's – ". . . well appointed, comfortable and commodious, M. McCarthy, proprietor" – and a few smaller guest houses, such as Kennedy's, Dykegate Street: "Good Fare, Comfort and Satisfaction at a moderate tariff, 5 minutes walk from the Railway Station. *Labhartar Gaedhilg sa tig seo.*"[5]

There was an Irish College in Dingle during the summer months, held under the auspices of the Gaelic League for those wishing to gain knowledge of the Irish language and culture, which was achieving notable success. They most likely paid it a visit. At that time the college was held in the licensed premises of Mr John O'Donnell in Bridge Street, down by the Holy Ground, and there were two sessions, one in July and one in August each year.

> The college is situated in one of the healthiest, most interesting and most beautiful spots in Ireland; and is one of the best staffed and most up to date and largest of Irish Colleges.
>
> The Professors are well known Irish Scholars and writers of the language.
>
> Outside the College, the students will have splendid opportunities of learning Irish among the people of West Corca Dhuibhne, which is the most Irish speaking part of Ireland.
>
> There will be special outings to visit Ventry Harbour, An Chonair, Ceann Sléibhe, Gallerus, Brandon Mountain &c.
>
> Sea bathing, boating and fishing.
>
> An Rúnaidhe, Coláiste an Daingin,
> Daingean Uí Chúise.[6]

Both Eibhlín and Máire were staunch and energetic members of the language movement known as Conradh na

Gaeilge, or the Gaelic League. The League had admonished its members to spend some time in the Corca Dhuibhne Gaeltacht during the summer, praising the area for the purity of its Irish as well as the beauty of its scenery. The area had already achieved fame in Irish language circles for the richness of its Irish. As Fionán Mac Coluim wrote in 1905: "Corca Dhuibhne is the most Gaelic area in the Province of Munster, and if we do not succeed in keeping the language alive there, there is a poor chance that we can keep it alive anywhere else."[7]

While a certain amount of Irish could be heard in Dingle, the more into the west you went, the more you would hear. "Gaedheal Óg" wrote in the *Kerry People* in 1907, after he had attended the Dingle Feis of that year: "We have heard Corca Dhuibhne written of and spoken of as the most Irish speaking district in Ireland, but there is nothing to indicate here that it is, but everything to point the other way. We have scarcely heard a word spoken but Béarla."[8]

As it is today, you had to go to the right places in Dingle to hear Irish.

The two young women spent about a week in the town. Dingle, the oldest town in Kerry, was founded in the early days of the Normans. It had, at one time, three castles, a sign of its importance as well as of its garrison influence. Elizabeth I granted it £300 in December 1585, after the Earl of Desmond had burnt the place, "towards the charge of walling their town with stone three quarters of a mile compasse",[9] to keep out the Irish. It was probably the only town in Kerry that was adorned with a wall, slight traces of which can still be seen. No doubt they saw the Holy Stone, named not for any Christian religious reason, but because of the holes made by the cup and circle patterns etched on it in ancient times, which were religious, though of a more primitive type. The Rice house, the oldest dwelling in the town, dating from the 1750s, was built by Thomas Rice, a Dingle wine merchant, and prepared in

1792 as a refuge for Marie Antoinette, Queen of France. The queen, however, declined the invitation at the last moment, preferring to remain on with her husband, Louis XVI, and children.

They visited St James' Church, originally St James of Compostella Church, with its Spanish influence, and saw the old tomb of Frederick Mullins, whose father had arrived and set up as the principal landlord of the area in 1666 and whose son Frederick II is commemorated on the earliest inscribed tomb in the churchyard, dated 1695 in the thirty-first year of his age.[10]

They probably saw the town crier as he travelled the streets ringing his bell and calling attention to all the forth-coming events that the citizens should attend. They would have seen the barefooted boys as they ran the dusty streets and the Gaeltacht people coming to town carrying their produce, fish, wool, rabbits, eggs and seaweed, calling out in their broken English as they walked the streets:

> The islandwoman: Madam *in áirde*, would you buy a *coinín*?
> The lady: Is it a hare?
> The islandwoman: *Níl, ná caoch. Is maith an dá chnap-shúil atá 'na phlaosc.*
> The lady: Is it fat?
> The islandwoman: *Ní hea, ná cat, ach coinín mór maith ón Oileán Tiar amach!*
> The lady: Would you take eightpence?
> The islandwoman: I wouldn't part with it without sixpence.[11]

After a week or so Máire returned to Dublin, and on 6 July Eibhlín transferred to Ceann Trá, a village some four miles to the west of the town. She took a sidecar, with her baggage, across Milltown Bridge, along the edge of Dingle Harbour, or Cuan an Daimh Deirg (the Harbour of the Red Ox), by the fine wood, the only one of its size in Corca Dhuibhne, planted by the nature-loving Lord Ventry, whose fine regal residence rose by the harbour's edge and could occasionally be seen through the trees.

The family of Mullins, who later changed their name to "de Moleyns", arrived in Baile an Ghóilín in 1666, the year of the Great Fire of London. They rose to prominence in the days when Ireland was a Protestant nation for a Protestant people, and were MPs for Dingle during much of that time. They became Barons Ventry in 1800, having given their vote in favour of the Union of Ireland and Britain. A son of Lord Ventry's gamekeeper, Pádraig Ó Siochfhradha, had a great interest in the old language and was awakening interest in the people. He taught Irish reading and writing to the local people and began to take down the old stories, songs and placenames, and later became famous for his work.

She passed through Baile Móir by St Michael's Well. A short distance from it, on the edge of the cliff overlooking the quay, stood the fine thatched house of Parson Goodman who, though a Protestant clergyman of English stock, had succeeded in gaining the affection of both contending religions. One of his sons, Séamus, a clergyman and a native Irish speaker, had become the professor of Irish in Trinity College, Dublin, and had made a very valuable collection of old songs and airs from Corca Dhuibhne, most of them dating to pre-famine times. Eibhlín had often heard of him and his work. He had taught, among others, John Millington Synge while he was a student of Irish at that college. Synge didn't think much of him as a teacher, and more's the pity. There was much he could have learned from Goodman, had he given him a chance.

If she stopped to chat for a moment with the old people she met on the way, travelling with a donkey, or driving a cow before them, she may have been told of Trant's Leap, a great leap across a cliff face taken by a man of a Norman family who had settled and built a castle across Ventry Harbour in Cathair an Treantaigh. English soldiers pursued young Trant on horseback as far as the cliff chasm between Ventry and Baile Móir. He urged on his horse to clear the chasm.

"My life on you, little horse," he called as they galloped towards the chasm.

The horse took the leap and found his four feet on the other side, and without stay or stop galloped into the distant west, leaving the English soldiers floundering on the edge of the chasm which still holds his name.

Ceann Trá or Ventry is a small village on the edge of the fine golden horseshoe expanse of Ventry Strand, famed for one of the greatest of our Fenian tales, the Battle of Ventry, where Dáire Donn, the King of the World, fought the Fianna in a battle that lasted a year and a day.

In pre-famine times the village consisted of a straggle of small cabins gathered where the old road from Dingle met the strand, where the traveller going further west had to cross the strand either to go back to Fán or over the Clasach to Dún Chaoin or to turn north to go to Ballyferriter by Ráthanáin, the castle of the Geraldines. Ceann Trá had then about 200 inhabitants. It had been badly stuck by the cholera epidemic of 1832 and was, according to Mrs Thompson, nearly wiped out. In 1844 the same Mrs Thompson, whose chief aim in life was to convert the ignorant peasants from the errors of popery, described the village:

> Ventry, lying in the centre of the district, became a gathering-place, and many converts from other parishes collected for strength and mutual support into this poor village . . . Ventry was superlatively wretched and squalid. Misery marked every countenance, the untenanted houses were falling into ruin, or become the haunt of lawless men, the place had what we call in Ireland, "a bad name!" It is situate at the head of a stretch of shore, called therefore, coun tra, "the head of the strand." Yet here, in this despised spot, had the Lord a people to bring from darkness to light, and from the power of Satan unto God.[12]

It had two rather dubious claims to fame. Its first was its connection to the family of Mullins, the Lords Ventry, and the second was that the small community had been singled out in the 1830s and 1840s by proselytisers in a great sweep of conversion to Protestantism that engulfed the peninsula. The headquarters and base of that drive was Ventry itself, headed by a local man of great charisma turned minister, Revd Thomas Moriarty, better known locally as Tomás an Éithigh or "Tom of the Lies". For a score of years the term "Ventryise" meant to apply pressure to make people change their religion. Some dozen cottages, referred to as "the Colony", were built to support and protect the families who had embraced the Protestant religion, who were ostracised by their neighbours. They were referred to locally as "soupers", and the term "soup" meant the Protestant religion, particularly the form introduced by the proselytisers of the mid-nineteenth century, when people were given food to convert.

The strand itself is known as Fionntrá, as is the parish, while the village is known as Ceann Trá, but was Anglicised to "Ventry" by the same proseltyising community, and was also known as "the Colony" by the locals.

Many of the people from outside the village didn't feel comfortable when they visited the village for business or entertainment, feeling they were being laughed at because they spoke Irish. It was also the administrative centre for the south side of the western peninsula, having the school, the post office and the constabulary or "Peeler's" barracks and the imposing Protestant church just outside the village. There was originally a coastguard station here, but it had been changed about four miles to the west across the harbour to Cuan in the middle of the nineteenth century. It also had two or three shops, the largest of which was Thady Kevane's, with a pub to complete the picture. There had been the parish Catholic church there in the old days on the site where the present National School stands, but in 1870 it was decided to build a new one.

The church, Séipéal Chaitlíona, was named from the patron of the parish, Saint Caitlíona, whose body was washed into Ventry Strand from Alexandria in the early days of Christianity. It was decided to move the church to Ard an Bhóthair, some two miles to the west, to get away from both the Protestant influence and from the pub which had lately been opened. Ever since then, even up to the time of the events described in this account in 1909 and afterwards, the clergy had been wary and suspicious of Ventry and visited it as seldom as possible.

Bearnárd Ó Lubhaing describes the village in which he was born and reared in the 1930s, over twenty years after Eibhlín's visit: "That's how it was when I was growing up, and though the old ways were ended, still there was the smell and the taste of the soup right over Ceann Trá. The village was left out of the official Gaeltacht and was a great source of suspicion to the priests of Dingle on account of the Protestant influence. The people were kind to each other again following the fierce religious clashes between the two sides, each claiming that they were the ones who had the true religion . . ."[13]

It was said by the old people that there was every trade in Ventry except that of the saddler. There was a tailor, a blacksmith, a shoemaker, a carpenter and a cooper. There was a post office run by a Protestant family of Sullivans out at Clochán on the new Dingle Road. There was a pub, and two or three shops where you could buy the simple necessities: flour, tea and sugar, meal, tobacco, a shovel and a four-pronged pike.

The barrel maker, Michael Long, known as Cooper Long, who had his shed in the middle of the village, had been born in Fán on the road to Slea Head. He had learned his trade in the Isle of Man and had come home and built a shed by the road in the middle of Ventry and was soon employing three other coopers in the skilful craft of making wooden barrels used for the storing and transportation of salted fish for the American market, where there was a great demand for Irish mackerel. They were boom times for the fishing industry, and mackerel were being cleaned and cured at many of the small harbours around the coast. Cooper Long, who was very involved in local politics, was an insatiable and bitter enemy of Lord Ventry. He was a member of the Dingle Board of Guardians, the forerunner to the County Council, and was also a member of the Congested Districts Board. He was among those who finally deposed Lord Ventry from his until then unassailable position as chairman of the Board of Guardians by uniting the members and voting him out of office. Ventry retorted by evicting him from his shed, but the neighbours gathered with their horses and carts, saws and hammers, and rebuilt the shed all in one day.

By 1909, the time of Eibhlín's visit to Ventry, the proselytising drive was still a memory, and there were people in the village who still possessed a copy of the *"Cat Breac"*, the simple booklet used for the teaching of Irish reading by the proselytisers. The fine red sandstone church still stood on the outskirts of the village on the new road to Dingle, and service was still held there on Sundays, though the school had been closed since early in the century.

Though there was plenty of reasons for disagreement and dissension among the villagers, religion wasn't one of them. They had come to terms with that. There were even families who, to make sure they were on the right side, had their children discreetly baptised in both churches. Still, it was obvious to anyone who studied the situation that the scales were turning slowly in favour of the old order and that the Catholics, and the nationalists, were taking over the village again.

Ceann Trá was one of the first villages in Corca Dhuibhne to realise the tourist potential of the area. It was a beautiful village situated above a spectacular strand, with a view across Dingle Bay to Uíbh Ráthach and Valentia Island. There were breathtaking views of Sliabh an Fhiolair and Cruach Mhárthan to the west, while the remains of an old Geraldine tower house, Ráthanáin, guarded the exit on the road to the north. The whole Ventry area was, and is, rich in archaeology, in scenic beauty and, above all, in the character of its people. Even in the early years of the century there were three guest houses in the village, bearing the fine holiday names of Sea View, Bay View and Mount Eagle View. Ventry had prepared itself for visitors well before the surrounding villages, and was equalled only by Dingle itself.

The late Victorians had considered leisure as necessary for health and well-being and had taken to travelling to the seaside resorts. The coming of the train had made it easier for people living near the sea to take day trips on weekends during the summer, and the better-off class could afford to come and stay for a week or two. It became fashionable, for city families that could afford it, to relocate the family to the coast, where the women and children could enjoy the sea and country air while the father remained in the city attending to the family business and perhaps joining them at the weekend. The emphasis was on recreation rather than idleness, and they believed that it improved both mind and body. Walking, cycling, swimming and golf were all recommended. It was in the late nineteenth century that the Saturday half-day was introduced, as well as other national holidays, or "bank holidays".

Since the coming of the Dingle train in 1892, visitors were arriving to west Corca Dhuibhne from places near and far. Irish was widespread in the parish of Ventry, the village excepted, and with the new interest in it people were coming to the Gaelic rural areas to learn by the firesides in the homes of the people. The Gaelic League had been founded in 1893 to promote the use and learning of Irish, and the interest was growing continually. The objects of the League were: "The preservation of Irish as the national language of Ireland and the extension of its use as a spoken tongue."[14]

The League had pledged to be non-political and

non-sectarian. A later added clause pledged the League to the promotion of Irish industry.

People were beginning to come to their own. The famine was past, as were the religious troubles of that period and the land troubles of the eighties and nineties. Life was getting a bit easier among the farming and fishing folk. Those who had gone before to the United States has not forgotten their people and had sent frequent remittances home. There were good prices for fish and farm produce, and money jingled in pockets for the first time since the famine. C.P. Crane, who had been here as sub-inspector of the police in the 1880s, returned as resident magistrate for Kerry in the early 1900s. He describes the change that had taken place, through official English eyes, since he had last been in Dingle:

> The generation of "moonlight" disorder and crime had passed away almost entirely, or if it still lingered in the minds of the rising generation, it was not made manifest in any untoward act. The beneficent legislation affecting congested districts was beginning to be felt. The Agricultural Board and the Congested Districts Board had, between them, wrought wonders in the country. Everywhere there was sign of improvement. Children better clothed and fed; the farmers busy reclaiming land; industries springing up here and there; all pointing to progress and giving hope that Ireland was at last going to fulfil her destiny and become a prosperous and law-abiding part of the Empire – a strength and not a weakness.[15]

It was to the Kevanes' Sea View – Radharc na Mara to the Irishers – that Eibhlín went to seek board. The great dramatist John Millington Synge had stayed in this very house on one or two of his visits to west Kerry and the Blaskets. He stated in the preface to his great play, *The Playboy of the Western World,* that he was very much indebted to the folk imagination of the herds and fishermen along the coasts from Kerry to Mayo: "Anyone who has lived in real intimacy with the Irish peasantry will know that the wildest sayings and ideas in this play are tame indeed, compared with the fancies one may hear in any little hillside cabin in Geesala, or Carraroe, or Dingle Bay."[16]

Synge had been listening with open ears to all that was said in the homes he visited. Kevanes' was a bilingual household, which because of his limited Irish was just what he wanted. Unfortunately his career was short-lived. He had just died in the spring of 1909, having paid his last visit to Ceann Trá the previous October.

Thady Kevane was more than willing to have Eibhlín as a guest, even though she had not booked and it was the busiest time of the year. Thady was an up-and-coming young businessman. He had moved from his father's house at Ráthanáin when he married Máire Curran from a well-to-do farming family in Cathair Aird, a short distance away on the old Dingle road. At first he rented a small shop in the village, but soon realised the business potential and built a fine, slated, two-storied home at the edge of Ceann Trá, an object of pride and wonder at a time when the greater majority of homes in the area were still thatched houses, with a room up and a room down. In 1902 he set up shop, as well as making part of the building into a small pleasant guest house. In his shop you could buy flour, yellow meal, fish, rat poison, a coil of yarn for making chair seats, salt, tobacco, tea, sugar, white bread and a shovel, life's essentials in those simple times. His shop provided a welcome service to the local people, saving a lengthy trip into Dingle for those everyday needs.

The Kevane shop was doing well, and so was the guest house, during the summer months. Máire Curran was a fine housewife, as well as being an assistant teacher in the local Ventry National School.

Thady himself was a character, full of mischief and fun, always ready with a story or a song as the occasion required. People loved to come and stay in his home. There was a visitors' book in the hall which contained comments and signatures in Irish, English and German, expressing guests' joy and satisfaction at having spent a while in Sea View, not to mention the wonderful care Mr and Mrs Kavanagh had taken of them during their pleasant stay, with wishes and promises of a speedy return to Ventry. The scenery was wonderful, the archaeology mystic and the beauty of the people so friendly and outgoing. As M. Kennedy wrote on 5 August 1902: "Ventry is a very bracing and pretty place, with sea, mountain and romantic scenery. Mr Kavanagh's house is a good one facing the sea and both he and Mrs Kavanagh are most obliging and anxious to please. The peasantry are very interesting and original."

General Neuber of the Austrian army and his good wife stayed in the Kevanes' in June 1904: "Mrs Kevane is a very attentif Landlady and Mr Kevane went out many times to bring home for us the really delicious Pollock, which Johanna, our little cook knows so well to prepare nicely. It is with pleasure that we will remember that simple little place with the many interesting antiquities which brought us here from Austria."

Johanna, sometimes referred to as Hannah and again as Siobháinín, with the word "beag" added, or even formally as Miss Curran, was Mary Curran's sister, who cooked for the guests. Obviously she was improving in her cooking skills as time passed, as was noted by Maolmhuire Mac Cárthaigh in his second visit in July 1904: *"Mí do bhíos annso an taca so. Go deimhin féin tá feabhas mór tar éis teacht ar an áit le bliain. Ar imeacht dom anuraidh bhíos sásta – an-shásta. Ag imeacht dom i mbliana táim lán t-sásta. Tá an Ghaoluinn chomh blasta ag Tadhg agus ag a bhean agus do bhí riamh agus tá Siobháinín na hana chócaire anois."*

("I spent a month here this time. Certainly a great improvement has been achieved in the course of the year.

When I was leaving last year I was satisfied, very satisfied. Leaving this year I am fully satisfied. Tadhg and his wife have the Irish as sweet as ever and Siobháinín is now a great cook.")

Another note from the Misses Warren and Powell from Dublin in May 1910 gives an indication of the cultural tourism of the time: "I spent nearly 3 weeks in this delightful country, the pleasure of the visit being much enhanced by Mr. Kevane's knowledge of fairy tales and legends and Mrs. Kevane's kindly hospitality. I hope to return at some future date and renew acquaintance with lovely Ventry."

Brian Gwinn and his sister from Clontarf in Dublin, who spent nearly a fortnight in Sea View House in September 1910, give us a further insight into Thady's personality: ". . . My sister and I can at least say with confidence, that nowhere else could better or more friendly entertainment be found . . . Mr. Kevane has a wide and entertaining knowledge of local history, from the exploits of Fionn M'Cool onward, while his prediction of the weather reaches the level of exact science."

Another visitor of far-seeing enterprise described Ventry as the ideal place for the main holiday activities of golfing, fishing and cycling, but recommended highly that bathing boxes be erected close to the beach for the ladies and that a golf links be developed along the strand and a pleasure boat be engaged to provide sailing trips around the harbour.[17]

Small wonder that Thady Kevane was a happy man. He had everything going for him and Mary.

This was the place for Eibhlín. She needed the break badly after a hard year's study. She had just completed her MA course in French, having achieved the same success in the German course the previous year. She had been awarded a travelling scholarship of £300 to France and Germany, remarkable at a time when both degrees and scholarships weren't easily come by; and for a woman it was even more notable. She became interested in the Irish language at an early date, as can be seen from *The United Irishman* of 20 September 1902, when she was still a student: "Miss Eve Nicolls, a pupil of Loreto College in Stephen's Green, took Irish instead of English in the Junior Exam senior grade. She was awarded a £4 prize for Irish composition."[18]

Thomas MacDonagh presented a copy of his first book of poems, *Through the Ivory Gate,* "To Miss Eveleen Nicolls from Thomas MacDonagh",[19] in the same year. To give time and energy to the study of Irish at that time was unusual and courageous, both on Eibhlín's part, on that of her parents and indeed even of the school itself. Though there was a great interest in the revival of Irish, there were many, even among the university alumni, who regarded it as a dead language and would prefer that it remain so, as they felt that its revival, if achieved, would result in dragging the people back into the ignorance of the Dark Ages. Frank O'Rahilly, a wonderful scholar from Ballylongford in Kerry, won a scholarship to Blackrock College, but when he said he wished to study Irish was told that there was no Irish teacher in the school. Rather than lose such a brilliant student, who would be a great asset, the college employed its first Irish teacher. The greater majority of the schools prided themselves in giving an education that was little other than a poor copy of the English system.

Eibhlín had begun her education at the Loreto Convent in Charleville Road, Rathmines. After completing her primary schooling, she went on to Loreto College at number 53 St Stephen's Green as a day pupil. She took learning seriously. Post-primary education at the time was called "intermediate" education and was run in connection with the Intermediate Board of Education. The board, which was set up in 1878, was financed by the Disestablished Church Fund, moneys that remained over after the Church of Ireland had been disestablished as the church of the state, and later from the revenue raised in Ireland on alcoholic drinks. The examinations were all written ones, with the exception of music and science. These exams were held in the middle of June. The subjects of study were English, Latin, Greek, French, Italian, German, Irish, Spanish, history and geography, mathematics, experimental science, music, shorthand, bookkeeping, trigonometry and natural philosophy. There was no provision for oral examinations. Indeed, a student might get full marks in a language and not be able to pronounce the simplest word. The Gaelic League always demanded that Irish be examined orally. It was, of course, a Dublin Castle board, and as such was very English orientated. It was criticised:

> There is nothing distinctly Irish in the whole system. No stimulation of patriotism. The whole outlook is English, and English in its most shallow and unreal form. Nothing taught about past, present, future of Ireland: about wants, capabilities, aspirations of Ireland. A bitter warfare in the press and strong agitation in this country were necessary before the Irish language got even the secondary place it now occupies. Other native studies of a real and practical and human sort will not be introduced into the system unless a similar agitation be raised.

Other criticisms of the Board system of education included:

> The Board represents nothing except an English official's view of how Irishmen may be tamed and rendered harmless and useful to England . . . The progressive elements of Irish life are suspected and disliked by the Board . . . It consists of men who have no experience of present-day Intermediate teaching . . . There is too much cram and too much competition . . . its system is unIrish, unpractical and a forcing or cramming system.[20]

Eibhlín would have travelled in on the tram, which remained horse-drawn until 1896, from Rathgar to St Stephen's Green. Dublin was only about a quarter of its present size with a population of about 300,000, but was still a bustling city, particularly in the centre. There were engravers, coopers, shoemakers, coachmakers and so many more trades plying in and around the centre. There were the street traders with their particular calls, selling fruit, fish, milk, coal and wood blocks. There were the ballad singers at the corners singing the great ballads peculiar to Dublin. At the same time there was grinding poverty. Many Dubliners suffered from hunger and disease in the slums that were groaning all along the old back streets, under the gaslights behind the city centre, and in the fine Georgian squares where fifty and sixty people lived in grand but crumbling eighteenth century houses.

The general feeling in Dublin during Eibhlín's childhood in the early nineties of the nineteenth century was that the people were content with being part of the United Kingdom, with the English institutions and the English language. What people wanted was more say in their domestic affairs and reform of the land system as sought by the Land League.

Ireland had undergone a great change during Eibhlín's youth. Parnell died in 1891 amid great heart-wrenching controversy that had split the country in two and lasted for many years. So many national movements had ended in failure, from the 1798 Rising, Robert Emmet's Rising in 1803, down to the Fenians in 1867, and now the great hope in Parnell had come to nothing. People, having lost their hope and interest in politics, turned their attention to non-political activities such as the language movement, the cultural movement, literature, sport, music, theatre and history. This had the effect of awakening the feeling of nationalism and belonging. People began to show interest in the Irish language, which was fast declining and had died our completely in many areas. Organisations such as the GAA and the National Literary Society were founded.

It was to the National Literary Society that Douglas Hyde made his famous speech in 1892 entitled "The

Necessity for de-Anglicising Ireland". In it he called on Irish people to turn away from things English before they lost for ever the sense of a separate nationality. He advocated that as much as possible from the past of our country be recovered: its language, its manners and customs, its games, its place names and surnames. The Irish should read works by Irish authors such as Thomas Moore and Thomas Davis – the precursors of Anglo-Irish literature.

According to many of the language enthusiasts, this did not go far enough, as it did not encourage reading in Irish. This led to the founding of the Gaelic League in 1893, with Douglas Hyde himself as its first president. A great revival movement spread all over the country taking in people of all creeds and classes. Since it was non-violent, many clergy of both denominations joined in the movement, as did many members of the professions. The Nicolls of Rathgar could be counted among those enthusiastic supporters. In the years following, the Gaelic League would become the most important movement in the country.

So it was that Eibhlín had begun to take such an interest in Irish. She was a special girl who could think for herself and who wished to become involved in the social problems of the age, such as the revival of the Irish language, the national movement for independence and the suffragette movement, which would achieve the vote for women. From the beginning Eibhlín excelled in her studies, and it was not unusual for her to win the first place in her grade, not alone in her school but in the whole of Ireland. In the senior grade she won an exhibition in modern languages and the first class prizes in Irish, French and German. In the matriculation she won first honours in Irish and Latin and a £24 exhibition. With such a record it is no wonder that she decided to continue on her studies to third level. That wasn't an easy task in the early 1900s. Women were not only discouraged from attending university but were barred from attendance at lectures. Their presence at lectures would have been regarded as a distracting influence to the male students and a threat to their virtue. University education for women was, moreover, considered an unnecessary luxury, causing social disruption and a waste of resources. Any efforts to change the system was frowned upon, in particular by the bishops and the university authorities themselves. The only way left open to them to pursue their studies was through one of the so-called ladies' colleges, like Alexandra College, St Mary's Dominican College and Loreto, St Stephen's Green, all in Dublin. Even there women were discriminated against educationally, as they were more likely to be taught by non-graduates. There were even separate examination rooms for men and women.[21] It was 1904 before Dublin University (Trinity College) allowed women to study.

Eibhlín pursued her studies through Loreto College, which had been teaching the Royal University course since 1893. In her first university examination she won first class honours in Irish, German, logic and Latin, as well as a first class exhibition of £36. She achieved the first place in Ireland in her BA results and won the prestigious Steward Scholarship, and a first class exhibition in modern literature of £40. Her achievements in the MA were second to none; she again achieved first place in the country, a first class honours and a scholarship of £300 to polish it off. She was the most notable student in the Queen's College (as UCD was called then) of her time. German, French, Irish and Latin were her forte, and each of them she had mastered. Her academic achievements were looked on as an honour, not only to herself and her family, but to her school also. There was sharp competition between the women's colleges, and particularly with Alexandra, the Protestant college.

Eibhlín spent some time both in Germany and France. During her time in Paris she studied old Irish under M. Jubainville, the great Celtic scholar. She was chosen to lecture in the subject in the University of Paris. Her work was not confined to study and research in Paris, as while there she reorganised a branch of the Gaelic League which had ceased to exist. She gave lectures on the theme of the Irish language in both Paris and Berlin. *The Freeman's Journal* once described her as: "One of these rare types that appear but at long intervals in the history of the nation."

She had become very involved in the Gaelic League, which was one of the first movements to welcome women. She became a member of the Five Provinces Branch and taught Irish classes there. George Moonan, a colleague, was to write of her: "No flavour of the atmosphere of the classroom attached to her work. She had an end in view; every available means was utilised by method and industry, every means was made available by tact and resource. Her industry was untiring When some additional work should be done she was the first to volunteer . . . that which she undertook to do was always done, and done well."22

One of the main arguments in the cultural circles of the time was what, if any, part would or should be played by the Irish language in the future teaching curricula of the universities. Needless to say, Eibhlín became very involved in the debate and spoke out strongly on the side of the language.

Back home from the continent, aware of the burden Ireland was carrying as part of the British Empire, she wrote in an article entitled "*An Bhan-Ghaodhal*" ("The Irishwoman") in *Bean na hÉireann,* a monthly magazine that first appeared in November 1908 to act as a voice for Irishwomen in public affairs:

> When I am residing in countries which have their own governments I become envious of the simplicity of life they enjoy. I suppose every English and every German person feels it more necessary to weigh up every action of his in comparison to those who do not have to keep up an empire. Little do they ever consider how difficult it is for an Irish person to be faithful to his native land. He has so much to do that frequently he has no idea how to even start the

process, or what is the best way to begin to help her. That is even made more difficult in the case of a woman who has to fight two battles, against the injustice to women and against the injustice to her country.[23]

Eibhlín was highly thought of in Dublin circles. Besides her usual Gaelic League activities, she had begun to express her opinions in writing in matters such as education and the language. Her writings had appeared in *An Claidheamh Soluis,* the journal of the Gaelic League. She was also the secretary of the Dublin Feis, a very important institution in the Dublin calendar of the time and, indeed, to the present day. The Feis of 1909 had been particularly successful, due in no small way to her efforts, according to the *Freeman's Journal:*

> Feis Bhaile Átha Cliath was brought to a successful conclusion with Coirm Cheoil na Feise, which was held in the Abbey Theatre on the 5th inst. The good order and method with which many complications were got through is very largely due to the care and attention of Eibhlín Nic Niocaill, who gave time without stint and untiring energy to the work of the Feis. The entries showed a big increase on those of last year. Under the heading of Intermediate Schools there were entries in 33 classes against 16 last year, while there were entries in 34 classes as against 9 for last year under the heading "National Schools."[24]

So she had been very busy, too busy perhaps, as there are indications that her health was beginning to be affected. She had fainted on a few occasions, something that had caused her worry. A long break would do her good, and where better to revive your health and spirits than in Corca Dhuibhne by the wild Atlantic among the native speakers of the language she loved. She had more than two fine, long months of freedom stretching before her, far from the city and all the pressures that went with it. A few weeks and everything would be fine again. She would be among those she most loved and admired, speaking and improving on her Irish. There would be long walks along the fine beaches and the windy hills, and swims in the late summer Atlantic, with songs, stories, music and dance late into the nights. Could anything be more reviving and invigorating?

CHAPTER 2

# The Bell-Branch

ON THE EVENING of 6 July 1909, another visitor from the capital, James Henry Sproull Cousins, arrived on his bicycle to spend a whole two months "in the more authentic part of the Ancient Kingdom of Kerry". He had come to Dingle by train, bringing his bicycle with him, and had cycled to Ventry. It was his first trip to Corca Dhuibhne to meet the saints and heroes, gods and goddesses and the reminiscences of a vanished world that now lay beneath the visitor's feet in the ancient monuments as well as in the imagination of the people. He dismounted from his bike near a wayside forge to ask an old woman with bright eyes under a shawl if he was on the right road to Ventry.

"Dyasmyrrygut!"

"Dyasmyrrygutfainrig!"

"You are indeed on the right road to Ventry if you go back about two miles." [1]

They walked part of the road together till they came to the top of the hill where they could see Ventry Harbour stretching away from them. There were about ten torpedo boats of the British fleet anchored in the bay, which Cousins would have much preferred not to be there. Not so the old woman, who was delighted to see them, and thanked God that the day had come when such a sight could be seen in Ventry Harbour. Cousins wasn't impressed. The movement hadn't made itself felt in these parts yet, he thought.

When he arrived at Thady Kevane's, he discovered that an unexpected visitor, Eibhlín, had arrived shortly before him and had already gone our walking on the fine, broad Ventry Strand.

He wrote: "I had booked a room over Thady Kevane's shop overlooking the strand round which the breaking rhythm of the Atlantic, softened by the intervening bay, made crescents of the phosphorescent radiance at night, with the dim bulk of Eagle Mountain blocking out a big share of the western skies."[2]

Were you to think from this piece of over-ornamented prose that Cousins was a writer, you would be correct. He was well-known, both as a poet and as a dramatist.

Thady was full of apologies in the true Kerry fashion: "A lady had come down to add Munster Irish to the other dialects she knew. And what could Mary do, Thady asked, (Mary being his wife), but take the great lady who had come expecting a place somewhere, and they being the only people that had a corner to spare. So Miss Eibhlín Nicolls M.A. . . . had been installed into the small room beside mine some hours before I arrived."[3]

Although she was slightly known to him, as they had met before in Irish circles, it would seem, from what he says, that Cousins might have preferred to have had the whole place to himself.

James Cousins was born on 22 July 1873 into a Methodist family of French Huguenot origin and of very modest means at 18 Cavour Street in the city of Belfast. They had a small garden in front of the house with two lilac bushes and a swing. His father worked at the deep-sea docks. Although James left school when just twelve years old, still he showed that he was bright and had an interest in going further by attending night classes. Having worked at several small jobs, including in a pawn office and as an office boy for a coal firm, he finally got himself an important position as the personal secretary to Mr Dan Dixon, the lord mayor of Belfast, with a handsome salary of £100 a year. Part of his work included the writing of the lord mayor's speeches.

James never enjoyed robust health, having a weak chest from his early days. In an effort to strengthen his body, he took up tough exercises like boxing and cycling. He tried to become a violinist, but got no farther than being able to scrape out "God save the Queen", the first tune that many unionist boys and girls tried to master at that time. His first book of poems, *Ben Madighan,* one thousand copies of which appeared in 1892 when Jim was only nineteen, was a remarkable achievement. Ben Madighan is the Irish name for Cave Hill, the hill high above Belfast.

On one occasion James attended a circus in London. Part of the performance, as was often in the case in circuses and shows of the time, was an act depicting and caricaturing the various nations and their people – the British bulldog, the American eagle, the French cockerel and the like. Jim was highly indignant at a caricature, such as those in *Punch,* of a stage Irishman riding around the ring on the back of a pig, shouting, "Begorrah! Bejapers! Bedad and Huroo!" to the great delight of and applause of the audience. He stood up and protested loudly at this racism, but was hushed by the audience and forced to sit down.

From that moment a change took place in James Cousins. He realised he was an Irishman. He began to take an interest in everything Irish, even extending as far as learning the Irish language, unbeknownst to his friends and relatives, even to his mother and father, whom he considered as prejudiced as any in Belfast, a wise move in that strange society where such an exercise might have had dangerous consequences. He became so interested in the language movement that he joined the Gaelic League in Belfast. He changed his name to "Séamus Ó Cuisín", and later changed it again to the more romantic Celtic "Séamus Mac Oisín", Séamus the son of Oisín. (Oisín was the son of Fionn Mac Cumhaill.) He found himself being drawn more and more towards Dublin and the new exciting cultural revival movement that was stirring there.

In 1897 he decided he had had enough of Belfast, left his fine job with the lord mayor and set off for Dublin, where he obtained a position as a clerk with Tedcastles and McCormack, a coal company that shipped coal in from England. There was an unusual perk in that he could travel overseas on the coal boats. That same year he published his second book of poetry, *Legend of the Blemished King and Other Poems.* He was beginning to make an impression, particularly on those involved in the movement.

He was happy in Dublin from the start and was won over completely when Douglas Hyde, the president of the Gaelic League, scholar and later president of Ireland, greeted him in Irish when he met him on the street a few days after his arrival: "*Beannacht Dé leat!* I always knew you had a southern soul in your northern body."[4]

He became acquainted with the poet George Russell (AE), who lived at Rathmines, and through him got to know those involved in the literary and language movement that was sweeping the country at the time. He also got to know William Butler Yeats. Cousins took a particular interest in the dramatic revival, appeared on stage himself and wrote a number of pieces for the Irish National Theatre Society, in one of which Willie Pearse, Pádraig's brother, had a part.

Up to the time of his arrival in Ventry in 1909, three of his plays had been staged – *The Sleep of the King, The Racing Lug* and *The Sword of Dermot* – and all had achieved modest success. *The Sleep of the King,* for example, was a poetic one act play in which a beautiful immortal summons a king's son to the Land of Youth, and contained these lines which were long remembered and used by people to lull their children to sleep:

> Rest, rest, sigh and jest,
> Wise and foolish, gay and grave;
> Down, down, sword and crown –

Sleep is master of King and slave.
Night with ruddy lip,
Sips the dregs of Day,
Swooning o'er the world in sleep,
Deep as the sleep of a child.[5]

James married Margaret E. Gillespie, or Gretta as she was better known, on 3 April 1903 in Sandymount Methodist chapel. James and Gretta had met for the first time in 1899 in Dublin, shortly after James' arrival from Belfast. Gretta was studying music at the Royal Irish Academy of Music. She was twenty-five and he was thirty. They formed an interesting and devoted couple, concerned and involved in the cultural and social questions of the day. Gretta described Jim – as she called him – as being small and fair and having a northern accent. By this time he had become a vegetarian, which was regarded as being very odd at that time. Gretta had thought it out, too, and come to the conclusion that James was right: "It is not necessary for health that I should demand living creatures small and large to be slaughtered and their flesh to be cooked for food for me – then it is murder, and a crime for me to be a party to such cruelty and wickedness, and as soon as I am free to order my own food I will be a vegetarian."[6] At the wedding reception, although there was a choice of meats for the wedding guests, Gretta took the opportunity to announce that she had decided to become vegetarian in support of her new husband.

They spent three days of a honeymoon, the Easter week-end, in Killarney. These wonderful days awakened both their interests in Kerry. The biggest problem they had was the vegetarian diet, of which little was known by the Kerry chefs of the time. Their meals mostly consisted of a mixture of cabbage, rhubarb and cheese. They enjoyed their stay so much that they revisited Kerry as often as possible. They loved the outdoor life, walking on the hills or cycling the roads, and spent several holidays in Donegal and Connemara as well.

They were very happy together in an odd sort of way. Gretta had very definite ideas regarding sex, which James, willingly or otherwise, seems to have agreed to. She described her early married life: "I remember that I grew white and thin during our first married year. People thought this was due to my being a Vegetarian. But I knew it was due to the problem of adjustment to the revelation that marriage had bought me as to the physical basis of sex."[7] They both agreed that the happiness of their married life would be based on love, knowledge of each other and spiritual aspiration, and that marriage would be secondary, not primary in their lives.

Many people thought highly of James' literary efforts, and he was spoken of in the same manner as Yeats and AE, yet it is clear that his poetry lacked bite. AE, his friend, in the *Irish Homestead,* described *The Awakening and Other Sonnets,* which appeared in 1908: "It is a book of 12 sonnets daintily bound and printed and dainty also in sentiment. There is little power in them but some fancy and melody . . ."[8] *The Bell-Branch,* a further book of his poems, was also published in 1908.

James Joyce had received much kindness from the Cousins, and was a frequent visitor to their home, often attending their Wednesday "at homes" and even spending the night of 15–16 June 1904 there, the night before the most famous day in Irish literature: Bloomsday, the day of the events of *Ulysses.* In spite of this, Joyce rather meanly lambasted Cousins in his jingly couplet poem "Gas from a Burner" (1912). On his way back to Trieste in Italy, Joyce wrote the poem in bitterness at his failure to find a publisher for *Dubliners* in his native city, and attacked everything to do with Dublin – the culture, the writers and the publishers, because none of his works were being produced:

> I printed mystical books in dozens:
> I printed the table-book of Cousins
> Though (asking your pardon) as for the verse
> 'Twould give you a heartburn on your arse. . .[9]

It illustrates the understanding nature of James and Gretta Cousins that they always spoke kindly of Joyce and remembered his departure without bitterness.

Yeats himself wasn't overjoyed with James' latest dramatic effort either. He found it rather vulgar. New work was needed. The dramatic movement had to move on, and Yeats, who had by now become a leading figure in the dramatic and literary movement, bypassed Cousins. No more of his plays would ever appear on the Irish stage. John Millington Synge was to take his place with his *Riders to the Sea, The Well of the Saints, The Shadow of the Glen* and *The Playboy of the Western World,* as would another young, up-and-coming Longford playwright, Pádraic Colum, with *Broken Soil.*

Without training or experience as a teacher, James was appointed to the staff of the High School in Harcourt Street, Dublin, as a geography teacher, a position in which he was so successful that he published a textbook in 1909 entitled *A Modern Geography for Irish Intermediate Schools.*

By 1903 both Gretta and he had become active in the suffragette movement. Gretta's life had changed abruptly when she attended a suffragette meeting in Manchester. From then on she devoted her energies to the cause of women's rights, both in Ireland and England and, later on, in India. In time she became prominent in the women's movement.

The first women's movement in Ireland, the Dublin Women's Suffrage Association, was founded in 1876 by Anna M. Haslam, a Quaker woman from Youghal, County Cork. The Association sought to improve the lot of women in work and education, to seek property rights for married women and, ultimately, the vote and the right to stand for election. They organised talks, campaigns and meetings, as well as the gathering, signing and presenting of petitions. They produced a newsletter, *Woman's Advocate.* The Association, because of the Quaker influence, was entirely peaceful and law-abiding. By 1904 the Association had almost 400 members. In 1896 they achieved a great victory when they succeeded in achieving the vote for women for the Poor Law Guardians election, and also a limited vote (for women of property) for the new county councils which were set up in 1898. But on the big one, the vote for parliament, there was no progress, the problem being put back rather than faced up to.

People like the Cousins and, in particular, Hannah Sheehy Skeffington began to feel that they were getting nowhere and that it was time to step up the pressure and become more active in their pursuits for the franchise.

But in Ventry in July 1909, here was James, alone with Eibhlín in the beautiful wilds of Corca Dhuibhne, while his wife Gretta was in London, lending her support to and learning from the English movement.

CHAPTER 3

# Fragments of a Dream

If James was uneasy at Eibhlín's presence in Sea View, that didn't last very long. As soon as he met the young woman with the happy, open countenance he felt at his ease, as most people did in her presence. The weather suddenly took a turn for the better and became bright, warm and sunny. Such a blessing turns the area into the most wonderful, magical, sparkling place in the world. The friendliness of the local people, and in particular of their hosts the Kevanes, helped them to relax and forget the stiff formalities of the time, not that they bothered much with them anyway. Besides, Eibhlín had such a relaxed, friendly personality, as well as being such a handsome woman. Their conversations at the breakfast table showed them that they had much in common and had, more or less, come to Kerry for the same reasons, to live the life of the people for a short time. Eibhlín wanted to become as fluent as possible in Munster Irish, while James planned to study the customs and culture of the district.

In a short time they were going on discovery walks together: "Common interest drew us together . . . and the discovery of deep affinities, also of stimulating divergences in the leisurely life when the soul has time and space for blossoming and revelation made our week together a round of intellectual delight."[1] Long discussions shortened the strolls on the broad strand of Ventry and on the surrounding hills and glens.

Just above the village at Mám an Óraigh, where the

ancient road to Dingle cuts between the hills down to Cathair Bó Sine, in the middle of a field, within a *lios* stands the ogham stone of Cill na gColmán, or the Church of the Colmáns. The stone is not a tall standing stone like most of its kind but is almost round. There is a cross of arcs surrounded by a circle with the ogham markings in Irish running around the edge, asking our prayers for "Colmán the Pilgrim". Was he on his ancient pilgrimage from the Skelligs to Mount Brandon when his journey was cut short here? Or while on his journey did he decide to remain and set up his little monastery to help the tired, hungry pilgrims?

Together they visited the Iron Age fort of Dún Beag, built at the very edge of a steep cliff above the Atlantic waves and dating back to the coming of the Celts. They saw the ogham stones at Baile an tSagairt and Gallán an tSagairt on Dunmore Head, second in antiquity, according to Cousins, only to Newgrange itself. Carved stones from other long gone eras of wonder were daily being dug out of ditches and crumbling field walls all over the peninsula. It was so important that they be safeguarded and protected.

They visited the mediaeval castle at Ráthanáin, a castle of the Desmond Geraldines who reigned supreme in west Munster for nearly four hundred years, built in the centre of a much earlier ring fort defence. A trip to Gleann Fán with its *púicíns, clocháns,* or beehive huts, presented a little unexpected difficulty, which, though small in stature, he overcame in his own direct way: "At Glen Fahan while inspecting some of the beehives, three young men approached and demanded 'trespass' money, two shillings. I need hardly say that I refused to pay this demand which was made in a threatening manner, and pointed out that these antiquities were under the control of the Board of Works."[2]

On another occasion they climbed Mount Brandon, Ireland's second mountain, the site of ancient pilgrimages, the last point on the mainland of Europe on which the sun sets. From the moment he set foot on the Dingle Peninsula, James had his eye on the mountain, and it seemed, according to himself, that Mount Brandon had its eye on him. He had to wait until the weather was fine enough to attempt the trip. There are but 100 days in the year when Brandon shows his proud head, being shrouded in cloud for the remainder.

At last the opportunity arose, and they took off on bikes, one that he had got a loan of from a priest, having already loaned his own machine to a neighbour who had not yet returned it. The bike was much too big for him, and he had to lower the saddle to its minimum. The brakes, too, he describes as being Kerry brakes: that if the front wheel really didn't mind, perhaps it would be so good as to pull up. They started off back towards Dingle, crossed Milltown Bridge and turned north until they came to Baile Breac, where they dismounted at the bridge and walked to the village on the rough track. It was a perfect summer's day, and having left the bikes in the house of a friend, they set off with the guide, appropriately named Brendan. They walked the Saint's Road, of which nothing remained but the name and the tradition, and with little difficulty climbed the 3,127 feet of Brandon, or Sliabh Daidhche, the second highest mountain in Ireland.

"The whole of the Dingle Peninsula lies below, and a marvellous sight it is, not so much for its impressions, as in its suggestions of a model world fresh from the hand of some master, just unpacked, with little bits of wadding stuck here and there between the excrescences that form the level that would be regarded as mountain peaks."[3]

On another occasion they walked back to Dún Chaoin over the Clasach together. Eibhlín was delighted with that western parish and was especially moved by the view of the Blaskets from the top of the Clasach, one of the most wonderful views of ocean and islands in the whole of Ireland.

The region west of Dingle is surpassing fair to look upon. Here are several pretty villages – such as

Ventry, Ballyferriter and Ballydavid – resting cosily between low hills on the ocean rim. This spot being the most westerly point of Europe, is popularly known as the next parish to America.

No place in Erin, perhaps, can equal Slea Head for the vastness of the ocean view. The sightseer who has not been to Slea Head is merely at the beginning of his career.[4]

Jim has left us a poetic account of some of these delightful expeditions, like the visit to the holy well at Teampall Mhanacháin, adjoining an ancient early Christian site at Baile Riabhach, a few miles to the north of Ventry in the parish of Kildrum, where he describes a man performing the pattern rounds. At that time, and way before it, the holy well was visited every Sunday in the year, and it was said there was not a better well in Munster at which to do the rounds. It was thought that a salmon and an eel occasionally appeared in the well, and if the pilgrim were lucky enough to see them, he would be cured of whatever ailed him. The well was supposed to be very effective in the curing of "Fairy Strokes", an illness brought on by the intervention of the fairies:

He dragged his knees from flag to flag,
And prayed for health with awe-struck brow;
Then hung his ill's discarded rag
On the oerhanging hawthorn bough.[5]

He loved meeting the people, talking to them by the roadside or joining them by the turf fire to talk of crops and fairy lore, of the weather and dress and old forgotten far-off things, such as when he sat by the fire of an old woman, who:

Half stifling reminiscent moans
She gossiped of the famine times;
Then sang in thin and wavering tones
Some ancient nameless poet's rhymes.[6]

He expressed his disappointment that he could not buy Irish-made goods in Corca Dhuibhne. Even a simple item like a box of matches was made in Liverpool with a picture of Marshal MacMahon on the box. He couldn't get Irish-made cigarettes either in the shop in Ballyferriter, where the English-manufactured Quaker Oats, Sunlight Soap, foreign jams and English papers were readily available on the shelves.

The cottages he describes as being poor and squalid, but no matter how bad they appeared externally, he found on entering that they were invariably spotlessly clean and tidy inside.

He wasn't too impressed with "Mr. T. B . . . our M.C.C." (Member of the County Council) either. The first fault he had was that he was the principal emigration agent in the district and had posters displayed prominently advertising passage to a new life in America to those willing and able to take the chance. This was not at all popular in certain Irish-nationalist circles, the opinion being that Irish people should stay at home and build up their own country.

Cousins went out to Ventry church one Sunday morning to hear "Mr. T.B." (obviously Tom Baker, also known as Lord Baker, who now has a restaurant in Dingle named after him) speak after mass. He described him as a "mean skulking fellow" and much preferred Lord Ventry, who was making some effort to improve life in the district. To him T.B. might have been Irish, but he was commercially English.

None of these disagreeable points took from his enjoyment of his holiday. It was an idyllic situation, and though there may not have been any romantic attachment between the two, it is clear that this was a very special time for James: "She was twenty five, tall, stately: an embodiment of sweetness and gentleness, but a sweetness that has no mawkishness in it, and a gentleness resting on fixity and fearlessness."[7]

As Jim himself admitted, it was a week of high delight.

Like her mind, Eibhlín's physical beauty had not gone unnoticed in Dublin, and even men such as Pádraig Pearse had been attracted to her. Pearse, whose father was an English stone carver, had moved over to Dublin from Birmingham in the early 1870s to find work in the new surge of church building that was taking place at that time. He married Margaret Brady, a girl of Meath stock, strong in the old Meath traditions, whose family had also moved to Dublin. The Pearses lived at 27 Great Brunswick Street, now Pearse Street, and it was there that Pádraig was born on 10 November 1879, which made him about five years older than Eibhlín.

Ernest Blythe, a Northerner, who had come to Dublin and had become involved in the national movement, had known her from the time he was in the Ard-Chradbh of the League and was speaking (in Irish) from personal knowledge: "It was she of whom it is said that Pearse was in love with. She was tall, handsome and very reserved in herself. She had a very attractive smile, but as a rule she would be as steady and peaceful as the face of a beautiful statue. If it wasn't that the word 'noble' might remind one of self-importance you might say that she was noble. But there was no sign of self-importance on her. She had a poetic strain. I enjoyed very much verses that she had translated from the German."[8]

There were great, merry nights in the house above Ventry Strand, with dances, songs, verses and poetry way into the night. The parish of Ventry was at that time rich in storytellers, *seanchaithe* and songsters. The Battle of Ventry and Trant's Leap were on the lips of storytellers such as An Saor Ó Loingsigh from Baile an tSléibhe, from whom the famed international collector Jeremiah Curtin had collected stories in 1891 when he handed out shillings and a glass of whiskey to every good storyteller in the neighbourhood. It was said that old Eamonn Sheehy from Dún Chaoin had crossed the Clasach on foot to Ard an

Bhóthair to get the ear of Curtin, and he well over a hundred years of age at the time. There were the local Irish songs, too, such as one from their own village, "The Lament for the Four Women", composed by Seán na bPaidreacha (Seán of the Prayers), a travelling weaver, on the drowning of five young women on Ventry Strand as they were picking *bairnigh* along the foot of the cliffs at Bun Fhána.

One day in particular remained in James Cousins' memory: the afternoon a travelling fiddler arrived at the house. For a two shilling bit, a feed of potatoes and a shake-down for the night, he provided music for a night's dancing. That was the night Thady entertained them with a bout of step dancing. The kitchen was crammed, and even the windows and doors were stuffed with heads and eyes. The table was pushed over into the corner while a turf fire blazed on the hearth.

> He removed his coat in Thady manner as if it was a millennial cosmic process; and as he stood on the hearthstone in shirt and belted trousers and heavy boots, he whispered an instruction in private Irish to the fiddler. From slow to middling quick, to "go tappy" (fast), the solo dance went to a crescendo of wild fiddling, drummed by deafening clashes of thick-soled boots on a stone slab that sounded like rhythmical rifle-volleys.[9]

The dance was as old as the language itself. It fused with the natural wild music and told in beat and motion of love and war and of the dew on sunny summer mornings. It told of the smell of turf smoke in the village, of death and life.

Everyone in the company froze as Thady came to the high point of the dance.

> Towards the end Thady presented the appearance of an unmoving body, poised above, legs moving so rapidly that they had almost reached invisibility when

the fiddle gave a final screech. The dancer's head all
but hit the ceiling that was John Synge's cracked floor,
and with a mighty crash he stood straight on the
stone slab – the imperturbable Thady.

I looked at the visitor. With bulging eyes he said,
"That's a miracle!"[10]

"John Synge's cracked floor" refers to the preface to *The
Playboy of the Western World*: "When I was writing The
Shadow of the Glen some years ago, I got more aid than
any learning could have given me from a chink in the floor
of the old Wicklow house where I was staying, that let me
hear what was being said by the servant girls in the
kitchen."[11] Cousins was suggesting, with a little light cyn-
icism, that Synge was also listening in through a hole in the
floor to the conversation of the Kevanes.

Corca Dhuibhne was a lively fun-loving place in those
early years of the last century. At the drop of a hat people
broke into song or lined out for a dance. Jim describes one
such impromptu gathering, complete with the priest breaking up the dance as seems to have happened regularly. This
was a different dance, the dance of the young men and
women of the village:

On another such occasion at Ventry when an itiner-
ant piper (piccolo player) gave up an hour of a
Sunday afternoon to an extemporised roadside
dance, a barndoor was lifted off its hinges and made
a floor for the single and double dances, and a swept
stretch of roadside for the rinka fada (long dance),
for which a boy chose a partner by touching a girl's
boot with his own. A line of a dozen pair of dancers
in heavy boots made a great dust. But protest in the
guise of the parish priest approached. The dance had
ceased; but the recumbent barn door and fifer and
boys and girls standing shamefacedly in rows on
opposite sides of the road told what was afoot. A
domineering beefy voice in local Irish beyond my

little knowledge was followed by the dispersal of the assemblage and the departure of the fifer to the next engagement.[12]

Irish was the means of communication everywhere. Even the cow standing in the middle of the road wouldn't think of moving unless addressed in Irish. Cousins was impressed:

> Before I was forty eight hours established at Ventry I began to wonder what the Irish language "Revival" was. When you run through your stock of book-learned phrases to a small farmer at Cahirboilg, a quaint village on the slopes of Mount Eagle, and then have to fall back on the services of his Returned American daughter as interpreter because her father has not a word of English, then it should be Irish language "extension" rather than "revival".[13]

James and Eibhlín loved the area. They could not resist the spirit of the place. Always Cousins would remember the seductiveness of the sea, the soft eye of a lovely child or the twinkling humour and swinging grace of an old man.

He loved Sea View and the view from his upstairs room: "From my room I see from South to North West a line of hamlets whose names, said softly and with feeling are as a poem, Cahertrant, Raheen, Kilvicadownaig, Caherbuilg, Ballincota, Kildorrihey, Rahinane. Every name takes you into the heart of mystery, the wonderful mystery which is Ireland."[14] The names sound even more poetic in Irish: Cathair an Treantaigh, Na Ráithíní, Cill Mhic an Domhnaigh, Cathair Boilg, Baile an Chóta, Cill Uru and Ráthanáin.

Eibhlín, too, was enchanted by the place, but the more she saw, the more she wanted to go farther west to hear the pure, untouched Irish. She had been to Dún Chaoin and listened to the people working in the fields and walking the roads with their donkeys, and she wanted to go back there and hear a lot more. Also, the room in Sea View was needed for other visitors who had booked in for the thirteenth, Thomas H. Mason, a photographer, and his wife, Meta, from Dublin.

It would be an opportunity for her to get to meet the people at the very end of the peninsula. "On July 13th Miss Nicolls set out to find a settled abode farther away from 'civilisation' where nothing but Irish would be heard."[15]

Although Cousins with his *cúpla focal,* spoken with the aid of a manual, was happy with the Irish in Ventry, Eibhlín wanted to make a deeper study of the language, so she bade a fond farewell to the Kevanes, promising that she would see them all in some six weeks or so and booking to stay overnight on her return. She then got the loan of a horse and cart from Thady, and James and herself loaded up her bags on it. Before they moved off, James assembled his camera and took a photograph of Eibhlín sitting up in the cart ready to start the journey. It would be fun to show it to her friends when she returned to Dublin.

James accompanied her and the horse and cart around Slea Head on his bicycle. The other road, the mountain pass from Ventry to Dún Chaoin, across the Clasach, although much shorter, would have been too difficult for the horse.

Again it was a lovely day, great fishing weather, with most of the boats gone to sea. The soft dust rose from the road. *Airgead luachra* (meadowsweet) and *créachtach corcra* (purple loosestrife) sparkled in the hedges. The road wove through the little villages by the sea: Ard an Bhóthair, Cathair Boilg, Cill Mhic an Domhnaigh, Fán and Sean-Ghleann. The scene as they rounded Slea Head was breathtaking, the Blasket Islands like jewels in the ocean, the small white houses beckoning them. Seagulls wheeled and dived, and black choughs with red legs plunged over the cliffs to be caught by the upward surge of the breeze. Small black boats fished out by Beiginis and around the Seanduine.

Eibhlín thought that she would get lodgings with the Kavanaghs in Baile na Rátha in Dún Chaoin (no relation to Thady and Máire). Friends of hers who had stayed there the previous year had had a great time and had recommended it highly. The Kavanaghs, however, had their own worries. There had been a death in the family, and they were unable to help. The best they could do was offer them a mug of milk. Milk was still the drink to offer the stranger; tea had not yet taken over. Jim left Eibhlín in the Kavanagh home sipping the milk while he tried some other houses in the parish to see if anyone would have her, but without success. Almost all the houses were small, thatched and unsuitable for visitors, without the basic facilities, each family large. Dún Chaoin was not yet ready for tourists. Indeed, there were very few homes in the west of the peninsula geared for visitors at that time.

Cousins was finally directed to the home of the Máistir Ó Dálaigh, the local schoolmaster, known locally as "the Common Noun". The Máistir, too, was very involved in the language movement, and was, himself, a well-known writer, contributing to *An Claidheamh Soluis* and *An Lóchrann* and to the local *Kerry Sentinel*. He had played an important part in keeping the language alive, not alone in the parish of Dún Chaoin, but in Corca Dhuibhne as well. He had taught classes in Irish writing and reading way back in the 1880s, and together with the principal teacher in Ballyferriter, Mícheál Ó Mainín, was among the first to do so in Kerry, if not in Ireland.

He had a two-storied slated house beside the schoolhouse, the finest in the parish, with six windows to the front, and had kept visitors and language enthusiasts under the careful attention of his wife, Nóra (Narrie) Ní Mhurchú from Fán. Unfortunately, it was the height of the season, the house was full, and he was unable to accommodate Eibhlín. He spent a while talking before noticing the name "EIBHLÍN NIC NIOCAILL" engraved on the travelling trunk in the horse's cart. He realised then that the lady

Cousins was speaking of was one of the great people in the language movement, "a proper noun" rather than a "common noun" like himself. Such a pity to send such an eminent person away from the parish.

The Máistir thought there would be a place for her on the island, in the King's house, which had been specially adapted for visitors by the adding of an extension. He was related by marriage to the King himself and had often visited that house and stayed there on holidays, on one occasion after a hard year in the training college. The islanders were famed for their generosity to the stranger, be he an escapee from a shipwreck or a visitor coming to learn Irish. Moreover, he thought that a spell on the island would prove a unique experience for Eibhlín.

Up to this Eibhlín had no thought of going into the island and, since there was no room for her in Dún Chaoin, was on the point of returning to Ventry. Few women visitors had gone alone, especially to stay overnight on the island. There was still a cautious fear of the wild, Irish-speaking, strange and "uncivilised" people.

Eibhlín answered that she would love to go to the island.

The Máistir would have enjoyed going in himself (it's always *into* the island). The King's wife, who justifiably might be called the Queen, was a cousin of his. He was a good hand on the oars and had brought many to and from the island, including Synge himself in 1905 and Marstrander in 1907. It would have been a delightful way to spend the evening, to row into the island in the company of this young lady whose fame had gone before her. He could have a mug of tea in the King's house. There would be singing and dancing, and they would row home in the twilight. Unfortunately, he was otherwise engaged. Besides, all the boats had gone out fishing, and it seemed as though Eibhlín would have to return to Ventry after all. Just then he saw Seán Óg Kavanagh, his own godson, some distance away and hailed him. It was to his mother's house that Eibhlín had just come hoping for a room. Seán came across. He readily agreed to go in if someone else could be got to share the rowing.

Seán, himself wrote: "The day she came to Dún Chaoin there was no *naomhóg* crew; they were all out fishing. After a lot of searching I found a boy who was willing, and we two rowed her over. I have often since asked myself what fate was it that made us meet on the road that day and she on the point of leaving when she could not find any place to stay nor a boat to bring her over. Life is indeed strange."[16]

The weather was fine and the tide favourable. Two oarsmen would suffice, and Johnny, the Máistir's son, was willing. Seán Óg and Johnny could divide the few shillings fare between them. Doubtlessly they, and in particular Seán Óg, took stock of the handsome young lady, the same age as himself. Very seldom did such strange beauty arrive in this place far away west.

They went down to the cliff and down the arduous steep and twisting path to the *cé*, where the two men raised the *naomhóg* from the stage and lowered it into the sea. They helped Eibhlín down along the green slippery edge and into the *naomhóg*, making sure she sat in the centre so as not to upset it. The luggage was stored, the oars were grasped and the *naomhóg* set in gliding motion.

She called out and waved farewell to Cousins, who was still standing on the quayside. He shouted out and promised that Gretta and he would come and visit her on the island just as soon as she arrived from London and had a few days to settle down after her long trip.

"*Slán, a chailín álainn!* Goodbye, lovely girl!" he called over the waves. It was the first time he had let his guard slip. He couldn't say whether she heard him or not, but as though she had, she raised her head and gave him a last happy wave.

"*Slán is beannacht leat!*" the voice returned.

"I waited on the edge of the cliff until I saw the curragh across the heaving sound so that I could report her safe landing to her mother."[17]

He threw up the bicycle on the horse's cart and jogged away home again around Slea Head. "It was a beautiful evening, a rare thing in the broken weather of July – and the islands lay like fragments of a dream in the slanting rays of the sun setting across the Atlantic."[18]

It had been a very strange week, a week spent in close proximity to a beautiful young woman who shared his own interests, a week he would always remember, even as an old man.

Gretta arrived from London a few days later, having, in spite of herself, kept out of prison. They were happy to be together again. More walks followed, not as adventurous perhaps as those with Eibhlín, but there were compensations. There was a piano, an unusual adornment in those early days, in Bay View, Máistir Curran's guest house close by. Curran was the principal teacher in the nearby national school and had himself an active interest in the archaeological remains of Corca Dhuibhne. The neighbours gathered in for a night's entertainment by the fire with songs, dances and stories. Gretta, a very accomplished musician, played a suitable selection on the piano, both popular and classical. James, who was a fine singer, sang well, in his Northern accent, that song of Thomas Davis', "The West's Awake", popular among nationalists at the time:

> But hark! A voice like thunder spake,
> "The West's awake! The West's Awake!"
> Sing, Oh! Hurrah! Let England quake,
> We'll watch till death for Erin's sake!

There was more dancing, stories and chatting, and cups of tea and fresh home-made soda bread and jam. As the night drew to a close, all rose to go and wished each other good night and *"Slán abhaile"*.

James and Gretta walked back together to Sea View arm in arm. They went the roundabout way, up the Cathair Aird road, turned left and down the lane back to the main road to view the stars and hear the murmur of the sea. They had gone a short distance when Cooper Long overtook them and confided to them in an intimate whisper that he would like them to know that there were strong, faithful men in the parish of Ventry, willing and able to strike a blow against the Saxon when James would call for action to show that the West was really awake.

James smiled to himself in the dark. Little did he think it would ever come to that.

CHAPTER 4

# Not the Same to Go to the King's House as to Leave

*Ní mar a chéile Dul go Tigh an Rí agus Teacht as*

"The traveller should not miss Dunbeg Fort, a fine relic of the hero days of Irish history; the Blasket Islands in Dingle Bay, which are a law unto themselves, with a 'King' elected by the islanders"[1]

BOTH SEÁN ÓG and Johnny an Mháistir were fine boatmen who could ply the oars with great skill. They had youth on their side, a blue sky and the sun dancing in the waves, and a fine young woman as company. The trip was delightful. The *naomhóg* bounded along, dipping into a valley between two waves and then mounting a breaker to delve down into the deep valley again in mid Bealach. Part of the thrill of the trip was the knowledge that between you and the bottom of the great ocean was but a thin skin of tarred canvas.

As the mainland drifted away and the dark bulk of the island bore down on them, they could see, tucked into the hill, the houses with their black felt roofs and turf smoke rising from the chimneys. Although it was warm, the supper had still to be cooked over the fire.

The Blasket Islands are a scattering of seven islands that grass grows on, but the biggest of them, An Blascaod Mór

64

or the Great Blasket, was the only one still inhabited in 1909. Three others, where people had once lived, had been abandoned. It is really a huge rock in the sea, three miles from Dún Chaoin, three miles long and one mile wide. The only village nestled above the beach and below the hill on the southern end of the island. There is little or no shelter from the ocean gales with the sea battering against its edges unceasingly. In that year, 1909, there were twenty-eight homesteads on the island, housing about 150 souls. Nine family names shared the island:

| | |
|---|---|
| Ó Súilleabháin | 4 families |
| Ó Dálaigh | 1 family |
| Ó Conchubhair | 1 family |
| Ó Sé | 3 families |
| Ó Guithín | 5 families |
| Ó Duinnshléibhe | 2 families |
| Ó Cearnaigh | 5 families |
| Ó Criomhthain | 1 family |
| Ó Catháin | 6 families.[2] |

It would be romantic to think that the then community had been established there since time immemorial, but that wasn't the case. Every family there could trace their roots to the mainland. A great many had come to the island from 1750–1780, mostly because it promised a better life than that on the mainland. There was turf, rabbits and sheep on the hill, the grass of a cow or two per family in the low land near the village, and plenty of fish in the surrounding seas. Their biggest worry was to get enough money to pay the rent to Lord Cork, a difficult task, but they solved that problem. Any boat that dared to approach the island to collect rent, or to take away the cows in lieu of rent, was met with a shower of stones from the overhanging cliffs, some of them big enough not alone to injure the attackers but to hole the boat, and so leave the intruders in a very precarious position. There were many stories of incursions like that, most of them ending with victory to the islanders.

They came through the famine intact, though the number of families had declined from twenty-eight to seventeen and population had fallen from 153 to 97.

The tradition is that nobody had died of starvation. That was in a big way due to the activities of Mrs Thompson and the Irish Missionary Society. A ship had also run aground in 1850 loaded with wheat, which when dried out could be ground for making bread and porridge, enough to keep the life in a body.

Irish was the language of the community, with scarcely a word of English from the youngest child going to school to the oldest sitting by the fire. The livelihood of the islanders was almost entirely fishing, with the exception of the schoolmaster and schoolmistress. The seas were fished both night and day for lobster, crawfish, mackerel and herring, which they sold to the fish-buyers in Dingle, and pollock and connor fish which they used for their own food.

The greater majority had also a small patch of land for a cow and a couple of sheep. A patch of potatoes and some vegetables were cultivated, as well as a patch of oats. Most families had a donkey to help in the field and for drawing home the turf from the hill in panniers. Around the house one could see a goat, hens, ducks and geese and a couple of dogs.

The menfolk had just emerged from what could best be described as a communal drinking problem. Given the circumstances of the life on the island, it is easy to see how such a problem could develop. It was rare for them to get their hands on alcohol. In most of the towns and villages around, including Valentia and Caherciveen, they were recognised, and the word went out to give them only one drink, as two could easily set them drunk. As early as 1892, Jeremiah Curtin, the folklore collector, went there expecting to find an untapped reservoir of stories and lore, but was disappointed:

> At the island we entered a cove similar to the one on
> the mainland. A curious, busy scene was before us.

We climbed to the top of the cliff, and there was the village, perhaps 20 straw thatched cabins, the thatch held in place by a network of straw ropes fastened down with stones. In front of each cabin was a pile of manure. Cattle are kept in the cabin nights. Each morning the earth floor is cleaned by shovelling out the straw, but it is not taken far from the house. It accumulates all winter, and in the spring is carried to the potato fields. The schoolhouse is the best building on the island. It has windows, and the outside walls were whitewashed.

Kate, our faithful servant, found the cleanest house on the island and asked of its mistress the privilege of boiling a kettle of water to make tea. The wind blew so hard that a fire could not be built outside. She made the tea, but we did not sit inside to drink it; the house was too dirty. I asked a man on crutches if he knew any Gaelic myths. His answer was, "I care more about getting the price of a bottle of whisky than about old stories." Another man said: "If you give me the price of a bottle of whisky, I'll talk about stories." I got no stories.[3]

The problem must have continued on and grown even more serious. Drinking bouts had to take place on the mainland, after which they had to row back into the island with drink taken, with all the accompanying dangers, as observed by Synge in 1905:

Some time afterwards, when a number of young men had come in, as was usual, to spend the evening, someone said a niavogue was on its way home from the sports. We went out to the door, but it was too dark to see anything except the lights of a little steamer that was passing up the sound, almost beneath us, on its way to Limerick or Tralee. When it had gone by we could hear a furious drunken uproar coming up from a canoe that was somewhere out in the bay. It sounded as if the men were strangling or murdering

> each other, and it seemed almost miraculous that they
> should be able to manage their canoe. The people
> seemed to think they were in no special danger . . .[4]

It was Fr Liam O'Connor, who spent little more than a
year (August 1906–November 1907) as curate in the
parish, who finally straightened them out, making them all
take the pledge. The result was an improvement both in
the general appearance of the place as well as in the standard of living for themselves, their wives and families.

Of course, there were stories. The long winter nights
were shortened by stories, many which went back in the
communal mind for generations. There were the heroic
stories about Fionn Mac Cumhaill and the Fianna, tales of
the history of the locality, such as tales of Piaras Feiritéar
and the Earl of Desmond, and a vast store of religious,
magical and romantic tales.

As the boat from Dún Chaoin drew in, there was a
group of islanders waiting on the Deck, as they called the
raised land above the quay, watching the approaching
*naomhóg,* to see if there was anyone interesting coming to
visit. The young men looked out for new strange girls from
the mainland or from Dingle, and the girls looked out
equally for strange young men, who would provide variety
for as long as they remained. They were fed up looking at
their own girls, and, conversely, the girls were equally fed
up looking at the same boys the whole winter. Then there
were the children, shy and barefooted. Their interest was
in sweets. Hopefully any stranger would also bring a bag
of sweets to be shared out among them. They crowded
around Eibhlín, examining her person and her fine clothes.
The men were there also, standing aside shyly with their
caps and navy blue fishermen's ganseys.

Eibhlín was led to the King's house and her luggage
followed.

They did succeed in getting lodgings for Eibhlín in
Peats Mhicí's (Pádraig Ó Catháin), the King's house, the
same house in which Synge had stayed some five years

previously and immortalised in his book, *In Wicklow and West Kerry*.

Almost all the houses were roofed with tarred felt by this time, instead of the earlier thatch. This was such an improvement, as the thatch roofs had to be repaired regularly and were always in danger of being blown out to the sea in a gale. Peats Mhicí had added an extension to his house for visitors. There was a felt roof on it, complete with a fireplace and a fine window facing out to the ocean with a view of Dún Chaoin, Mount Eagle and Cruach Mhárthan across the Bealach. His was the first house on the island to keep visitors. The new room doubled up as a classroom for those such as Marstrander and later Robin Flower, who were taught there by the Islandman himself, Tomás Ó Criomhthain.

When the rowers had partaken of refreshment and listened to a few tunes on the fiddle, they set out again to row home across the straits. Eibhlín waved them goodbye from the Deck above the pier where she could watch them until they disappeared out of view.

\* \* \* \* \* \*

From the moment Eibhlín set foot on the island, she felt at home, and it didn't take long for her to get to know the people, both young and old. The King's daughter, Cáit an Rí, remembered her many years after at the nightly gatherings in the island homes at the storytelling, the music and the dancing: "At all the gatherings Eibhlín was the life and soul of the party. She was so light on her feet, a withered leaf would not be crumpled by her."[5]

The year 1909 was a good one on the island. The people had become owners of their land since 1907 when the Congested Districts Board had bought the holdings from the landowner, the Earl of Cork, for £500. The land was theirs now, and as Seán Ó Criomhthain, the son of the Islandman, said: "Bess and Clara were under the sod and the young Island people were dancing with music on their own native sod. So turn the great wheels of the world."[6] (Bess and Clara were two notorious land agents of Lord Ventry and the Earl of Cork from earlier, tougher times.)

Seven children were born on the Blaskets in that year, one being Máire Ní Ghuithín, or Máire Mhaidhc Léan, named from her father Maidhc and grandmother Léan. The fishing was good and the market demand was good. There were five new houses being completed by the Congested Districts Board on the Sleán Bán. There were twenty-nine houses and between 150 and 160 people living there. The school was thriving and had lately been upgraded to a two-teacher school.

Mrs Méiní Dunleavy remembered Eibhlín's arrival on the island, and told Mícheál Ó Gaoithín, Peig Sayers' son, years later: "I was a good while married on the island when the noble lady, Eibhlín Nic Niocaill, came on holiday to the island. She was a great scholar. She was not in any way standoffish or ostentatious but a gentle girl."[7]

She soon got to know the Cathánaigh, the King's family, the father, mother and the young ones, Cáit and Seán. They had another son, Maidhc, but he had gone to America a few years previously; and then there was Máire (Synge's "Little Hostess" who was the model for Pegeen Mike in *The Playboy of the Western World*), who was married to Mícheál Ó Guithín and lived next door. Synge had been attracted to her when he visited in 1905. At that time she had taken care of him in her father's house. Now she had two or three young children, including the baby, Máire, who had been born on the ninth of last June.

Cáit, later known as "Cáit an Rí", or "the Princess", became very friendly with Eibhlín. The Blasket people spoke of Eibhlín as "*an* Lady" on account of the fashionable clothes she wore, something entirely new to the Blasket girls who had never seen the likes before. She was the first lady visitor to have spent any time with them since way back, when Mrs Thompson had visited them in an attempt to make them change their religion back in the days of the famine.

Eibhlín found joy and satisfaction in everything: the evening *céilithe* down at the sandbanks, the chats by the fire, the Irish, and her own writing in Irish. It must have been a great joy to her to experience the island ways, the lack of hurry and pressure and the courtesy practised by all. Thomas Mason, who visited the island on a few occasions around that time, remembered:

> In some of the inhabited islands of Ireland, in an especial degree in the Aran and Blasket Islands, I have found a courtesy that is impossible to describe; the inhabitants may now be peasants, but they are remnants of ancient races and are gentlefolk in the literal and highest meaning of that phrase . . . The visitor must not make the error of mistaking natural courtesy for a sense of inferiority; it is widely different, in fact I would go so far as to say that the inferiority complex would be with the visitor. If he repays courtesy with courtesy and respects the islandman as one man should respect another, he will have nothing but pleasant memories and will learn much. If, on the other hand, he feels and shows a sense of superiority, he will have a dull time and learn nothing. These people "size one up" very accurately, and if they feel that you are attempting to patronise them the door is closed.[8]

She would spend long periods sitting on the sandbanks staring out to sea at the waves as they came in breaking on the beach or pounding against the rocks. She might walk to the hill with a young group bringing home the turf in the panniers. There were up to thirty donkeys on the island, but the absence of any wheeled vehicles had the effect of a peaceful silence. She visited the Tráigh Bhán a few times every day and walked up and down. The women gathered at Tobar an Phoncáin (the Yank's Well) every morning to fill the water pails. They stood there waiting their turn, chatting and laughing like, as Tomás describes them, "a flock of coloured birds". The men might gather there, too, to fill their buckets or copper sprayers to mix bluestone to spray on the potatoes for fear of the dreaded blight. They, too, could be easily recognised, not by their colours, but by the fog of blue smoke that rose from their pipes. Eibhlín met them all and stopped for a while, joking and chatting. The weather was fine and she took to swimming, unusual for girls in the narrow moral climate of Ireland at the time. Soon she started teaching swimming to the island girls on the White Strand. Even though most of the men and boys could swim across the mouth of the strand from side to side, this was unknown for island girls at the time. It was to strike another blow for the freedom of women that Eibhlín wanted them to be able to swim.

Women swimming on the beach did not go unnoticed by the young, and not so young, men in the sandbanks above. Tomás Ó Criomhthain, who above all the islanders wrote with the courage and confidence to tell of life as it was, described one such occasion when twelve young women went swimming on the Tráigh Bhán and Tomás watched from his work in the field:

> The twelve threw off what clothes they were wearing and appeared just as they were born, and I could take in my fist to Cork all that was left covering them. The four big girls rushed into the sea first, and because they were of age, I can tell you, they had fine arses. Off they went swimming just like porpoises.
>
> As they were coming in, one of the big girls was stooping clearing the sand from her feet. Just as the girls were passing her one of them gave a slap of her palm on her bottom which sounded as loud as the ship's siren which we heard earlier on in the day.[9]

Girls had a good happy life on the island before the responsibilities of married life and motherhood were placed on them:

And then during the Summer they used be very happy, working away. Sometimes they had to spread the manure on the fields. The men had to go fishing, and the girls had a great life. All they had to do was go on the hill and bring home a load of turf. They used be singing together as they went on the hill. They thought the Summer would never come till the strangers would come visiting, because there would be dances in the houses and on the Sandbank. They had a fine life as long as there were people on the island, even in the winter when they would be going from Peig's house to Peats Tom's . . . or the Dáil. Sometimes we would be playing cards or marbles, and we often used to rise up against each other.[10]

In the summer twilight there would be dances in the houses or down by the cliff out by Cuas Dall away from the watchful eyes of the parents. The island people entered into the set dancing with gay abandon. The Dálaighs, the Sullivans and the Keanes were master musicians on the fiddle. Tomás describes such a night:

There was four types of music there and seven different dances, all held in the Gaelic manner. There were songs sung there the finest ever sung. It was no wonder, for there was the sound of the ocean, the echo of the cliffs and the sound of the voice rising over the hill . . . it was like a small Oireachtas. It was seldom to find so many people together and to have no blackguard among them. But neither a foot nor hand was raised against anyone until everything was over.[11]

Cáit an Rí had many happy memories of those days with Eibhlín, as Imelda Hallahan wrote in 1914:

But the picture of Eibhlín I liked best was when Cáit described how one morning she stood outside the cottage, throwing handfuls of crumbs to the seagulls as they swept in over the headlands. "She was laughing:

she called to me to come out; the gulls were causing an awful noise as they swooped down; she pointed out one big fellow with his beak open and he beating his wings to scare the others off. I remember her words to this day – 'Look Cáit, he is a bully, he wants the whole world for himself, even in his world there is that sort of thing, the strong crushing the weak, until a day come when the weak will unite and take their rightful heritage' – as she finished, she flicked the tea-towel at him, and he rose squalking into the air.' " In a long sigh Cáit finished, "A Ghealla, my brightness, for that is what she had become to my days."[12]

Back in Ventry, Cousins wrote: "Reports of the doings of the 'Lady of the Blasket' reached me at intervals. It was clear that she was happy and that the people had grown to love her."[13]

A trip was made to the Tiaracht, a sharp rock on which the lighthouse clings, some six miles from the main island. It was a special treat for the young island fishermen and their girls to row out there on a day trip on fine days in summer. They would be given a tour of the rock and have a session of card playing. Their names were recorded in the guests' book in the lighthouse, their signature acting as a disclaimer in case of accident. Eibhlín and the islanders signed their names: Eibhlín *as Gaeilge* and the islanders all in English.

Great indeed was the sport and joy on the island: "Every Sunday *naomhóga* used come from the South, from the parish of Ventry, from Dún Chaoin, from the North, Baile an Chalaidh and Cuas na nAe and they would stay here dancing until the day was dawning."[14]

Others to visit the island from time to time included the people from Uíbh Ráthach, the next eastern peninsula, from Valentia Island to Caherciveen. They often came in on Sundays and other days in the summer and were very welcome. Tomás himself liked to see them, echoes perhaps of family connections with that peninsula way back. They always brought sweets and fruit like bananas and oranges for the children, and they spoke beautiful Irish. The islanders used to visit Caherciveen from time to time also, selling rabbits and fish. Blasket rabbits were very popular with the Uíbh Ráthach people. The islanders enjoyed the trips to Valentia and to Caherciveen even more than a trip to Dingle.

And as far as Irish was concerned, Fíonán Mac Coluim said in the year 1905: "I would say that the place is as Gaelach today as it was in the time of Piaras Feiritéar . . . there are none, be they young or old but speak fine rich Irish."[15]

Small wonder Eibhlín enjoyed this land of magic. She confided to Cáit an Rí, "As long as I live, I will return here."[16]

There was no resident priest on the island. If there was a priest visiting or on holidays there, they would have Sunday mass in the school. Otherwise those who were able, mostly the menfolk, would row out to the mainland to mass in Dún Chaoin, weather permitting, while those remaining at home said the rosary in the school. There were not enough *naomhóga* to carry everybody, so usually the women and children remained at home. Mass was celebrated at the very late hour of twelve, midday, to give the islanders a chance to row across the Sound. So it was on Sunday, 8 August.

The morning was fine, so the islanders, men and a few women, and Eibhlín, in five or six *naomhóga* crossed over the waves to mass. They made their way in a scattered group from the cliff top down the winding road through Baile Ícín to the church at the bottom of the Gleann Mór, some half a mile away. There the people were hurrying in, having come from Ceathrú and Com Dhíneol, men on horses, women and children walking, and old women in donkeys and carts. Some of the menfolk waited outside talking until the priest arrived on horseback. The islanders waited out at the cemetery also, Eibhlín among them, chatting. As the priest began the mass, they all crowded into the sturdy little chapel, built in 1857. With a mixture of shyness and fear of enclosed spaces, it was the custom of the island people to remain at the back of the church. Eibhlín went further up, but instead of going to the women's side as was the custom for women at the time, she went among the men on the right side of the church. People looked at each other. That was something that had never before been seen in Dún Chaoin chapel.

Eibhlín was active in the women's movement. That and the Irish language movement often vied for her attention. She wrote an article in *An Bhan-Ghaodhal* in February 1909, in perfect Irish:

> The other day I was speaking to a friend, one of those who believes that we should neglect everything else until we would have achieved success in the women's cause and she asked me to go to a meeting to support that aim. I told her that I was unable to attend as I had to be at another meeting that night about Irish in the National University.
>
> "Ah," says she, "you are no different than many of the women of this country; you have more interest in other matters than in the women's fight! But I tell you one thing, we will never get justice unless we leave other matters aside until we solve this problem."
>
> I told her that it was my opinion that the women who were working for the Irish movement were also working well for the women's cause, and that I was certain that the men whom we were helping now would see justice done to our cause as soon as it was within their power.

She did, however, waver in her conviction and faith in men occasionally:

> When the night of the two meetings arrived and I was there among the Gaeil I happened to be talking to three or four men, and one of them drew down

the way that women were rising up all over the world.

"If so," says one of the men, "that doesn't affect us. Our Irish women are too womanly to be trying to get votes and the likes."

I objected, but not one man there agreed with me.

"Maybe," says I to myself, "that I am at the wrong meeting."[17]

During the mass in Dún Chaoin, James and Gretta Cousins arrived but remained outside until mass was over. Gretta then chose a high bank at the edge of the cemetery with a good view of the emerging congregation, and mounting the bank, she addressed them in English on the subject of the universal franchise.

"Fellow Irishmen and women," she began, and then continued on about such subjects as "justice and freedom", "natural rights" and the like. The people, particularly the men, gathered around listening because the like had never been seen before, a woman speechifying. Her speeches, though, were always well received, being vivid, fiery, forthright and never too long. She never indulged in rabble rousing.

There were few present who had any idea of what she was saying, but that she considered them worthy of her words was, in its own way, a compliment to them. Eibhlín busied herself distributing badges to everyone, and they were delighted to pin them to their jackets and shawls.

The Cousins had come to meet Eibhlín, but Gretta could not miss the opportunity to speak to these, the most western people in Europe, the women of which, she considered, should be part of and would add greatly to the great equality movement. Cousins, though giving full support to Gretta, rarely got involved himself in her protests. As she was speaking, the priest, having divested himself, arrived out from the sacristy and approached Cousins to ask what was going on when he saw the badge pinned to his jacket – "VOTES FOR WOMEN!" He disappeared quickly, declaring that surely the end of the world was nigh when the day had arrived that the women had forsaken the home and faced the public life. Women speaking in public could not and should not be encouraged. And as for voting rights, you never know where they might stop.

The people of Ventry and Dún Chaoin had something to talk about that night by the fires.

As soon as Gretta had finished and the people had dispersed to their little thatched cabins, James, Gretta, Eibhlín and the Blasket people called into Kavanaghs' house, which was on the way back to the quay. This was Seán Óg's home, and a shop besides, where sugar, tea, candles soap and flour could be bought. Máire Sheosaimh de hÓra, the woman of the house, had a special affection for the Blasket people. Her brother Seán from Cloichear had married one of the Dálaigh sisters from Inis Mhic Uíleáin, one of the small Blaskets. She was married to Seán Kavanagh, whom everyone knew as Seán Dhomhnaill or, even more so, as Nack, as it was said he had the knack of hiding whiskey from the excisemen. There was never an island person let go from that house without a cup of tea, a mug of milk or better. Her home was a favourite stopping place for everyone, especially the islanders. Her fame spread far and wide as a woman with a great heart whose main aim in life was to help her fellow travellers through life. When she died, the beggars of Kerry arrived from all quarters to attend her funeral, which, it was said, was four miles long. One beggar arrived, having got out of his sick bed to attend. "I couldn't miss Máire Sheosaimh's funeral," he announced to everyone.

It was while they were at Máire Sheosaimh's that Eibhlín asked Gretta and Jim to come in to visit her and spend an evening on the island. They both thought this a good idea, so it was arranged there and then with Seán Óg that he and one or two other rowers would row them in on the following Friday, the thirteenth, weather permitting.

Then they all walked together back to the slip, talking

and laughing, the island girls stopping here and there to pick early blackberries at the roadside, a delicacy not to be had on the island. They went down the steep winding way to the water's edge. Eibhlín entered the bobbing *naomhóg*, oars were splashed, and she bade farewell to the Cousins. They watched and waved as the men heaved and the black *naomhógs* disappeared into the waves. Gretta, as everyone did, had taken to Eibhlín, even in the short time they had spent together. Both Gretta and James looked forward to the trip to the Blaskets and to meeting Eibhlín again on the following Friday. Gretta intended, if possible, to address the islanders, the women in particular, on the subject of the franchise for women. Didn't they have the same right to the vote as the women of Dublin or Dingle? True, she would have the problem of language, but Eibhlín would be able to translate her words into Irish.

*＊ ＊ ＊ ＊ ＊ ＊*

The annual Oireachtas and Ard-Fheis, the main gathering of the Gaelic League, took place during that very week in the Rotunda in Dublin. Eibhlín should have been there herself but chose to remain on in the Blaskets. *An Claidheamh Soluis* remarked on the fact on 14 August: "Eibhlín Nic Niocaill has been elected a member of the Executive Committee (Coiste Gnó) of the Gaelic League. She was on the Great Blasket during the Ard-Fheis. She stayed in the King's Court while there."[18]

Her election to office was a great achievement, not only as a woman, but also as the youngest ever to have been elected to that committee of four women and eleven men. It is difficult for us today to understand the importance of the Gaelic League at that time. The main driving force of the Irish nation, it would within a few years become the main instrument for the achieving of complete independence from Britain. It was a tragic irony that she died before receiving the news that would have been the high point of her career.

CHAPTER 5

# The Gift of Patience

## *Grásta na Foighne*

TOMÁS Ó CRIOMHTHAIN had been a widower since his wife's untimely death in 1904. He came to be known as An tOileánach, the same name as the book which made him famous both in Ireland and over the seas. But that would be far into the future. Although he had had in all a dozen in family, by 1909 his family had been reduced to seven: Pádraig, Eibhlín, Tomás, Cáit, Domhnall, Muiris and Seán. Seán, the youngest son, wrote: "It was in my uncle's house that this girl stayed, and what do you think, but didn't my sister, Cáit, get to know and become friendly with her, so much so that the two of them used be coming and going everywhere together. This new girl got to know our Domhnall as well, and she used be on hill and mountain in his company."[1]

It adds greatly to the romance of the story to speculate that Eibhlín and Domhnall were in love, and there are stories in the island folklore that Domhnall said to Máire Uí Ghuithín on Friday morning, "She is my woman, be she dead or alive." But it is generally conceded that if there was love, it was unrequited on Eibhlín's part. Domhnall was only eighteen while Eibhlín was twenty-four. As Méiní later told of them:

> In those days there was a young boy on the island whose name was Domhnall Criomhthain. He used always be playing tricks on Eibhlín, whatever notice

he took of her above other island boys. Eibhlín was delighted with this young lad and used take him with her to the top of the strand so that she could be learning the Irish from him. She understood him better than his sister Cáit who would always be with them and another girl who was related to them whose name was Cáit Ní Chatháin. She would not go on hill or strand without having him with her. The noble lady became friendly with them for as long as she would be among them, but God knows, that wasn't to be long. She would not go on hill or strand without these three, and like children, they took to her and they loved the kind mentality she had and they went everywhere together. It's often Domhnall would say that he would never have any other woman but her.

"I'm happy with that," she would say, half jokingly.[2]

On the Thursday Seán Óg cycled from Dún Chaoin over the Clasach to Ventry to the Cousins. He explained that he thought that the following day would be suitable for their trip and that they should be back in Dún Chaoin ready to sail around one in the afternoon. He also explained that Fíonán Mac Coluim would join them on the trip. Seán is remembered as being the first local to have a bicycle, bought with money earned by rowing visitors into the island.

A fine day dawned on the Friday, 13 August. The sea was calm. Every rock was black. The *naomhóga* went out to their lobster fishing into the rosy dawn. Tomás went out with his brother, Paddy, who had been fishing with him since his arrival back from the States. Paddy had been a great support to him and had helped him over the loss of his wife. He was also a great worker. They had fixed up a small *naomhóg* between them and had taken to fishing lobsters with twenty pots. "It would do your heart good," Tomás tells us, "to see us ploughing the waves." While some of the boats went farther from home, to the little

Blaskets – An Tiaracht, Inis Tuaisceart and Inis Mhic Uíleáin – Tomás and his brother fished close to home, around Beginish, so they could be home for the morning meal, the potatoes in the early afternoon and the evening meal.

Affairs has taken a turn for the better for Tomás: "Tomás was very happy at that time. There was nothing in the world he needed. As you might say, 'everything was going his way.' Indeed it's often he said afterwards that it was three times worse to be knocked from the top of the ladder than from half way up. And he knew, if anyone did."[3]

His son, Seán, afterwards remembered those days: "So it was that Tomás used spend the lobster season. Gone at five in the morning, come home about one o'clock in the day and away again between three and four and home about nine at night."[4]

All the *naomhóga* had gone that fine day, and only the women, the old folks and the young people remained behind. Domhnall Ó Criomhthain didn't go fishing that day. He stayed minding the family and doing the daily chores.

Eibhlín spent the morning walking around the village, calling into the houses or stopping to chat with the old men sitting outside their doors in the sunshine. Then she went to her room in the King's house and translated a poem from German. She wrote two letters, one to her brother George in Galway, and another to Jasper in Argentina. The letter to George contained the translation of a poem by Heine from the German that she had just made:

> I enclose a translation that I have made of a German poem by Heine. It is almost word for word and is in the metre of the original.
>
> > *Thug buachaill óg grá do chailín;*
> > *D'fhear eile thug sise a croí,*
> > *Ba chuma leis-sean ise,*
> > *Agus phós sé cailín nach í.*

*Bhí stuaic ar an gcailín, is phós sí,*
*An chéad fhear bhuail uirthi, ochón!*
*Níorbh é an buachaill thug grá di,*
*Is fágadh eisean fé bhrón.*

*Sean-scéal sea an scéal seo,*
*Ach cia déarfadh nach bhfuil sé nua?*
*Is an té go dtiteann amach air,*
*Ní lúide, más sean a chumha.*[5]

She signed the letters and laid them aside to give to the King, the island postman, who, as it was Friday, would be going out to the mainland later with the post. There was a postal service on Tuesdays and Fridays.

About one o'clock a patchy fog slowly descended and wrapped the island in a soft, thick, grey blanket. Yet both the sea and the weather remained quiet with scarcely a breeze. This can happen in the summer when it becomes so warm that a fog falls on the island and the coast all around, while a mile or so inland the weather could still be clear and sunny.

This was the time that she usually went swimming with the island girls, but she had put off the swim because she was expecting the Cousins. Outside her window the mainland could not be seen, though in patches the sun shone brightly through the mist. It was still warm with no breath of wind, and the sea could be heard clearly as the little waves broke on the sand.

Meanwhile, out in Dún Chaoin, the Cousins had arrived, having cycled and walked across the Clasach from Ventry. They called to the Kavanagh house to meet Seán Óg, as arranged. They took with them a box of oranges and bananas that had been sent by Eibhlín's mother in Dublin to Kavanagh's house with the request that they be delivered to Eibhlín when they would be going into the island. The mother had been anxious about her daughter's diet and thought that the addition of fruit would help to balance the island fare of potatoes, fish and rabbit, with occasionally mutton from the island sheep. They probably were given a cup of milk and a piece of bread there in Máire Sheosaimh's generous home. Seán Óg joined them with one of his brothers. When they arrived at the quay, Fíonán Mac Coluim, an old friend of the islanders, was there waiting, intending to spend a few days on the island.

They had no intention of letting the fog stop them, especially as the sea looked calm and gentle. The young men thought themselves experienced seamen and knew the course well. They raised the *naomhóg* from the stage and carried it down on their shoulders to the water's edge. The three passengers were helped in and placed in the most suitable places to keep the craft balanced. They pushed off, heaved the oars and disappeared into the mist. The fog seemed to become denser. There was no view of the surrounding islands or cliffs, though there were patches of bright sunlight here and there.

Seán Óg, or Seán an Chóta as he would be later known, was to write much later, "As we approached the island a thick blanket of fog lay on the water, though the sun was shining brilliantly through the fog in patches."[6]

They began singing, Jim entertaining them with his fine tenor voice that carried across the quiet waves. He sang the "Lament for Owen Roe", one of Ireland's great heroes of the seventeenth century, of whom much was expected, but was taken away in an untimely death:

Oh, black breaks the morrow in tempest and gloom,
When we bear to our sorrow Owen Roe to the tomb.

In on the island Eibhlín waited and wondered and finally came to the conclusion that the fog was too heavy and that her friends had not sailed. Maybe tomorrow or Sunday, which was Assumption Day, a traditional day for visiting the island. She decided, since it was not cold, to go swimming to the Tráigh Bhán with her friends and give them some more instruction. Taking her swimming gear, she went out as far as Cáit an Rí's house. Imelda Hallahan recounted the story Cáit told her in 1969: "Eibhlín wrote to Dublin for a swimsuit for Cáit. When the parcel arrived there was great excitement. The floor of the kitchen was littered with wrapping paper and twine. How Eibhlín laughed at Cáit's remarks, 'It would be the pity of the world to get sea water on that; the salt of the sea would fade the colour.' "[7]

Cáit, however, had a toothache and did not feel like swimming, but she said she would go to the beach with her.

They called into the Guithín household, and Eibhlín took Máire Uí Ghuithín's tiny baby, Máire, not yet three months old, in her arms from the cradle and was playing and cooing to her. They then went to the Criomhthain house and told Cáit they were going to the strand. Cáit an Rí gave her new swimsuit to Cáit Criomhthain, who was just twenty years of age. There was another young girl, Máire Ní Chatháin, fifteen years of age, who also came along. The four of them set off merrily from the village, down Port an Eidhneáin, arm in arm, as was the custom with the island girls, skipping and laughing down to the beach. It was about a quarter to two by the few island clocks. Soon the fishermen would be arriving at the quay to go up to their homes for the potatoes, fish and new milk.

"On a fine day in the month of August Eibhlín Nic Niocaill dropped in to my sister, Cáit, and they went together down to the White Strand, and out they went swimming. They were a little out in the water screaming in fun at first, but it wasn't long till mocking came to catching," Seán said years later.[8]

Méiní, remembering back sadly, gave a slightly different version of events:

> A fine day came at the end of summer and you would think that such a beautiful calm morning was far from any harm doing to anyone who might be lying on the bright sand sunning themselves with the fine sun that shone on land and ocean spreading joy and happiness in all sides. But it is near to hand that harm arrives, God save us. Eibhlín went on the

strand sunning herself. She had no desire to swim. No indeed. She had a cold. But in case she would she had brought her swimsuit with her and an air tube. She used have that when she was teaching the girls how to swim.

When the two other girls saw Eibhlín walking down the top of the strand on the edge of the waves, down with them after her through the fields down to the strand. . .

A soft fresh fog began to come in from the sea, and in the space of a minute not a bit of the island could be seen, but through this summer fog the sun could be seen shining and the weather beautiful.[9]

The three undressed at the Cloch Fhada and ran down Cúltráigh an Fhíona. The houses could not be seen from that point as it was under the cliff. The sea was so quiet that scarcely was there a wave big or small breaking on the strand. The three entered the water at about 2.45 P.M. They began to splash about for a while before Eibhlín started teaching Cáit Ní Chriomhthain by the edge of the water using the air tube as an aid. After a while she told Cáit to go in on the strand and she herself went out into the deeper water. Máire Ní Chatháin just went in a short distance, and she didn't stay in long.

Cáit an Rí gave an account a few days later to *An Claidheamh Soluis*, probably speaking to the editor, Pearse himself:

> Eibhlín would go other days swimming alone. She said today that it was not enjoyable to go swimming alone and that she would like to have others along. She asked me to come along. I went to the strand with her, but I had a toothache and would not go out into the water. On our way we asked two other girls, Cáit Criomhthain and Máire Ní Chatháin to come along, and they did. Eibhlín and the two girls went into the water and I stayed on the strand watching. About

2.15 we left the house and it would have been at least 2.45 before they entered the water.[10]

Máire Ní Chatháin didn't go far out. Eibhlín was showing Cáit Ní Chriomhthain how to swim, and Cáit was making a good attempt at it.

> Suddenly a wave knocked Cáit Criomhthain. The water entered her mouth and she began to scream. Cáit an Rí who was on the strand reading a book called out to Eibhlín to come to her aid. Eibhlín came back in to help Cáit.
>
> It was then that the tragedy happened. Cáit grabbed Eibhlín and tore off her swimming cap. Eibhlín had long hair which fell down on her face and she was unable to do anything. Both girls began to drown.
>
> "O, Cáit, come out and help us," Eibhlín screamed again and again. Cáit was almost losing her mind on the strand. She scarcely could swim herself yet, and although they were not far out, they were still too far out for her to get any grip on them – and the tide was bearing them away. She was shouting at the very top of her voice.[11]

Watching all that was enfolding before her eyes was Cáit Bhán Ní Chonchubhair, the schoolmistress from Cill Mhic an Domhnaigh across the Bealach, who was on a visit to her relations, the Criomhthains. She was sitting on Rinn na Sileach knitting a stocking. She raced down to the water's edge and stretched her shawl out to Cáit an Rí, who was in the water trying to catch Eibhlín. Cáit caught the shawl and tried to throw it out as far as she could to Eibhlín, and though it went very close to her fingertips the sweep of the water bore it away before she could grab it.

Cáit an Rí remembered:

> Eibhlín and the two girls went into the water and I stayed on the strand watching them . . . Máire Ní Chatháin didn't go out too far. Eibhlín was showing

Cáit Criomhthain how to swim, and Cáit would make a good attempt at it . . . They had been in the water about twenty minutes when everything went wrong.

Cáit Criomhthain was further out than Eibhlín at this time, and whatever happened to her she began to scream. Eibhlín swam out to her and they became stuck in each other. Eibhlín never succeeded in bringing her in or in reaching the ground. Eibhlín's hair became entangled in her mouth. I saw Domhnall Ó Criomhthain, Cáit's brother, running down towards the place at his best. I went into the water as far as my waist. It seemed to me that the girl was no more than about five feet away from me, but I knew that it was no use for me to go out any farther when I felt the water catching my clothes. The boy stopped me from going out further. He did not take off his boots or trousers or anything else but plunged into the water between the two girls, and they became entangled in each other. The boy went down under the water. Eibhlín kept afloat just a few minutes afterwards when she went under the water. I lost my mind then in the way that I didn't know what was happening after that.[12]

Cáit an Rí told Risteárd Ó Glaisne years afterwards, "Without any delay Domhnall Criomhthain was on the strand. He was trying to get his boots off.

"You have no time to take off your boots," says Cáit to him, "they will be drowned if you do not go to them at once," and he plunged into the sea, boots and all.[13]

By this time Méiní, whose house was near the strand and who had heard the screams, had run to the top of the cliff where she could see what was happening:

They were down by the edge of the waves when I was coming from the field with potatoes for the dinner.

Domhnall Criomhthain was out in the yard before his own house. I used have to go by the gable of

Tomás' house because that is the way the path to my own house went. I could see from the path anything that was happening around Tomás' house. Domhnall was fixing the front of the pannier or some such job, I'm not sure, but that's what I thought at the time.

He throws it aside as if he was thinking of something. He shakes himself and looks up and down. He went down to the quay. That wasn't too far away from him, maybe looking for crabs . . .

He was too young to be fishing lobster. Maybe he went fishing conner, or looking for bait or maybe to see if the *naomhógs* had arrived.[14]

Méiní was the only witness as to Domhnall and what he did. Therefore, although it has gone into tradition that Domhnall was digging potatoes for the dinner when he heard the screams, according to Méiní, this was not so.

Cáit Criomhthain's brother Seán related (as he heard afterwards):

They [the girls] both moved to the White Strand, and out with them swimming. It wasn't long before the joking became serious, and whatever look back Domhnall took when he was digging the potatoes for the dinner, he noticed the two going under the water. Away with him and out. He caught Cáit first as she was the closest to him and he dragged her in. Then he went back out again after Eibhlín, but from the exhaustion that had come on him, he could do nothing for her but to grip on to her hair and fall with her down to the bottom. The two of them were drowned together, and the two bodies were shoulder to shoulder when Tomás and Paddy came home in the middle of the day.[15]

Méiní says:

I hadn't washed the potatoes when he [ Domhnall] was back up again and a hurry on him that was not too happy. He had his cap in his hand and he was running.

"Domhnall, what's the hurry now?" I called.

But he didn't speak to me. He ran through the potato gardens and never yielded to anything. He ran the short cut down to the strand by Cúltráigh.

That was the last sight that I got of Domhnall Criomhthain in this life because when I saw him again he was dead without life or breath.

I went out below my own house to see what was amiss. From there I could see the strand and poor Domhnall running at his best to his doom. He was running across the strand when next I looked at the middle of the strand.

O, God be with us, it is how the two women were drowning, entangled in each other just a few feet out from the strand. And, oh, God save us, the groan of despair they made from them with every scream as they called for help.

I saw Domhnall going out fully dressed into the sea separating them from each other. In that separating he and Eibhlín went down to the bottom. What a loss and tragedy.

Cáit remained a short while on the top of the water after the two had gone down. Just as Cáit was slipping down, what happened but that she came down on the two and they kept her head above the water as the water was not deep enough to cover her, and she remained like this until help arrived.[16]

By this time Eibhlín was caught in the returning tide and was being drawn towards the Inneoin, the island quay.

Peats Tom Ó Cearnaigh had been out since early morning, himself with his two brothers, Mártan Tom and Seán Tom, fishing lobster. About this time they brought in their catch and put it in the store pots at the mouth of Tráigh Earraí. Then, instead of rowing around to the quay as they usually did, they left the *naomhóg* and, disembarking, walked home the narrow track westwards to the village. Just as they were leaving, another *naomhóg* arrived and they helped them transfer the lobsters to the store pots before that *naomhóg* set off home rowing across the harbour. They would go home for dinner and then set off again for the Ród in the evening. Peats Tom was a married man of thirty-two at the time, with a wife, Neilí Jerry Ní Shé, and three children.

As he passed above the strand on his way home, Peats Tom heard the screaming and saw people running down to the strand. He spoke to *An Claidheamh Soluis* a few days later:

> As I was returning from fishing I noticed five or six from the village running towards the strand. I knew something must have happened and I too ran towards the place. When I reached the strand I noticed a girl out on the top of the water, about forty feet out. She was still, given up on the top of the water, her mouth and face downwards. I thought it was Eibhlín as I could not imagine any of the local girls out swimming as I had never seen any of them swimming before. I went into the water just as I was, trousers and heavy boots on me. I swam towards the girl and caught on to her. She had gone about a foot below the water when I caught her. I caught her by the back of the head. I recognised that it was not Eibhlín that I had. I didn't succeed in making land, as I had but one hand to swim with, the other one being under the girl's oxter. I kept her head up until a naomhóg came to help. They were in that much hurry coming that I was afraid they would sink us and I told them to take it easy. They eased off on the hurry then and they came up to us on the outside. They brought in the girl and placed her on the strand. I knew then that Eibhlín was drowned. I saw the boat going out searching for the other two. They had a priest with them. I went home to put on dry clothes,

and I returned immediately to the place where the people were gathered on the strand. When I arrived back they had found the boy. The men in the boat said they had seen Eibhlín but they had no means to take her in because the water was too deep. I then got a fishing hook and three others and I went out in another *naomhóg*. I went into the boat in which the priest was, taking the fish hook with me. I saw her underneath me. The second time I threw the hook it caught into her. I drew her up then and the priest took her into the boat. There was about three quarters of an hour between the time I saved the girl and the time that we got Eibhlín.[17]

Three *naomhóga* had gone out to help. The first one brought Peats Tom and Cáit in. The crew were Eoghan Sheáin Eoghain Ó Duinnshléibhe, Muiris Cooney Ó Catháin and Mícheál an Phoncáin Ó Cearnaigh. That was the *naomhóg* that had left the lobsters in the store pot at Tráigh Earraí and was making its way home across the harbour. The second one brought Domhnall in, and the third, the one that had the priest on board, was the one that took Eibhlín in.

A shout of alarm had gone around the island. Women left the cooking and ran to the strand wrapping their shawls around them as they ran. Others hurried down to the quay. Men threw down their tools and headed for both the strand and the quay to their boats to row out to help.

Cáit Ní Criomhthain tells us in her account in *An Claidheamh Soluis* that she lost her footing as she was trying to swim and that she fell back on her back into the deep water. Eibhlín swam over to help her, but they were being drawn farther out. Eibhlín then put her hand under her chin in an attempt to keep her head above water. Eibhlín then swam out a little to take a rest and came back to her again. Then her brother Domhnall came into the water to her. Eibhlín then let go of her. Domhnall went down under water and rose on the outside of her once before going down for good. She couldn't remember anything more.

We have one more account, that from Peats Tom that he gave to Seán Ó Dubhda, the folklorist, in September 1956, forty-seven years after the event. Peats Tom was at that time living with his daughter, Siobhán, who had married Muiris Ó Sé and settled in Na Gorta Dubha in the parish of Ballyferriter, having left the island for ever. He remembered coming with his fishing partners along the pathway until they came in sight of the Tráigh Bhán. They heard the noise and screaming:

> "So," said we to each other, "something has happened and that's for sure: the Dublin lady must be drowning."
>
> Every one of the four of us ran, and I jumped down the short cut so as to go to the strand the quicker, and a boy of the Kearneys who was there said, "I think you are going to have a go at it . . ."
>
> When I came to the strand I threw from me my gansey and I made an attempt to throw off my boots, breaking the laces, but I had to leave them on as they were, strong heavy nail boots. So, I went out towards her where the event had happened and she was no more than forty feet from the edge of the water. I started out and I thought I would be close enough to her before being out of depth, but indeed I hadn't gone far out when I was up to my neck. I had to use the arms then for maybe a yard or more, but I grabbed her as she was going down, I grabbed her hair. I took up her head, and just then I saw the other one on the bottom below me. That is Eibhlín Nic Niocaill.
>
> So, I caught her by the head and I kept up her mouth and nose in case the sea water entered them, and it was three minutes before I did anything or was able to do anything. I twisted her hair on my left hand and turned it around her, because I wanted to be sure

not to let her mouth or nose into the water. I was moving and moving with the right hand and moving along nicely . . . There was an old man of the Dunleavys in on the strand and he was giving me great encouragement, saying that I was doing great and that it wouldn't be long till I was there and not to give up now because I had only a short way to go. In the end a *naomhóg* came out to me . . . I called on the three crew to stay calm and not to hurry, in case they would bring the *naomhóg* down on me in their hurry.

They took it easy then, and they backed into me and as they did that I could feel my feet on the ground. We brought her in then together, and we placed her up on the Tráigh Bhán, and she stretched out, the girl.[18]

As Peats Tom left the strand, people were trying to revive Cáit by rubbing whiskey to her lips. On his way up he met Father Tom Jones, who wanted to find out where exactly Eibhlín was. Peats Tom returned and directed the priest down to the strand. After he had returned home and changed his clothes, he ran over to the slip and boarded another *naomhóg* that had just come in for dinner.

By this time the tide had turned, taking Eibhlín with it.

I came out and saw a *naomhóg* over where the woman had gone down and they were trying to get her. There was a naomhóg with a mast and a hook on the end and the priest thought he would be able to catch the swimsuit with the hook. The mast was thirteen feet long but the water was fifteen feet deep. I took a naomhóg and I went west and I took a fish hook with me with a stone fixed so that it would sink. . . . When I went out I went into the naomhóg in which the priest was and he was keeping her in sight below him as the evening seemed to be getting dark and the priest was anxious in case it would get so dark that we could not see her . . .

"I'll go down," says the priest.

"Yes, Father," says I, "take it easy a few moments till I try this."

He took it easy then, and I threw the fish hook in across where I had seen the body below, and I was drawing steadily till I felt the hook getting a grip on her swimsuit and then I felt the priest catching me by the shoulder.

"By gor!" says he, "you have her."

"I have, Father, thank God," says I to him.

Then we took her into the *naomhóg*, myself and the priest. When we had her in the *naomhóg* you would have no idea that she had no sign of being drowned, her face was so nice, so shining as she was ever before she went swimming, lighting up.

Wasn't it the first inquiry the priest made of me, "Does she live?"

It was difficult. I knew the opposite. I knew it would be difficult for her to be alive, that she couldn't still be alive so long underwater.

I answered the priest, "If it is God's will, Father, maybe she will come to yet."[19]

Cáit an Rí looked on in horror as the bodies were brought in: "When the bodies were recovered Cáit was waiting on the Tráigh Bhán. She recalled, 'I knelt on the sands holding her in my arms, her head resting on my breast, the sea water dripping from her hair. All the time the sea thundered among the rocks. Oh, that black, black day.' "[20]

Peats Tom continued, concerning Domhnall: "He drowned just before I went out. I saw his boots going down as I was making my way out, but he was gone down as I was approaching them. He was taken up with a fish hook."[21]

At the same time as the tragedy was unfolding, Seán Óg's *naomhóg* was skimming over the waves bearing the Cousins and Fíonán Mac Coluim. Fíonán sang a song in Irish to which Cousins replied with "Dark Rosaleen", the translation by James Clarence Mangan of the classic "*Róisín Dubh*":

The Judgement hour must first be nigh
'Ere you can fade, 'ere you can die,
My Dark Rosaleen,
My own Rosaleen . . .

He sang loud so that Eibhlín, wherever she was in the village, would hear, know they were coming and come down to the quay to meet them. The others sang out, too. It was the custom, in fog and when very dark, to call out and whistle as the *naomhóg* approached the island to let everyone know that everything was all right, that they had arrived safely. Those waiting would come down to the slip and help pulling in the boat and carry up anything they had brought.

"I thought she would hear and come – and she came – my God, she came."[22]

Cousins would always remember what happened: "We walked to Dunquin early in the afternoon of August 13th. A thick mist obscured the islands, but there was no wind and the sea was calm. Seán Óg escorted us in the curragh. As we approached the island landing place I observed that another boat appeared to want to reach it before us. Shouts in Irish were exchanged and the stunning news reached us across the water that an accident had happened, and that Miss Nicolls was being brought ashore in that boat."[23]

The two bodies lay on the quay. Men and women arrived running with blankets and coats which were wrapped around the bodies while the water dripped from them. The priest was on his knees praying and trying to revive them. This memory also remained with him. He wrote about the tragic evening on 13 August 1946, thirty-seven years after the tragedy, and a year before he died himself:

As we approached the island a heavy blanket of fog covered the water, though the sun shone through in patches. Little did I think . . . the spectacle I would see at the island quay in another five minutes. Instead of friends meeting and shaking hands there would be women wailing and clasping their hands.

So sudden the whole scene appeared before us. It came to us through the fog, as if it had been hidden under a curtain. I was standing on the slope for a short while before I had any inkling of what had happened. As though in a dream I saw the crowd gather on the slope with bended heads. I heard the talk and the crying. I didn't realise anything until I saw the bodies of Eibhlín Nic Niocaill and Domhnall Críomhthain. My heart gave a terrifying leap. I saw a priest praying. I saw Domhnall's father crying. And I stood there without moving.[24]

When Tomás Ó Críomhthain and his brother Paddy came into the quay, sorrowful indeed was the sight that met them. Afterwards people said that Tomás knew right away that it was Domhnall, his own son, who had drowned. He could see the soles of his boots and the pattern of the hobnails. He had repaired the boots himself. He ran to the body of his son and gave out a great cry of sorrow and horror that could be heard all over the village.

Méiní was watching: "Great was the sorrow felt for Tomás Críomhthain that day when he returned home from fishing and found his son drowned before him on the quay, stretched in quiet death, it gripped his heart, the young man that he had left at home, a man that was just on the point of being a help to him in life."[25]

Seán, his son, remembered:

That day struck a blow on Tomás' health that took a long time for him to recover from.

"It isn't too bad," said he, "if the other woman lives."

When he was told that she lived and was out of danger, he never did anything else but to go on his knees and kiss Domhnall on the mouth and then kissed Eibhlín's hand as well.

"I leave everything else for the God of Glory to lay out the road for you both to the Kingdom of Heaven," said he, "and to give me the grace of patience to carry this cross."

When all the arrangements had been made and the two bodies prepared, he said, "This isn't my affair alone, but also that of the poor people who have lost their beautiful girl in this unfortunate place. God and time will heal our wounds."[26]

# CHAPTER 6

# And There Were Present. . .

## *Agus Bhí i Láthair. . .*

IT TOOK SOME time for Seán Óg to feel the full extent of the horror that had fallen on the little bunch gathered there on the quayside. Even worse, he felt guilty that he had played a major part in the tragedy that had just unfolded. That feeling of guilt was to remain with him till the end:

> I felt that I was the cause of this great sorrow. It ran through my mind that she would not have been stretched there in death had it not been for me. The old man [Tomás] looked at me. I think he tried to say something, but silence was all the result. And I felt guilty! Guilty! I thought he would say, "You are the one responsible for today's sorrow."
>
> Instead of that he grasped me by the hand to let me know that he did not hold me to blame.[1]

By this time a good crowd had gathered on the quayside, both the islanders themselves and visitors. A boat from Uíbh Ráthach, the next peninsula, had arrived bringing people in on a day trip. The local curate, Fr Tom Jones, who had taken part in the rescue attempt, had arrived earlier in a *naomhóg* from Cuas na Nao in the parish of Ferriter. Accompanying him were Mary and Agnes Manning, both teachers in the girls' school in Ballyferriter and daughters of the famed Mícheál Ó Mainín, the principal teacher, who had been a great force in the survival of the language in the peninsula till his death in 1904. Fr Jones, who had lately come as curate in the parish, had decided to pay a visit to his parishioners on the Blaskets to introduce himself.

According to Peats Tom Ó Cearnaigh: "When we went to the proper quay underneath the Inneoin it is how it was full of people from Dublin and everywhere, five or six *naomhóga* having come from Dunquin with them during this time. They had no idea that anything had happened. Many had come to find out what had happened. But she was taken up and she was given every treatment possible in an effort to revive her. But what is, is."[2]

Fr Jones anointed Eibhlín and Domhnall there on the quay. Eibhlín was wrapped in blankets and coats. The priest then made a great attempt to revive Eibhlín. He spent up to four hours with her, according to Cousins. According to folk memory, the colour was beginning to come back into her cheeks again, until a woman present said it was no use, that she was gone. The priest rose and said, "A great pity you did not keep your mouth shut."[3]

From then on the battle was lost. It is also reported that what the woman said was, "Look how everybody attends to the daughter of the gentleman but nobody gives any attention to the son of the poor man."[4]

Needless to say, there are two tellings to every story, and in this instance there are more than two.

Méiní said:

> They spent two hours trying to bring back the life into her. The body was drifting towards the quay all the time, and it good and deep. When they succeeded in getting the body it was brought to the quay, and the body was laid out beside Domhnall's body. Fr Jones did his best to bring back the life into her. He got a basin of hot water from a woman and rubbed her all over with it. There was a little tinge of colour appearing back in her cheeks and there was a woman there with a watch who said, "She's coming at two

seconds." Then a woman who was present said,
"Why should we bring back life to one and not to the
other?"

The priest straightened himself up, "Who said
that?" he asked. When he got no answer he put the
question the second time, and then the third time,
but he got no answer. He then gave up the attempt
entirely.[5]

There is still another telling that mentions that the
woman asked, "If Domhnall is dead, is not Eibhlín dead
too?"[6]

It would indeed seem from all the accounts that Eibhlín
was getting priority treatment, while at the same time little effort, if any, was made to revive Domhnall, even
though it would seem there would have been a better
chance with him as he had not been in the water as long as
Eibhlín. Eibhlín was a woman and a visitor, and that may
have accounted for this preferential treatment, but it must
also be said that poor, simple peasants were generally given
little importance in those times. The island people also
thought of themselves as peasants, and almost all references to her in island literature speak of her as "*an* Lady"
or "*an Bhean Uasal*", the noble lady – or as Tomás calls
her "An Óigbhean Uasal", the noble young woman. On
the other hand, the amount of information we can gain
about Domhnall is very limited and of a general nature,
such as would apply to the great majority of the island
boys. Class consciousness was rife all throughout early
Edwardian society.

Even by this early stage the Blasket tragedy was taking
on the characteristics of an old folk story: for example, the
asking of the three questions with no answer.

The people believed also in the special powers of the
priest, not least in the powers of Fr Tom Jones. They
thought that he even had the power to work a miracle to
bring someone back, if not from death itself, at least from
the brink. There is one story about him when he was

parish priest in Glenbeigh. There was a young girl in grave danger of death. He prayed to God to spare the child and take him instead, and so, God being pleased, both were spared. It is also said that he had the *Ortha an Bháite*, the special, ancient mixture of Christian and pagan prayer that could rescue a person from drowning.

When Fr Jones ceased his effort to revive Eibhlín and gave her up for dead, it was then that James Cousins took over all Eibhlín's affairs. He it was who made all the arrangements, and everyone obeyed his authority. Leslie Matson remembers hearing from Méiní that many of the island people were of the opinion that he was a relation of hers, and when they heard the name "Cousins", they took it that he was Eibhlín's cousin.

Eibhlín's body was raised on a door – the usual form of island stretcher – and taken to the King's house, and Domhnall's body was carried to his own home. It made a sorrowful procession as they were carried up the steep way to the clifftop.

Cousins took his pen and paper at the first opportunity and prepared a press release for the Dublin and the Kerry papers. He then wrote a telegram to Eibhlín's family which he entrusted to Fr Jones to be dispatched as soon as he reached the mainland. Then he looked on Eibhlín in the bed and he had time to think of the reality of the terrible event that had occurred. He saw her there, "a picture of infinite peace, with the beautiful composure of her face and the delicate smile around her lips kept us all from madness."[7]

He thought of those who had been through the last terrible hours and was filled with admiration and gratitude:

> The pictures of that wonderful night pass before me and fill my heart with an awful pathos. I cannot yet write of them with control.
>
> Nor can I find language sufficient to express my gratitude and admiration for the part played by the islanders and Fíonán, Seán Óg, his brother and

friends, Fr Jones of Ballyferriter who was ready to do anything, from plunging to raise the body to taking telegrams to the mainland in the falling darkness, Mr. Savage, the island headmaster, the Manning sisters and Mrs. Cousins.[8]

Darkness had fallen and it had started to rain. Seán Óg with his crew were the last to leave the island, taking Fr Jones with them. Everyone was anxious and worried that they might go astray in the dark, but they reached Dún Chaoin safely.

According to Muiris Kavanagh (Kruger), Seán Óg's younger brother, they came to the Kavanagh home in Baile na Rátha when they landed at the mainland. Muiris was at the time a strong sturdy youth of fifteen or sixteen. Although there had been a post office in Dún Chaoin since 1899, it did not have the telegraph equipment. Muiris was given the job of running to Ventry, a distance of some five miles, to the post office there. This he did barefooted and in the darkness over the mountain pass known as the Clasach. In Ventry he ran to the Post Office in Clochán, run by the Sullivans, and they, rising from bed, sent the telegram to Eibhlín's parents in Rathgar in Dublin, explaining that there had been a tragic accident and to come without delay, but not telling them that she was dead.

That night there were two sad wakes on the island. The people gathered in huddled silent groups, whispering and weeping. Cousins described them: "A second wake was simultaneously held in the cottage of the boy who had shared the destiny of Miss Nicolls. Between the two houses Gretta and I made our way in a chain of hand-clasped men along the edge of the cliff."[9] The King's house was one of the highest on the island, while Tomás's house was the lowest. The way was dangerous and steep between them, especially in the dark of night. There was no light except that of candles in the windows. The men stood along the way helping those who travelled between the two houses.

Cousins could not remember the name of the boy who had been drowned when writing. Later he mistakenly called him "Donough", instead of "Domhnall", so that he is more often referred to afterwards in the papers and reports as "Donough". Nor did he know Tomás Ó Criomhthain, his father.

Cáit Criomhthain was recovering slowly. She remained weak and was confined to bed for a long time. She had been taken from the sea, apparently dead, but after about half an hour's attention she began to recover.

Peats Tom said, "To the Guiheens' house, to Mary Pheats Mhicí, Mrs. Guiheen, her first cousin, Cáit was brought, because Domhnall's body was being waked in her own home."[10]

Máire Ní Ghuithín, who was that very baby that Eibhlín had taken in her arms the morning of her drowning, got the full account from her own family afterwards: "Cáit Criomhthain was brought up to our house, and she was put in bed there, and Cáit Bhán was taking care of her . . . Cáit Bhán Connor (Mrs. O'Shea) she was."[11]

Tomás, Cáit's father, wrote: "I don't think I would have ever recovered were it not for my uncle Diarmuid, along with God's help, because the daughter that was in the sea, there wasn't great hope for her that she would make any recovery either, there was only the shade in her. If I was sure she would come to I could accept that things weren't too bad for me."[12]

Again Máire Ní Ghuithín: "When my father came in from fishing that evening and it dark, he couldn't figure out how there was light in the bedroom below, with the woman sitting on a chair beside the bed and another woman in it. He told my mother that he got a great shock, because he knew something had happened, and he thought it was his own dead mother, that was sitting in the chair taking care of the other woman in the bed."[13]

Peats Tom told Seán Ó Dubhda:

The other girl lived, Criomhthain's daughter, she

survived. She came out of it. It wasn't that morning and evening were spent trying to revive her when she was brought in from the sea, but she had to be brought home on the men's shoulders that evening. You can see, so, that she was in a fairly bad way, but she had life in her always, and she came to in a bed of the neighbours, because her brother's body was in her own house and they did not like to bring her there into her own home.[14]

As Méiní said, "She revived, but Lord save us, it took a long time for her to come to."[15]

As for Eibhlín, Peats Tom remembered:

She was brought in reverence to the house in which she was staying since her arrival, that is the King's house. She was given every attention possible there. A table was placed under her and white sheets were placed above her and she was arranged as fine as could be, and there was one person, a stranger from Dublin who remained there as long as the body was there. The name of this person was Mr. Cussen . . . and he stayed inside at the wake until the body was taken out.[16]

It was Méiní, the island midwife and unofficial nurse, who laid our Eibhlín's body. It was she who saw many of the islanders into the world and, in many cases, out of this world also.

A curious note regarding the date, Friday the thirteenth, a day that traditionally has a great deal of superstition surrounding it as being a day of misfortune, and a day which people are glad to see pass with a sigh of relief: on Friday, 13 August 1976, another drowning with close island connections occurred. Tomás Ó Catháin from Baile Ícín in Dunquin was drowned while returning to the island in a dingy late that night. He, his wife, Eibhlín, and their three-month-old baby, Neilí, were staying on the island for a holiday, and Tomás had gone to the mainland to Kruger's pub for provisions.

It is true, however, that even though the islanders had plenty of superstitions of their own, Friday the thirteenth was not one of them. Nor was it in Dún Chaoin, though it is now.

The following day Cousins was up early. He had not slept a wink, nor had anyone on the island. A heavy, lonely cloud remained over on the village and over the Tráigh Bhán that could not be adequately described.

Cousins wrote:

> I finish these notes at 4 in the morning – the first faint indication of the approaching day is in the sky. 150 feet below the Palace I hear the increasing roar of the Atlantic breakers. My crew is ready, and as soon as the light permits we shall make for the mainland with sadder hearts than we sped singing across in anticipation of a happy day with our dead friend at the fireside of the good, kindly, heroic race that eke out a precarious but apparently contented existence in this island of the Atlantic.[17]

A quiet anger spread through the community, as though the island, the Tráigh Bhán and the sea were responsible for the outrage. There had not been a drowning for more than forty years, but now the sea had taken its price with a vengeance.

Years later, Seán Óg wrote:

> There is something about a drowning that moves a person in a way that no other form of death does. The tragedy is so unexpected. The opinion is formed that there was a conspiracy, a sort of horrid disappearance.
>
> Never before had I seen a crowd of people so overcome and so angry as I saw on the island that evening, and in Dunquin the following day. The cover of sorrow that the fog brought on the island that evening spread loneliness; you could scarcely see your hand in front of you, it had become so dark.
>
> The people moved about like shadows, with as

little conversation as possible. You would imaging
that some great power was seeking redress.[18]

Méiní also felt this great covering of misfortune that had
descended on them: "'Tis how it was, that it was not sorrow we felt but terror . . . The island is a small close-knit
community and the little cabins were built so close to each
other, and the people were so close and so supportive to
each other that it took but little to happen among them to
upset them."[19]

In the early morning Cousins was brought by *naomhóg*
to Dingle, and this time he sent a telegram to the nuns in
Loreto College in St Stephen's Green, telling them of the
tragedy and asking them to tell Eibhlín's mother of her
death. They contacted Máire de Buitléir, Eibhlín's friend
who lived a short distance away in Leeson Street at the
time, and asked her to go to Eibhlín's parents in
Kenilworth Road with the tragic news.

Peats Tom remembered: "It took a few days on the
island before everything could be arranged as to what
might happen, with telegrams coming and going between
the island and Dublin. Myself it was that was mostly travelling in and out, myself and two others, a Keane and a
Guithín. We were going in and out, you see, expecting
word at any minute to remove the body to Dunquin."[20]

On Saturday evening, word came that Eibhlín's mother and father had come as far as Dún Chaoin and that the
funeral could be held on the following day, Sunday, 15
August, Mary's first day in autumn (*Céad Lá Muire sa
bhFómhar*). Before Máire de Buitléir could reach them,
the parents had left Dublin on the 9.15 train on Saturday
morning, not knowing whether Eibhlín was alive or
dead. The mother was hopeful, but the father was very
doubtful. Eibhlín's mother was sixty-four at the time and
the father sixty-five. They readily accepted God's will and
the cross that had been placed upon them. Cousins was
very impressed with their spirit of acceptance and their
strong faith.

While Cousins was in Dingle he bought a coffin for Eibhlín and another for Domhnall, and he sent them back to the island in the *naomhóg* while he waited there. He met Eibhlín's father and mother in Dingle from the train, and they all hired a coach and came back to Dún Chaoin where they spent the night.

\* \* \* \* \* \*

Sunday, 15 August, dawned cloudy and showery. A crowd gathered early on the high cliff top in Dún Chaoin at the place called the Seanbhaile, probably because of a long lost village that once thrived there before slipping into the sea. A view could be had right across to the island, lying calmly in the ocean.

Meanwhile, overnight, a small crisis had arisen, as Peats Tom related:

> The big people in Dingle went talking to them [Eibhlín's parents] and they made out that the island people did not have a boat suitable for taking out the coffin, that they were not equipped for doing that sort of thing at all; the way they worked it out was to get a fine trawler from Dingle, there were no engines out then; there were no boats but rowboats and sailboats. Four men came rowing from Dingle as a crew and I think there were two strangers from Dublin with them in the boat. They left fairly early and set out for the island, fourteen miles of sea probably, and just as they were approaching the island the funeral was leaving the island and making for the Bealach on its way across to the Quay at Dunquin.
>
> The two funerals travelled together.[21]

The funeral left the island quay at eleven o'clock. The old women gathered round the two coffins on the Deck, and the ancient traditional lament began rising and falling in a sad wail. The call was taken up by a lone dog. A seal surfaced and looked around curiously before disappearing into the waves. The coffins were then taken in procession down the steep, windy slope and each placed in a *naomhóg*. The other *naomhóga* were boarded, word was given, and all began to move out to sea. The lament followed them over the waves.

Cousins, who was waiting on the clifftop, was the first to spot the funeral coming: "With my field glasses I could make out the two funeral boats leading the fleet, one going ahead alone, the second being flanked by two curraghs, the remaining boats following irregularly, some hoisting a sail."[22]

The procession had formed the figure of a cross, with the King's *naomhóg* bearing Eibhlín's body, followed by the Criomhthain boat with Domhnall's body, with a *naomhóg* on either side forming the arm of the cross. The Kavanagh boat followed immediately behind Domhnall, with the remaining *naomhóga* following in a line behind. There were more than twenty *naomhóga* in the full procession.

The twin funerals of Eibhlín and Domhnall were the greatest funerals to have left the island ever.

Peats Tom also described it, though his account differs from Cousins':

> I would think there were twenty two naomhógs altogether there. There were thirteen or fourteen from the island and all the Dunquin naomhógs were there except, maybe one or two. And to be sure, the Dingle people were amazed to see that she had been taken out at all until they came themselves, but, upon my word, there were people in the island at that time who were able to draw in and out with the boats they had, the naomhógs, when I am sure there are very few boats in existence that could do what they did, and that in rough seas close by rocks with a good crew. I do not think there is any boat of its kind that would beat the naomhóg. She would come through in a place where other boats would be lost.[23]

Domhnall's father, Tomás Ó Criomhthain, wrote: "It was the biggest funeral ever held in the parish of Dunquin. They remained as one funeral until they divided and headed, each one for their own native burial place."[24]

"All gazed with grief from the high cliffs of Dunquin as the long curragh funeral crossed the Blasket Sound," said Cousins.[25]

Another eyewitness account of the melancholy event is that of Thomas H. Mason, the Dublin antiquarian and photographer, who was one of those who waited at the top of the cliff for the arrival of the remains of the two:

> Many years ago when I was staying on the adjoining mainland a visitor (Miss Nicholls) lost her life in a gallant attempt to save from drowning an island woman who got into difficulties. I was told that shortly before the tragedy a "phantom ship" had appeared, a sure forerunner of misfortune. The funeral procession of curraghs across the Sound – there is no burial place on the island – reminded me of a funeral that I saw in Venice where black gondolas take the place of the mourning coaches.[26]

The quay and the cliff top in Dún Chaoin were thronged with people from both the locality and from many parts of Ireland. The two coffins were raised from the *naomhóga* and placed on the sand there. Some of the boats hoisted sail as a last salute to the tragic pair. There to meet them was the parish priest, Fr Tadhg Griffin, who recited the rosary for the repose of their souls. He had met Eibhlín briefly the previous Sunday when she had been to mass in Dún Chaoin, when she was handing out the badges.

The two coffins were then borne on the shoulders of the men up the long, steep, difficult way to the top of the cliff. The long wail of the lament mingled with the perpetual roaring of the waves. On the top to meet them were the women of Dún Chaoin, who made their own share of the lamenting, spreading sorrow and loneliness on all sides as the dark crowds pushed and mingled.

One question remains unanswered: was Pádraig Pearse there among the crowd that received the bodies of Eibhlín and Domhnall as they were taken from the *naomhóga* and carried to the top? And was he more lonely than most there present? It has been part of the local tradition that he was there. Cáit an Rí always believed that he was there. But if so, it was indeed his first, and except for a further visit on the occasion of a *feis* in Dún Chaoin, his last. He would set his sights on Conamara for the future.

The two coffins were then borne by the men on the narrow road to the small church in Dún Chaoin, through Baile Ícín to Baile na Rátha, where they turned south to go through the narrow Bóithrín na Marbh (Road of the Dead) by the Kavanagh home, the traditional funeral way, till it came to Crosaire an Bhainne (Milk Cross) at the top of Bóthar Chéilleachair. There was until relatively recent times a grass triangle in the middle of the crossroads there known as the Triantán na Marbh (Triangle of the Dead). The coffins used to be placed there in olden times to give the bearers a rest. The coffin would be placed on the toes of the boots, to make it easy to lift on the shoulders again, while a few prayers were uttered in rapid Irish.

Here is an extract from the account given to Imelda Hallahan by Cáit an Rí:

> When Eibhlín's parents came to Dunquin they asked Cáit would she go with them to the church. They were having the coffin opened to see their daughter before burial in Dublin. They wanted Cáit to tell them if that was the way Eibhlín looked when she was taken from the sea. Cáit agreed.
>
> As she gazed upon her friend she was able to confirm Eibhlín looked just as lovely and peaceful as when she held her body in her arms when it was taken from the sea.
>
> It was Cáit's last gesture to Eibhlín.[27]

It is said then that her mother cut a lock of her hair with a small scissors to keep as a memento.

Domhnall Ó Críomhthain was buried in the family plot in Teampall Dhuinín in Baile an Teampaill, just across from the church entrance. The exact location of the grave remains a mystery. The grave in which his father is buried, very well marked by a fine sculptured stone executed by the famous sculptor Séamus Murphy, is a new grave.

While Domhnall was buried, Eibhlín's coffin was placed before the altar in the church. It would seem, according to accounts, that the body was then transferred to another coffin. Peats Tom could not be sure: "So, the two bodies were brought into the quay at Dunquin and she was brought east to the church, and she was placed inside the church for a time, and, even though I was present, I cannot be certain was she transferred to another coffin in the church or not, or was there one waiting there for her, but to the best of my recollection she was transferred to another coffin in the church."[28]

Cousins tells us:"The boy's body was buried in the little graveyard of Dunquin . . . While we waited for the burial Gretta explored the vicinity for flowers and made a cross of blue hydrangeas which she placed on Miss Nicoll's coffin."[29]

Cáit an Rí did the same: "I mind how she loved the Fuschia, the red leaves and the purple bell-like flower; 'Deora Mhuire', we call it here, 'The Tears of Mary'. I stole into the chapel the evening before she left and placed a bunch on her coffin."[30]

Peats Tom said:

> Her mother and father were speaking to me – someone had told them that I had been present and that it was me who saved the other one, the girl who lived . . . but if so, I had no English to make myself understood, but I made an attempt to give something to them, and I said that I was sorry that I had been unable to save them some of their trouble, that I had

not got the chance, and had I got it, I would have
acted, and that there was nothing I could do, and
that I was very sorry that I could not have spared
them their trouble, and so forth, in the kind of
English I had, and that wasn't much, because I never
had the opportunity to use that language, nor anyone that went before me, for that matter.[31]

There also was Tomás, whose son had shared in the
tragedy. He shared the sorrow with the Nicolls, though of
the opinion that it was on account of Eibhlín that
Domhnall drowned: "They both came to me in Dún
Chaoin, the father and mother, and I had to be introduced
to them. I hope they did not think I held anything against
them since it was on their daughter's account of that I had
lost my son. But I was always more understanding than
that. If it was on account of her, it wasn't their fault."[32]

The horse-drawn hearse from Dingle was waiting.
Eibhlín's coffin was taken out of the church and placed in the
hearse. The funeral then proceeded from the church in Dún
Chaoin to Dingle, by the oldest roads, as was the custom.

At every crossroads sorrowful groups of people waited,
knelt as the funeral passed and then followed walking in
the procession: "From Dunquin to Dingle the body was
escorted by a procession of sidecars, and by many men and
women on foot. At crossroads the coffin was laid on the
ground and prayers chanted. Halfway along food was provided in the house of a priest near a roadside chapel. Mrs.
Cousins, although a Protestant, was put at the head of the
table to preside over the meal."[33]

Cousins does not name the generous priest who provided the refreshments, buy we can be sure that it was
through Ballyferriter that the funeral passed, as it is the
only road that had a priest's residence. We can be sure also
that it was the parish priest, Fr Griffin, and his curate, Fr
Jones, that provided the repast. It surely was a nice gesture
on their own behalf and on that of the people of the parish
of Ferriter.

The funeral continued and turned south at Crosaire an tSean-Chnoic over Mám na Gaoithe past Caisleán Ráthanáin down into Ceann Trá. "People walked from Ventry and shouldered the coffin from Milltown to Dingle where it was met and keened by some of the oldest women of the town."[34]

Eibhlín's remains rested in Dingle church Sunday night, and early on Monday morning, after requiem mass, were taken in procession to the station. An immense crowd of people lined the street in an expression of sympathy with Mr and Mrs Nicolls as they followed the coffin. Arriving at the station, the coffin was placed in an especially laid out carriage. There was a last prayer of farewell, and the train pulled quietly, slower than usual, from the small station at 10.30.

"She lived like a true patriot, she has had the funeral of an Irish Queen," reported *Sinn Féin*.[35]

*The Kerry Sentinel,* Wednesday, 18 August, stated:

> The funeral took place to the mainland on Sunday morning, every boat connected with the island following in sorrowful procession. The remains followed by hundreds of the natives were placed in the Catholic Church. Mass on Monday morning was celebrated with a large congregation. The remains were then brought to the train followed by an immense crowd. The parents of the dead girl were present. The remains were then conveyed to Dublin on the 10.30 train.[36]

Great was the contrast between the departure and that beautiful evening six weeks previously when Eibhlín first set foot in Corca Dhuibhne, her heart full of gladness and excitement, as a fine carefree holiday stretched before her.

The Dingle train pulled away from the platform and started its sad journey to Tralee. The people waited for a while in silence, and then in ones and twos slipped silently away.

An early harvest was in full swing all over Kerry in ideal conditions, according to *The Kerryman*:

> Harvest operations have been carried out in the above district [south-west Kerry] for some ten days or so under conditions of tropical heat. There has been practically no trouble in saving the hay which is all, nearly now, in winds in the greater portion of the district. Potatoes have ripened rapidly, and on the whole, promise a good all-round crop. The oat crops are looking well on good deep soils, but on the hillsides and exposed uplands the great heat has scorched both soil and crops.[37]

The Blaskets alone lay under a black cloud.

Another great crowd was waiting at Kingsbridge station in Dublin when the Tralee train steamed in at 4.20 P.M. Thousands, of all classes and creeds, gathered to meet Eibhlín's remains, among them the important officials of the capital city, all come to pay their respects and show their deep sorrow. Present also were the leaders of both the freedom and the language movements, but the ordinary Dubliners were most represented. The clergy, along with the plain people of Dublin, lined the quays along the Liffey to see the cortège pass and welcome home their child. The men doffed their hats and caps as the funeral passed. Many of the women and not a small number of the men wept. The funeral extended for two miles, followed by pedestrians and carriages at a slow walking pace.

The beautiful oak coffin, which was covered with a profusion of floral tributes, bore the following inscription in Irish:

*Órait do*
*Eibhlín Nic Niocaill,*
*Do thug a h-anam ar son Dé,*
*13 Lúnasa 1909.*
*R.I.P.*[38]

Present also was Joseph Holloway, a friend of Pádraig Pearse, who later that day wrote in his widely quoted diary: "Rare sorrow was felt at the loss of this fine young girl and wonderfully clever scholar – many looked on her death as a national loss – she took a practical interest in the Gaelic movement and was becoming such a power in the organisation . . . a solemner funeral I was never at – a nation wept for her lost child as well as those who knew her in life."[39]

Pádraig Pearse was there, too, also weeping bitterly. Desmond Ryan, his pupil and later his biographer, thought that Pearse was so moved that it proved that he was in love with Eibhlín. This seems to have been an effort on his part to over-romanticise the tragedy and the relationship between the two. He translated and adapted Louis Le Roux's French biography of Pearse:

> It is true that before he reached his 30th year he had felt attracted towards a young girl – Eibhlín Nichols – a UCD graduate, as ardent a patriot as himself, and as true a Gael and as fair as any colleen could be. Her courage was equal to his own and, she, too, was drawn towards him. The young woman was an expert swimmer and she one day dived into the sea at the Blasket Islands to save a girl from drowning. Through her gallant act the girl was saved, but she herself perished in the stormy and treacherous waves.
>
> At her funeral some of the bystanders bore away the memory of the grief in the face of Pearse and the tears in his eyes.[40]

But there were so many who wept that day.

Eibhlín's funeral continued on to Glasnevin cemetery, the main national cemetery for the Gael. It is there that many of our statesmen and patriots are buried, including Daniel O'Connell and Charles Stewart Parnell. It is strange that Eibhlín was buried in Glasnevin, although living on the south side of the city. Perhaps it was because Glasnevin

was increasingly being recognised as the nationalist cemetery, or maybe it was because Eibhlín was a native of Eccles
Street on the north side.

Prayers were said in English and Irish at the graveside
before the oak coffin was lowered into the earth.

Fíonán Mac Coluim had accompanied Mr and Mrs
Nicolls from the Blaskets. The chief mourners who stood
by the grave on that sunny early autumn evening were her
father and mother, Archibald J. and Mary Nicolls, her
brother George Nicolls, Revd P. Head, SJ, her uncle, Miss
Helen Nicolls and Mrs O'Connell-Murphy, her cousins.

Her friends and relations remained for some time after
the grave was filled in and mounded up. They left then sor-
rowfully in ones and twos and started for home. The flowers gleamed in the late summer sunshine as the day faded
and night approached. Among the floral wreaths the card
of one read:

To Eibhlín,
With sincere sympathy,
Mr. and Mrs. T. Kavanagh.
Ventry.

Cousins finished his account for the *Freeman's Journal*
with an item that was not given much importance at the
time. He seems to be a little doubtful on the cause of
Eibhlín's death. He apologises to his readers for the little
inaccuracies of his first accounts and says: "No inquest has
been considered necessary by the authorities. Dr.
O'Donoghue who saw the victims on the island is of the
opinion that since the body of Eibhlín was found in an attitude of swimming, she had been overtaken by heart failure
– no indication of a struggle – or pain on her face – with a
faint trace of a smile until the last."[41]

"Found Drowned" was the reason given for her death
according to her death certificate, with Peats Tom Ó
Cearnaigh cited as the witness.

One would have to remember the words of Peats Tom
many years after the event: "You would swear by all the

117

books that were ever printed that there was no marks of drowning on her, her face was so nice, so flushed as she was before she ever entered to swim, lit up."[42]

The Blasket people also held the view that she had been stricken by heart failure. Cáit an Rí remembered that Eibhlín herself had mentioned that she used to experience periods of weakness:

> One night as the rain beat from the Atlantic the two girls drew their chairs close to the fire. As the gusts swept around the cottage Cáit noticed the uneasiness in Eibhlín. She would lift her head in a listening attitude, or glance towards the door. Then she spread her hands before the fire and spoke as if to herself. She told Cáit she had two blackouts before she came down – one on the stage during the rehearsal of a play, the other in her bedroom. Seeing the concern in Cáit's face she impulsively caught her hand and assured her, telling her not to worry; it was only over-tiredness, she was involved in too many activities in Dublin.[43]

Thinking back over the years Cáit could recall a change coming over Eibhlín: "A great quietness was on her; how shall I describe it, it was as if a cloud had shut out the sunlight." She spent more time in the house, and seemed less inclined to join the gatherings in the neighbouring houses. Often Cáit came across her seated at the table, her finely fashioned hands clasped around an unopened book.[44]

In the year 1964, Risteárd Ó Glaisne spoke to Cáit an Rí: "Cáit said that Domhnall had taken a great deal of water, but that Eibhlín had taken none, and that she had no froth at her mouth when she was taken from the water. Could it have been that she had heart failure?"[45]

He also spoke to Peats Tom: "Peats Tom said that it was his opinion that she had a heart attack before she went down to the bottom, and that there was no water in her lungs when the doctor examined her later, and there would be none if she had died before she went below the water."[46]

Cáit also recollected that Eibhlín did not rise to the top when she had gone down. This, too, led her to believe that she had suffered a heart attack.

Now, nearly a hundred year later, with greater knowledge of postmortem findings, we know that the features noted on her body by witnesses at the time are, in fact, not incompatible with drowning. As stated by forensic pathologist Bernard Knight: "the classical postmortem appearance of waterlogged lungs and air passages filled with froth are seen in less than half the cases of bodies recovered from the water. The so-called 'dry-lung' drowning is frequent and the actual fact of drowning is often impossible to prove."[47]

However, Cáit an Rí's recollection of Eibhlín's two blackouts also suggests the possibility of a form of epilepsy known as "petit mal" – partial seizures – during which a person does not completely lose consciousness and fall, but stares ahead and is unresponsive when spoken to. If she had such a seizure in the water, she could have drowned.

Although it is unusual for someone of Eibhlín's age to have a heart attack, there is a slight, though less likely, chance that she could have suffered from a form of cardiac arrhythmia, or irregular heartbeat. This could explain the episodes of weakness and could have caused a cardiac arrest brought on in her frantic efforts to save Cáit.[48]

From this distance in time, it is really impossible to say precisely what caused her death.

# CHAPTER 7

# Beyond the Wash of Waves

NEWS DID NOT travel as quickly in those days, and it took about a week for the full news of the Blasket tragedy to spread around the nation. The edition of *An Claidheamh Soluis* of 21 August was the first that dealt with the tragedy:

> It is long since any story as great as that has happened in Kerry last Friday, that is Eibhlín Nicolls to have drowned in an attempt to save another girl. Her action will be remembered as one of the bravest actions in our time. It will fill every Gael with sorrow, but it will fill them with pride as well as sorrow. Sorrowful indeed, without doubt, this fine young most intelligent woman to have been whisked away from us with her friends and relations in great sorrow, but a reason for great pride and courage to us to say that the blood of heroes still flows in the veins of the Gael, and that there are noble girls in Ireland yet who do not shirk their duty though it risks death itself!
>
> Ireland is a better place as a result of the death of Eibhlín Nic Niocaill. All of us who knew her during her life span are the better for it. She was our star and our heroine in her time, and her light will live on after her life has been extinguished.
>
> God rest her noble soul. May Mary the great mother of mercy give solace to her father and mother.[1]

The writer, Pádraig Pearse himself, goes on to describe the Blaskets, and it is surprising that so little was known of it except that it had bore few of the marks of modern civilisation:

> The Great Blasket is a lonely island about three miles from Dunquin. There is neither priest nor church, courthouse nor barracks, policeman, tavern or shop there. There is a school there, however, with half a hundred children attending. There are twenty seven or twenty eight houses on the island, and about one hundred and fifty people there between young and old. Irish alone is spoken on the island.[2]

Because of the tragedy of 13 August, the island would become well-known, but perhaps not in the way the Blasket people themselves would have preferred. Besides being of a place of beauty, of music and stories, it would be also remembered as a lonely, sorrowful place in which one of Ireland's best known and best loved young women was drowned.

The *Freeman's Journal* wasn't exactly flattering in its comment on 16 August:

> The people are a most primitive people. They are exclusively Irish speaking . . . Until the Gaelic revival they had never seen a visitor, but in recent years enthusiastic students like Miss Nicolls had visited the island every summer for some weeks or months in order to study the old tongue at its purest source where it has suffered no corruption from contact with English, where the idiom is preserved pure and unsullied from the earliest times.[3]

Pádraig Pearse was the editor of *An Claidheamh Soluis* at this time. It was well-known that there was a very close friendship between himself and Eibhlín, and there were people who were of the opinion that it was much more than a friendship, and that they had intended to marry.

There were others who said their friendship arose from the work they did which brought them together so often. We cannot be sure as to their relationship, but it is clear that Pearse had a great personal affection for Eibhlín:

> There are times when journalists and public men experience a trial more cruel than others can easily imagine. It is when they are called upon in the course of their duty to write or speak in public of things that touch the innermost fibres of their own hearts, things that to them are intimate and sacred, entwined, it may be, with their dearest friendships and affections, awakening to vibrations old chords or joy or sorrow. The present is such an occasion for the writer of these paragraphs, and this must be his excuse if he does not pay to Eibhlín Nic Niocaill such tribute as readers of An Claidheamh Soluis will expect. It is not in human nature to write a glib newspaper article on a dead friend. One dare not utter all that is in one's heart, and in the effort of self-restraint one is apt to pen only cold and formal things. Therefore we will discharge as briefly as may be the duty that falls upon us.
>
> First we would voice the sorrow or our organisation for the death of one of its most brilliant and heroic members. We have often spoken in the name of the Gaelic League, but never have we felt ourselves peculiarly at one with it as thus making ourselves the mouthpiece of its tribute to Eibhlín Nic Niocaill. We knew her well, and she was the most nobly planned of all the women we have known. The newspapers have truly spoken of her as the most distinguished student of her time. Gaelic Leaguers will remember her as an incomparably strenuous worker during her brief but crowded career of active service. But it is neither as a student or as a League worker that her friends will think of her. Her grand dower of intellect, her gracious gift of charm and sympathy, her capacity for affairs, were known to all, but those who knew

her best know that all of these were the least of her endowments. What will stand out clear and radiant in their mental picture of her is the loftiness of her soul, the inner sanctity of her life.

The close of that life had been worthy of it. If she had been asked to choose the manner of her death she would surely have chosen it thus. She died to save another, and that as a young Irish-speaking girl. Greater love than this no man hath than he give his life for his friend. To Eibhlín Nic Niocaill high heroism was native. Her life was consecrated to the service of high things. And without seeking reward she found rich reward in the enthusiastic love of hundreds. She gave much love and received much love. Not many have been carried with such passion of grief and affection as that which thrilled in the keenings of the Kerry women as the curraghs forming her funeral procession moved across the sound:

"Mo ghroidhn tú, a Eibhlín,
Mo ghroidhn do mháthair,
Mo ghroidhn go bráth í!"

they said. In Dublin her comrades, and fellow-students, grief was not articulate, but no one who witnessed it could doubt its poignancy. Our second duty is to offer respectfully the sympathy of her and our co-workers to her father and mother and brothers. The memory of her life and death will be the greatest treasure in the years that are to come. And for them the treasure will be none the less though many thousands of her people claim a share in it also.

I bhfochair an Uain go raibh a hanam ar feadh na síoraíochta![4]

It is very clear from the above words that Eibhlín's death had a profound effect on Pearse. Which brings us back to the obvious question: was there a romantic attachment between them? The belief that there was, was widespread, and some even claimed that there was an understanding of marriage between them. But it must be said that all the real evidence, as opposed to rumour and romantic imagination, points to the fact that neither of the two had any intention of marriage, and that it was after Eibhlín's death and, even more so, after Pearse's execution in 1916 that the romance was given full credence. And then, of course, the Blasket people, being great ones for a story, may have added to the story, though from my own personal knowledge of the islanders that was not the case. They did not hold that there was any intention of marriage between them.

Without any doubt, in light of what followed in the next decade or so, it would enhance the cause both of the struggle for independence and the language movement to associate romance with Pearse. Were the people of Ireland to chose a partner for Pearse, the hero of the 1916 Rising, who better than Eibhlín Nic Niocaill, a beautiful woman, scholar and Gaelic enthusiast who died in an Irish-speaking island in an attempt to save the life of an island girl? True, they shared much in their work and in their opinions on the vote for women, the revival of the Irish language, customs and culture, the freedom of the nation. Given that, there were also great differences between the personalities of the two. Pearse was quiet and retiring while Eibhlín was open, cordial and friendly. Many had the opinion also that Pearse was too idealistic to have any time for romance, that he was really happily married to Ireland: that his romantic idea of Ireland was above the ideal of marriage or the love of a woman. One of his lifelong friend and teacher colleagues in Scoil Éanna, Eamonn O'Neill, remembered: "Pearse almost wept with vexation on hearing of Eoin MacNéill's then approaching marriage. Pearse felt it might lessen the activities of a man who was the light and inspiration of our work."[5]

Looking back on old copies of *An Claidheamh Soluis*, during a campaign to collect money to erect a memorial to an tAthair Mícheál P. Ó hIceadha, late lecturer in Irish at Maynooth, Eibhlín's name is entered as donating £1 on 21

Lúnasa 1909. Directly under it we see the name of Pádraig Mac Piarais and a subscription of £1 from him also. Is it a coincidence or did they send the two subscriptions together? It is anyway a further indication of how much they had in common. They were both Dubliners, involved in the revival of Irish, interested in education, and independence, had both taught Irish and had both degrees from UCD.

Eibhlín, in spite of being such an attractive woman, had never been known to have any attachment to a man, and it would seem that in this, she may have been of the same opinion as Pearse. She was married to Ireland.

In the article by Imelda Hallahan on Eibhlín, "The Girl Who Was Loved by Pearse", which is based on the information she gained from Cáit an Rí, she tells of Eibhlín in the island as they sat by the fire late into the night, chatting and sharing secrets: "After a few minutes she pushed her chair into the shadows and said to Cáit, 'Tá fear i mBaile Átha Cliath, ach ní phósfaidh mé é.' (There is a man in Dublin, but I will not marry him.) No more was said. Cáit never questioned her again on the subject."[6]

Risteárd Ó Glaisne asked Cáit some pertinent questions on that subject in 1964:

> She told me that he was interested in her, but that she would never marry him, Cáit told me.
>
> "And why not?" I asked sentimentally.
>
> "I couldn't say, but that is what she said," said Cáit. "She said that he used be coming to her home, and that her father and mother had a great liking for him. He is a fine man, a noble man, said she, but I will never marry him."[7]

We may get some hint of Pearse's love for women in *The Singer*, a play he wrote just before the Rising in 1916.

MacDara, thought by many to be Pearse himself, who has come home to see his mother Máire, his friend Sighle and his brother Colm before going into the fray against the Sasanach, tells of the love he has for Sighle:

Macdara: . . . yes, she is very beautiful. I did not know a woman could be so beautiful. I thought that all beauty was in the heart, that beauty was a secret thing that could be seen only with the eyes of reverie, or in a dream of some unborn splendour. I had schooled myself to think physical beauty an unholy thing. I tried to keep my heart virginal, and sometimes in the street of a city when I have stopped to look at the white limbs of some beautiful child, and have felt the pain that the sight of great beauty brings, I have wished that I could blind my eyes so that I might shut out the sight of everything that tempted me. At times I have rebelled against that, and have cried aloud that God would not have filled the world with beauty, even to the making drunk of the sight, if beauty were not of heaven. But, then, again, I have said, "This is the subtlest form of temptation; this is to give to one's own desire the sanction of God's will." And I have hardened my heart and kept myself cold and chaste as the top of a high mountain. But now I think I was wrong, for beauty like Sighle's must be holy.[8]

According to Geraldine Dillon, the sister of Joseph Plunkett, one of the leaders of the Insurrection of 1916, who knew the Nicolls family, Eibhlín's brother George stated that Eibhlín herself would never marry because of a drink problem in the family, and that she did not wish to leave her mother to deal with that problem alone. In the absence of any personal papers, who in the family had the problem is another question. Certainly, Eibhlín would be falling back on the traditional role of carer for the rest of the family in time of crisis or illness, as so often happened to daughters in Irish families at the time. Geraldine Dillon may well be correct regarding the drink problem, and we may get a further hint of that problem from a statement made by Fr Paul, a member of the Capuchins of Church Street at the memorial meeting for Eibhlín held in the

Mansion House on 8 September and presided over by the lord mayor:

> The Rev. Fr Paul supported the motion [to establish a Memorial Fund to enable girls to visit the Irish-speaking districts and to erect a local memorial]. He said he only knew the young lady by her successes as a scholar; but it was a satisfaction to him to know that one of his best and oldest friends was her worthy father, Mr. A. J. Nicolls, and the Fr Matthew Hall might be said to be in a large extent associated with his honoured name in his exertions to perpetuate the good work of Fr Matthew . . .[9]

Fr Theobald Matthew (1790–1856), a Capuchin friar from Tipperary and founder of one of the total abstinence associations, carried on a hugely successful crusade against alcoholic drink during the 1840s, resulting in up to 5 million taking the pledge, thus improving the lot of many poor families. In 1905 the Assembly of Bishops in Maynooth requested the Capuchin Fathers to preach another temperance crusade throughout the country. This, too, was highly successful. The Fr Matthew Memorial Hall in Church Street, Dublin, was built at this time, as a centre of social, educative and temperance work, to provide passtime and entertainment for people who wished to stay away from the pub.

An article in the *Freeman's Journal* of the 17 August 1909, which was then reprinted in *An Claidheamh Soluis* on 21 August 1909, written by George Munan, a member of the committee of the Feis Ceoil, tell us much of Eibhlín's personality, ability and dedication. He had worked with Eibhlín when she was secretary:

> The tragic event which has brought to an early close the brilliant career of Eibhlín Níc Niocaill, will be sincerely mourned by thousands who knew of her only as a distinguished student and as a zealous worker in the Language movement. But to the smaller circle who enjoyed her personal acquaintance, who were

her colleagues in work, and who came into contact with her admirable and exalted personality, the sense of loss will be accompanied by deep personal sorrow. Her absolutely selfless life of earnest study and practical effort have been crowned by a final act of noble self-sacrifice. Her end has a tragic fitness; but none the less will the event be mourned as an irreparable National Loss and a source of the deepest grief. Her intellectual attainments are borne testimony to by a brilliant series of academical distinctions. Her record of successes in scholastic fields shines brightly before the eyes of the public. Her career in the Intermediate and the University, her achievements in Paris and Germany, her enthusiastic visits to Aran and the Blaskets – these are obvious things by which all may recognise the ability and energy of the patriotic young heroine. They may, however, be recognised and fully appreciated without realising the nobility of character and the beauty of soul which accompanied such mental capacity. These inner and more admirable qualities were known to those alone who were in active communication, who were her colleagues in her practical work, or who otherwise had the privilege of her personal acquaintance.

The chief work with which Miss Nicolls was associated in the Gaelic League was in connection with the Dublin Feis. She had been known as a distinguished student, as a teacher in the "Five Provinces" branch, and as a quiet but observant representative of that branch at the meetings of the Dublin delegates. At one of the meetings some criticisms were made by, perhaps, some workers already overstrained as to the difficulty of securing practical assistance in their efforts. Soon afterwards a modest note came from Miss Nicolls intimating her readiness to give help. She was allotted to the Feis Committee and was appointed its Honorary Secretary.

. Eibhlín Nic Niocaill at her graduation

2. James H. Cousins in later life

3. Archibald J. Nicolls, Eibhlín's father, shortly before his death in May 1924

4. Eibhlín photographed by James Cousins as she started out from Ventry on her journey to the Blasket, 13 July 1909

5. Sea View, Ceann Trá, where Eibhlín stayed from 6 to 13 July, 1909

. Peats Tom Ó Cearnaigh down at the cliff, *c.* 1924; his wife, Neilí Jerry is in
the background

7. The King, Peats Mhicí Ó Catháin outside his house, with some members of his family

The King's House with his cow and some members of his family, *c.*1928

Caladh an Oileáin, the Blasket quay

10. *Naomhóga* at quay

11. An Tráigh Bhán

2. Three islandmen examine a tree trunk at the Tráigh Bhán

3. The landing of Eibhlín's body and the body of Domhnall Ó Criomhthain : Dhún Chaoin,15 August 1909

14. Loading a cow onto a *naomhóg* for transport to the mainland

15. Peats Tom Ó Cearnaigh, with his wife, Neilí Jerry Ní Shé, proudly wears his medal outside his home, 1937

To this new field of work Miss Nicolls came without any record of experience. The appointment, it may be admitted, was an experiment dictated by necessity. Yet never was an appointment so fully and thoroughly justified. As Secretary of the Dublin Feis she had to deal with a varied and intricate mass of details. Upon them she brought to bear all the precision and energy of her clear and active intelligence. She had the unusual gift of being able to apply to practical matters, with equal efficacy, that keen intellect which she had displayed in scholastic fields. No flavour of the atmosphere of the classroom attached to her work. She had an end in view; every available means was utilised by method and industry, every means was made available by tact and resource. Her industry was untiring. When some additional work should be done, she was the first to volunteer. The writer, as Chairman of the Committee, was often forced to remonstrate with her for undertaking new duties. She would, however, persist with a quiet determination – and that which she undertook to do was always done, and done well.

She was an absolutely selfless and impersonal worker. She never wasted words. When she spoke, her low tones impressed one by their earnestness and their conviction, born of sincerity and careful thought. Her adaptability was wonderful. From a day's hard study in the Library, from listening to an erudite lecture on Old Irish, from some hours' teaching to Gaelic League classes, she would come to committee meetings and conduct the business until late at night with practical skill – and extraordinary patience. Her brilliant lecture on "Nationality and Education" was composed at the busiest time of the Feis. To withdraw herself so easily from worrying details and to produce so eloquent an address with every sign of careful thought bespoke a power of detachment which was remarkable. She was an advanced Feminist, and destroyed many a reputation for politeness by insisting upon such points as paying her own tram fares. Yet there was no trace of the "blue stocking" about this tall, distinguished-looking, vigorous young girl.

Her work, alas, is over. In death, as in life she has been selfless. Her brilliant life has ended in a glorious act of heroic self-sacrifice. Thousands mourn for the sad blow that fallen upon a talented, a cultured and a patriotic household; a household united by domestic affection and by community of national feeling. May one measure of her reward be that the blow be alleviated.[10]

The following letter from Eibhlín's father, Archibald, dated 23 August 1909, was printed in the *Sinn Féin Daily* the following day and taken up by many of the provincial papers during the following week:

> Sir,
>
> The vast numbers of kindly letters etc., that have been sent to us since the drowning of our daughter would be acknowledged separately, were it possible for my wife and myself to do this. Especially, we desire to thank those who took part in the funeral from Great Blasket Island to Glasnevin, and the numerous societies and public bodies that mourn the loss of a true daughter of Erin.
>
> If you will be so kind as to publish these lines I should be glad if Provincial Editors would reproduce them, as if addressed to themselves; for from every province in Ireland my family have received most affecting and welcome tributes to the memory of Eibhlín Ní Niocaill.
>
> > Archibald J. Nicolls.
> > 23 August 1909.

Eibhlín's death was a great loss in particular to the Gaelic League for which she had worked so hard. At their next meetings, the various branches both in Dublin and around the country passed motions of sympathy in Irish at the death of Domhnall as well as that of Eibhlín, such as: "The following proposal was passed at the last meeting of the Keating Branch: It is of great sorrow to us, i.e. the members of the Keating Branch, how Eibhlín Nic Niocaill met her death down in the Blaskets and we sympathise with her family on her death. And also it is the cause of sorrow to us that the brave boy, Domhnall Ó Criomhthain, was drowned in an attempt to save Eibhlín from death."[11]

Back in Dingle a motion was passed by the Irish College, also expressing sympathy with the relations of Eibhlín and Domhnall, and Éamonn Ó Donoghue wrote a fine letter in Irish to *An Claidheamh Soluis* expressing the sympathy of the people of Munster on her death.

Eibhlín's mother wrote to *An Claidheamh Soluis* on 4 September 1909:

> Sir,
>
> I feel that my dead daughter is at my side, gazing at me with her thoughtful eyes, urging with voiceless entreaty that I, her mother, shall make known her last message to the Ireland that she loved so well. A few days before she went to Kerry she said: "I do not consider the political freedom of Ireland to be the most urgent question for today. When I look back upon the greatness of the many empires that have passed away, and see that their glory was but a point in time, I realise that for nations, as for individuals, true greatness lies in goodness. The Gaelic League is training the people to lofty ideals, to temperance, to industry, self respect and self reliance, and when their character is moulded on this basis, God will send freedom in his own good time."
>
> On the day of her death she had already lived six weeks among the simple, loving, true-hearted peasants of Kerry. She hoped to stay with them for many more weeks, in order to gain increased proficiency in

the language that must be recovered if Ireland is to maintain her claim to nationhood.

One of her last acts was to send a cheque to the Committee charged with promoting the testimonial to the Rev. Dr. Hickey, in recognition of the great services rendered by him to Ireland. She believed, as he and thousands of cultured and thoughtful Irish men and Irish women believe, that to make a study of the Irish language essential in the National University is of immediate urgency, not merely for the success of that institution, but for safeguarding Catholic Faith in Ireland, and for the development of National character of the best type.

In some moments of despondency she felt that if – even at this eleventh hour – the agency of the Irish language be not invoked to help in saving our young men and women from the filthy literature of England, their souls and minds shall sink lower than the level of English slum-life. She felt that a nation cannot live in the traditions of its glorious past and that Ireland must cease to boast the glory of her saints and scholars if their children fail in their duty now.

Still more she felt that the people must arise, with quiet but mighty resolve, and that it is for them to say that Ireland must not, and shall not become the bedraggled and mire-stained tail of a decadent, unjust and hypocritical empire.

Mary Nicolls,
25th August 1909.

The letter may seem strange, coming from the wife of a Dublin Castle official who was on the committee to welcome Queen Victoria to Ireland in 1900, but it is a good indication of the changes that had taken place over the previous years. It gives a further indication of Eibhlín's dreams and aspirations for Ireland, and again we can see the closeness of her point of view to that of Pádraig Pearse.

We get another glimpse of Eibhlín from a surprising

source, in a letter written to *An Claidheamh Soluis* on 4 September 1909 by District Nurse B.V. Hedderman, the Jubilee Nurse on the Aran Islands, published by her in 1917 in a book entitled *Glimpses of My Life in Aran*:

"We'll never be drowned as we have escaped this night," were the words Miss Nicolls uttered as she stepped ashore one dark, very dark, evening at Inishmaan. We had set out for South Island that Sunday morning accompanied by two friends, one a priest who had come to study Irish, and after Mass re-embarked again and voyaged to Kilronan where we stayed a little time . . . [I]t was late when we reached the Inishmaan coast. As the boat belonged to Inisheer and the crew knew absolutely nothing about the danger points surrounding that rugged island, the night was too dark and far advanced to effect a landing at the quay . . .

Happily for us, there was on board an Inishmaan man who had in some way got separated from his own crew, but the others took no notice of his directions. He kept pointing to the Caladh Mór as a possible landing place, while they were following a different course. This shouting caused a panic among themselves while Eveleen Nicolls remained perfectly motionless. I have never since forgotten her calm sweet voice as she tried to lull our fears at an extremity when we were nearly on the rocks. At length we prevailed upon the Inisheer men to permit the Middle Islander to steer. We landed in utter darkness and, with difficulty, succeeded in hauling up the boat, Miss Nicolls and I carrying the oars, for owing to the lateness the Inisheer men could not journey onwards.

Eibhlín Nicolls came to Inishmaan immediately after matriculation. The people loved her, and simply idolised her. No words can do justice to her character nor adequately express the sweetness and gentleness of her manners amongst us. I have seen her sit patiently for hours many days soothing the wounded spirit of an old crippled woman afflicted with rheumatism, reminding me of one of Raphael's angels. Hers was truly a noble and heroic soul.

Here is another account, dated 24 August 1909, from the people of Inis Meáin, Aran Islands, where she had been formerly a regular visitor:

A Chara,

The people of the island came together after Mass on Sunday on account of the death of Eibhlín Nic Niocaill.

They asked me to forward this letter to her people to explain to them the sorrow and regret they felt when they heard of Eibhlín's death.

There wasn't present either young or old that did not have a close knowledge of and friendship with her; she has not been amongst us now for a couple of years, but if so, we know well that she had not forgotten us. Although we are far removed from anywhere we used hear of Eibhlín and of her work.

We are sorry and experience great regret, that we, your people and all Ireland have lost you, Eibhlín.

May God have mercy on your soul and may He raise the sorrow from her father, her mother and her brothers.

We are,
In sorrow,
The People of Inishmean
through Tomás Ó Conghaile.[12]

We have one more account of her stay in Inis Meáin in a letter from someone signing herself "Bean Tighe", the "woman of the house":

It is impossible for words to tell of the love that Eibhlín had for the "fisherman's garden." She always liked to be at the edge of that garden looking at her flowers, though it was it that was to shorten her life, but heartily welcome be the grace of God! Those who ploughed that garden had the same love for her, for she was indeed gentle, friendly and fair. She never put a frown on her forehead on seeing the customs and methods of the ploughers. Though they are a peculiar people she delighted in spending her free time with them every year, and from the first time she ever got to know them she had a love for them. She loved the Gaeil, regardless of where their home was.

I well remember when she first came to Inismean, six or seven years ago. It was little the Irish she knew then, but she had great interest in learning it and in a short time she had good knowledge. She had a great interest in the people and they had a great interest in her. They were never shy with her because she could banish that shyness with her fondness and affection. She had love for the small person as well as for the great. She was not very talkative, and the people often said that she was a shy girl, but if she was sometimes shy, she had her own reasons for it. Little or no English did she speak as long as she remained on the island – particularly when she wished to speak to the people themselves. She spent a month or so like this, before she grasped properly the feel of the Irish, and until she achieved this, she said little, little more than to greet people. In the end she felt that she could speak the Irish freely and without mistakes. It wasn't long till she was as fluent as the people themselves. Then you would often hear the old people saying, "My God, isn't it amazing the way she caught on to the Irish, and she learning is for such a short time." Surely, Eibhlín didn't lose a chance, as there was nothing in this life that she wished more than to learn Irish, and it wasn't any half learning either.

At the end of her holidays, as she was leaving, the people would be so sorry to see her go, as though it were among them that she was born and reared. She was like one of themselves. The day she would make her way towards the quay she would be made to promise, "And will you come again, Eibhlín, next year, with God's help?"

"I will, certainly," she would reply, and she would come.

Both the day she arrived and the day she departed were holidays on the island. From a month to six weeks she would spend on the island each year.

One year she paid two visits.

She had a great liking for rowing and fishing. She wasn't a great swimmer those years, yet in no way was she afraid of the sea. She often used give good advice to the youth, finding fault with America, and the way the people must work there, the poor pay and unmerciful masters over them.

She never rested but was either reading or writing. She took down many old stories. Indeed, great was her interest in them. If she did take them down, I don't think they have been put in print yet.

Eibhlín had no desire to speak English until she had mastered Irish. She stayed silent until then. And every visitor who comes to the Gaeltacht should do the same. There are those who go to the Gaeltacht at this time with a little of the language, but with no confidence to speak it, and because of that they speak English to the people without thinking of the harm they are doing. That is a serious blow to the language in that place, and a great victory for English. Let them do as Eibhlín did. Don't speak to the people until you are able to speak to them in their own language (except of course for special reasons). Stay silent. Listen to them and you will enjoy the results of your efforts much better in the end.

On behalf of the people who loved Eibhlín so much, we are sharing with her people who are feeling sorrow, and may such sorrow and darkness never come their way again, nor such a weight of sorrow ever descend again on Ireland.[13]

Eibhlín was known far and wide across the country. Here's an account from Donegal:

> There is a dark cloud over St Columcille's High School itself since the news has arrived that Eibhlín Nic Niocaill is dead in the south of Ireland. But Úna Ní Fhaircheallaigh said that there was no use in being in despair, as it would do nothing to help now but to say a prayer to God above to grant the peace of Glory to her soul.
>
> Late in the evening the scholars of the College gathered in the chapel in Gort an Choirce where the Revd Ó Muireadhaigh said the De Profundis and offered up the Rosary for the repose of her soul.[14]

An account in *An Claidheamh Soluis* of the 1 October 1910 tells us that mass had been offered in Bolivia for the repose of Eibhlín's soul on her anniversary on behalf of Jasper, her brother. He was working there as a doctor and, true to the family tradition, had founded, in 1907, a branch of the Gaelic League, of which he was the secretary, for the Irish community there.[15]

Meanwhile back in the Blaskets the people were slowly recovering after the twin shock of 13 August. A new fear of the sea had been generated, and it was a long time before anyone went swimming on Tráigh Bhán an Oileáin. As Méiní remembered:

> 'Tis often when I would be walking west by the edge of the Tráigh Bhán just as night was coming on when the waves were breaking on the strand that I would imagine that the waves were lamenting Eibhlín Nic Niocaill and the young man that gave his life for her. He was right. He said he would never have any other woman but she, and he hadn't. He had lost his life for her.

The strand was very lonely for an long time afterwards. People never liked to be there alone or even near it.[16]

\* \* \* \* \* \*

The sad summer was drawing to a close. School would be starting soon, and it was time for James and Gretta Cousins to be getting back to Dublin. They left Sea View and Thady and Máire Kevane on 20 August. Before he left he recorded this message in the visitors' book, still a valued possession of Thady's grandson, Noel:

> We came to Ventry strangers, and we have lived in Ventry as part of the people. We leave with the greatest regret, having made fast friends among the people. We have been housed and catered for by Mrs. Kevane with complete comfort. Her friendliness and the friendliness of Mr. Kevane have put us at perfect ease, and enabled us to enter into the life of the country. Our one regret is that we have not been able to converse in Irish. But this disadvantage had been compensated to us by the richness of the district in legendary lore, and in valuable and most interesting relics of an ancient civilisation and of Early Christian settlements. The people of the district are the essence of hospitality. We shall certainly come back to enjoy the repose and pleasure, the friendliness and repose of Ventry.
>
> James H. Cousins. July 6th to Aug. 20th 1909[17]

He could not depart without mention of Eibhlín:

> Miss Eibhlín Nicolls M.A. of Dublin stayed here from July 6th to 13th, and proposed returning here on her way home from the Blaskets. Unfortunately it was otherwise decreed. She died in an effort to save another girl from drowning at the island on the 13th August. During her stay here she frequently expressed

her satisfaction at everything in the house, and was specially pleased with the unique advantages for practising the speaking of Irish, and with the dances which were given by the boys and girls of the district.

James H. Cousins.

20th August '09[18]

They left Ventry on their bicycles that Friday afternoon and went as far as Dingle, where they remained for the following two days.

On the next day, Saturday, they went around Dingle among the busy crowd distributing leaflets on the suffragette movement, announcing that there would be a meeting the following day at Hudson's Bridge, which would be addressed by Gretta, and inviting everyone to attend. The meeting would be held at "one o'clock sharp" when the people would be on their way home from last mass.

The meeting was covered by *"Duine do'n tSluagh"* for the *Kerryman,* and the rather mocking report appeared on 28 August under the headline "SUFFRAGETTES ON THE WARPATH". That was the general atmosphere of mocking disregard and ridicule that the movement met with, both here and in England. "Suffragists" was their proper title, but more often they were jokingly referred to by the press as "suffragettes".

A large crowd had assembled at Hudson's Bridge, named from Doctor Hudson who lived beside the bridge in the last house in the Holy Ground, beside what is now the pub Tigh Uí Fhlaithbheartaigh. The house still stands though the bridge has been changed beyond all recognition and a roundabout stands in its place. The writer wondered whether the large crowd assembled because of sympathy or curiosity.

Gretta Cousins, the brave little woman, hon. treasurer to the Irish Women's Franchise League, faced the audience alone and spoke out eloquently and earnestly for at least three quarters of an hour. According to the account, "many had come to scoff, but stayed to pray", such was the impression she made on her tough west Kerry audience.

The meeting ended to enthusiastic applause, while Jim, on the sideline, went about selling the badges calling for "VOTES FOR WOMEN". The crowd then dispersed to their usual Sunday evening activities; some made their slow way home to their frugal dinner. Some made it to the pub, while others hurried to the football match between Dingle and Lispole.

Jim and Gretta fixed their bags on the male and female bicycles, and readied themselves for the journey. Jim fixed on the bicycle clips and Gretta tied back her hair. They walked together out the Mail Road to Tralee, past the small train station. Then, mounting the bikes, they set off at a brisk pace way out by Baile an tSagairt and Baile an Ístínigh. The night would see them in Killarney in Tomey's Wood at the foot of Purple Mountain.

There were more poems to be made, new places to be seen, battles to be fought, fresh fields and pastures to be visited.

I think they knew they would never see Dingle or Ventry again:

> From far-off peaks in summer drowned,
> The river rushed past you and me,
> And in an ecstasy of sound
> Leaped straight into the sea!
>
> With faith as firm, and equal mirth,
> May you and I, in time to be,
> Leap from our edge of crumbling earth
> Into the Spirit's sea.[19]

At the fireside by nights the people remembered Eibhlín. Her early days after her arrival were fondly recalled and the signs that had taken place shortly before her arrival. A sailing vessel was seen leaving Dún Chaoin quay, facing north, skimming over the water without touching it as it glided silently out into the ocean, a sure sign that someone important was going to die. Something very strange had happened in Sea View, Ventry, on the night that Eibhlín was drowned. It was late at night. The people of the house and the residents were asleep, and the house had fallen into silence. A faint noise was heard down in the kitchen, as if someone were preparing a snack before retiring for the night, a custom that was widespread then and afterwards to those who were on holidays. Then footsteps were heard ascending the stairs softly, so as not to disturb anyone. The bedroom door was opened and then closed. That bedroom was empty that night. And in the morning it was still empty. It was the room in which Eibhlín had stayed before her visit to the island. It came as no surprise to Thady and Máire when the news broke in the morning that Eibhlín had drowned on the Blaskets.

Other legends grew up around Eibhlín with the passing of time. It was said on the island that Eibhlín's bedroom in her home at Kenilworth Road remained unoccupied, spotlessly clean, with the bed comfortably dressed and everything laid aside waiting for its occupant who would never return.

Another tale tells of Eibhlín and some of her friends gathered in conversation one night by the fire. The subject was the way they would all like to die. Eibhlín mentioned that the way she would most like to die was in an attempt to save someone from drowning.

Cousins was able to add that he had heard that Eibhlín had lately received a present of a typewriter, but had not the time or opportunity to learn how to use it. Her mother instead took to learning it and practised by typing texts from the Bible. When the sad news of Eibhlín's death arrived, the mother was in the act of typing a text from the Book of Job: "The Lord giveth, the Lord taketh away. Blessed be the name of the Lord."

# CHAPTER 8

# Behold the Perfect Life

MAIDHC PHEATS MHICÍ Ó Catháin was an accomplished musician on the fiddle. It was enough for him to hear a tune once or twice to recall and play it. It is often he used to rise in the middle of the night to play a tune which was coming between him and his night's sleep. He emigrated to America about 1906, but his interest in music continued on even stronger than before in memory of home. He was in great demand to play at *céilithe* in Springfield where he lived and in other parts as well where the Irish used to meet up. He was getting on very well. One letter that he sent home to the island was remembered. He described how he had been playing music in a room and that same music could be heard simultaneously by many people in many other places in the area and all that was needed was a small machine like a box. The box could be turned in, and the music or speech could be heard right there in the room. His father Peats Mhicí, the King, read this letter and puzzled over its meaning and finally came to the conclusion that his son had drink taken when he wrote the letter if they expected him to believe that he could play the fiddle in one place and that it could be heard in another place far from home. It was the first indication of the radio.

A further letter arrived from Maidhc saying that he was planning to come home for a few weeks, looking forward to meeting them all and saying that he would bring his fiddle and they could be sure of a few great nights of music and dancing.

He arrived on the Dingle train one evening in the autumn of 1909. He made his way to Martin Keane's house and pub in Goat Street. Martin was an islandman himself and a relation of Maidhc's. It was to Martin's house that all the island people used go when on a visit to Dingle, and if necessary they would stay there overnight.

Martin welcomed Maidhc back to Kerry. He filled a drink for him and Maidhc asked him, "Any news?"

"There's no news," says Martin. "Everything is very quiet since the two were drowned on the island."

Maidhc had heard nothing of the island tragedy, and it came as a great shock to him. Martin had to tell him the whole story from start to finish: how Eibhlín had come to the island, how she made friends with the young people, her swimming classes, and how the girls went swimming and that Cáit Criomhthain got into difficulties, and that Maidhc's own sister, Cáit an Rí, was watching as Domhnall Ó Criomhthain and Eibhlín were drowned.

Maidhc listened to every word in a state of shocked surprise. When it was time for him to leave, Maidhc gathered his belongings and then got his fiddle case and approached Martin.

"Would you ever keep this for me until I return to Dingle on my way back to the States in a couple of weeks?" asked Maidhc.

"Leave it here and I'll put it in a safe place and you can have it on your way back. But why won't you take it with you now?"

"I would much prefer to leave it here rather than take it over to the island. According to what you have just told me, the island is no place for music any more."[1]

But what's the use in always lamenting the dead. Life must go on. Slowly the little village gathered up its courage and accepted the will of God. Méiní explained it thus: "It is certain that a better place was set aside for their souls by the Almighty, a much happier place than this life."[2]

Everyone felt so sorry for poor Tomás Ó Criomhthain:

"Tomás Criomhthain got his share of misfortune in this life if anyone ever got it. But God gave his help to the poor unfortunate man to carry his cross, and carry it he did."[3]

Méiní was right. From the day of his marriage to Máire Ní Chatháin, the King's sister from Barr an Bhaile, on 5 February 1878, he was dogged by fate and misfortune. Seán, his firstborn, fell over a cliff to his death while out gathering gulls' eggs when he was just six or seven. Two other children died in an epidemic of measles.

> Ten children were born to us, but misfortune followed us, God help us! The first child of ours that was ever baptised was six or seven when he fell over a cliff and was killed. From that out they were dying faster than they were coming. Two died with the measles and there wasn't a disease that didn't pay us a visit. Domhnall was drowned trying to save the noble lady on the Tráigh Bhán. I had one other fine boy growing up. It wasn't long before he too was taken.
>
> The sorrow of all these affected the poor mother, and she was taken from me. I wasn't properly blinded till then.[4]

By the next census in 1911 his little family was scattered and broken, and there would be none left but himself and a brother, Paddy, who had returned from the States, as well as three sons, Pádraig, Muiris and Seán. Life had been too much for his wife, Máire Ní Chatháin, the King's sister, who had died in 1904 at just forty-four years of age. A sad little entry in the ledger of John Long, grocer and spirits dealer, Waterside, Dingle, on 29 June 1904, notes:

**Thos. Crohan Blaskets**
*Goods for Wife's Wake*

| | |
|---|---|
| Bread 3/-, ½ lb tea, 4 lbs. Sug. 1/10 | 4s. 10d. |
| 1 Bt. Whiskey 3/4 2 lbs. butter 2/- | 5s. 4d. |
| 1 Gal. porter 6292 | 16s. 0d. |
| | £1. 6s. 2d. |

| By Cash | 10s. 2d. |
| Bal | 16s. 0d.[5] |

Then for his son Domhnall to have drowned and his daughter Cáit to have been close to death was a further cross for the poor *ainniseoir*. Cáit died young, in 1922, in childbirth. To add further to his misfortune, another son, Pádraig, or "Denny" as he was known, died in 1913 in Dingle hospital as a result of a strain received in lifting a *naomhóg*. He was thirty-two and Tomás' main support. Still another son, Muiris, left for America. As he said himself, "As bad as things were, the grave beat them all for misfortune . . ."[6]

At the end of his days, as he was writing his books, he was left with one son, Seán, and his brother Paddy. Seán, who was to become one of the Blasket writers himself, married one of the Sullivan girls, Éilís, who wrote those now famous letters to George Chambers in London in the 1930s. Seán, his wife and young daughter, Niamh, left the island in 1942 and settled in Muiríoch.

\* \* \* \* \* \*

The death of Eibhlín moved many of her countrymen and women to poetry, some of it in the archaic and clichéd style she disliked, but some of higher quality. Cousins himself wrote "Death and Life", dated 13 August 1909, which he dedicated to her memory.

> Death and Life.
> The long dark slope is topped with mist,
> But here the sun is on the grass.
> Beneath, the sea waves break, and twist
> Backward like snakes of molten glass.
> Across an ancient sand-heaped wall
> The foot through graves forgotten goes,
> And stops where old old voices call
> Through generations of repose.
> But where a sorrow of today

Has set a freshly fashioned mound,
A bird slides down his airy way
And makes the silence ring with sound.

What gloom might now our spirits balk
Fades out before that high reproof;
And through the fabric of your talk
Go light and shadow, warp and woof,
With something deeper than the word,
Some stately certitude of faith
Whose eye at life had never blurred
Nor quivered at the eye of death,
But saw in that swift woman's way
Through changings to the changeless Whole.
And life and death as waves that sway
Across the ocean of the soul.

Then when the hill was lost in mist,
And in the sea the sky was glassed,
We wandered home in amethyst;
And you upon the morrow passed
On that last journey to the west
Whose end was in the Atlantic wave,
Where, on your youth's triumphant crest,
One stroke, another's life to save,
With glory crowned your life complete,
Proud as the horsed and pluméd seas
That laid your body at my feet,
A wonder past Praxiteles.

Oh! bear her body by the crest
And past the fields of fallen ears
On its last journey from the west
This holy Lady Day of tears.
But yet, though heads are bared and bowed,
And down the road the keeners keen,
Some spirit-music, deep and proud,
Slips out their shrill thin cries between;
And, like the bird that other day,

That made the silence ring with sound,
It floats along the sunset way,
A joy above our sorrow's mound.

What grief might now our spirits balk
Fades out before that high reproof;
And through the hushed and wavering talk
That fills the streets from roof to roof,
A fire from your high altar shines,
A kindles through our dusk of strife
A faith whose inner eye divines
That Death is minister to Life,
And all our years a moment's dream
In one vast Mind that grasps the whole.
And life and death but waves that gleam
Along the ocean of the soul.[7]

Probably the finest poetic memorial to Eibhlín was that of Pádraic Mac Coluim, better known in later times as Pádraic Colum. Pádraic's star was steadily rising at the time, and he was to reach great heights with poems such as "The Old Woman of the Roads", which is still recited today, and, of course, "She Moved through the Fair", one of our best known love songs. He knew the Cousins, and very likely knew the Nicolls, too, having been born in the Longford workhouse, where his father was gatekeeper and Eibhlín's grandfather was medical officer. The poem appeared in *Sinn Féin* on 21 August 1909.

Eibhlín Nic Niocaill *(i gcuimhne)*

And who was she so brave
And thus to challenge death,
And who was she who gave
Life for a sister's breath.

One who had grace with ease
And youth with dignity;
And one, being self-possessed
Had all integrity.

A sister with fair looks
With clear and tranquil gaze,
We straightaway were the friend
Of those who spoke her praise.

Resolve was in her mien
And knowledge on her brows,
And all the virgin will
Was in her deep repose.

The merits of a house
Were centred in this child,
The virtues of a name,
Were in her reconciled.

A paragon of maids,
Dear for her gentleness,
And one to Ireland gave
Her youth and nobleness.

We would have given store,
If all we had sufficed,
If gold could have redeemed,
Or high hopes sacrificed.

It may be we do no wrong,
Crudely to interpose;
Behold the perfect life
Hath its own perfect close.

We cannot grudge that she
Her character less brave,
We cannot wish unborn
The high impulse to save;

We cannot deem it vain
The high heroic will,
Beyond the wash of waves
She moves untroubled still.

Unto some finer task
She moves with look serene,

With solace on her brow
And comfort in her mien.

Although we say goodbye
We shall not sorrow, friend.
May all who think so high
Meet with so fair an end.

I have not succeeded in coming across any verse from
an island poet.The great poet Seán Ó Duinnshléibhe had
died some twenty years previously, as had another
referred to as Old Sullivan. There were younger poets on
their way, particularly Mícheál Ó Gaoithín, Peig Sayers'
son, though he would have been but eight years at the
time of the tragedy. Years afterwards he did record another drowning tragedy, also through swimming, that of
Liam Berkery, a young clerical student, who was drowned
on Clogher Strand in August 1953. Tomás Ó Criomhthain, the Islandman himself, was known to have composed some fine verses, but it does not appear that he
recorded the tragedy in poetry.

Another poet, a woman this time, Katherine Tynan, also
composed a poem in memory of Eibhlín. She was a very
popular poet in the first twenty years of the century. Her
best known poem, one we all learned in school, "Sheep
and Lambs", begins:

All in the April evening,
April airs were abroad . . .

She, too, like Gretta Cousins and Eibhlín herself, was in
her early life very involved in the women's movement, as
well as in religious matters and the national freedom movement. It seems likely that she was also acquainted with
Eibhlín. Certainly she knew James Cousins and Gretta as
she had two sons attending the High School where James
taught. In October 1909 she composed this lament for
Eibhlín which she had published in the *Irish Monthly*, a
magazine to which she frequently contributed:

## The Glorious Girl

How wise to take the easy way,
The easy way so hard to find,
While yet your life and work and play,
With songs of joy in every wind.

Why, men have toiled with ache and sweat,
Abjured all things that men hold dear
To win some little glory yet
Like you, you girl of twenty years.

Wise girl, not yours to toil and strive
In sandy deserts, fire and frost,
Who saved your happy soul alive,
Nor ever stayed to count the cost.

This man would scale the highest heights,
That one would vanquish fell disease,
Another by the Northern Lights
Survey a frozen world just his.

You child without a grief or care
Have found your easy place on high –
Further than glorious men may fare,
You who could only love and die.

Why, Eibhlín, 'twas bravely done,
Before your garden noon stole out.
The swiftest runner passed, outrun,
And – hear the people, how they shout.

Perhaps the most poignant reference of all was that of her old friend Máire de Buitléir, who had accompanied her to Dingle that first day. Máire became a very popular writer in her time, particularly through her two novels, *The Ring of Day* (1906) and *The Price* (1909).[8] *The Price* was serialised in the *Irish Weekly Independent* beginning on 9 October, less than two months after Eibhlín's drowning and concluding on 10 January 1910. In *The Price*, the heroine, Beatrice Burke (Eibhlín), has returned to an island to visit the grave of her dead lover, Eoin O'Gara. She goes walking to the other side of the island where she had walked with Eoin in happier days. There is a deep lake lying in a hollow on that side of the island. A young boy has followed her to be with the *"bean uasal álainn"*. Going over to the cliff edge to pick flowers to present to her, he slips and is left hanging over the precipice clinging to a small bush. Beatrice succeeds in dragging him back, but in doing so loses her balance and falls over the cliff herself.

A priest, Fr Conroy, comforts her family when they arrive. Beatrice is dead, but she has found happiness. They are the ones left behind who will miss her sorely. He makes a brave attempt to gain some good from their heavy loss:

> To love something more than one's self is the secret of everything which is great; to know how to live outside of one's own personality, that is the object of every generous instinct. That principle was the mainspring of Beatrice's life and it has also been of her death. She died in saving the life of a child, and as her whole life was spent in the service of the children of her motherland, inspiring them with something of her own brave, beautiful spirit, putting part of her very self into them, it was fitting that in the end she should give her life in order to save one of them from death . . . From Beatrice's death life springs. Not only her own supernatural life, but other human lives, the physical life of the child whom she has saved to begin with and then the spiritual life of her race which she has quickened into being by her vivifying influence. Beatrice is the mystical mother of many, the mother of the mind and spirit of her race.

Beatrice's spirit will always be there on the island, contented and happy, whispering in the west wind her joyous message: "You shall possess the land."[9]

# CHAPTER 9

# Her Fame Will Live

## *Mairfidh a Cáil*

A T THE END of August 1909 the following letter was sent to the secretary of every branch of the Gaelic League:

An attempt is being made to keep the fame and notice of Eibhlín Nic Niocaill alive among the people of Ireland. If this effort succeeds it will do good in two ways. Not alone will it keep Eibhlín's name in affection and honour but it will help a poor family which is suffering sorrow and heartbreak.

What it is planned to achieve, and Eibhlín's parents and family are in agreement, is that the most recent picture of her will be put up for sale, and whatever profit that will accrue will be put aside in aid of the family whose brave young man gave his life in an effort to rescue Eibhlín. Whoever will purchase the picture, not alone will he be helping in this worthwhile work, but he will also be doing his best to spread the fame of this noble young woman around the nation. There is no doubt but that Eibhlín herself would be totally against this project, seeing that she was not a person who liked to put herself forward in any way. One of these pictures should be in the home of every member of the Gaelic League in Ireland. The measurements of the picture will be about nine inches in length, and six inches in width, and it will cost only eighteen pence.

Send word, please, of how many your branch will
need. The money and the orders for the picture can
be sent to the Treasurer of the Blasket Relief
Committee, 25 Rutland Square, Dublin.

Mise le mór-mheas,

Pádraig Ua Séagha,

("Conán Maol.")[1]

It could be said that Seán Óg, or Seán Mac Murchadha
Caomhánach, or even Seán an Chóta, as he was later
known, represented the opinions of the people of Corca
Dhuibhne in the letter he sent to *An Claidheamh Soluis* on
26 August:

I saw by the letter from "Conán Maol" that the
image of Eibhlín Nic Niocaill will be available before
long from the secretary of the Gaelic League and that
the profit made will go to the aid of the people of that
brave boy, Domhnall Ó Criomhthain, who gave his
life in an effort to save his sister and Eibhlín from
drowning. This is a very praiseworthy venture without any doubt and the Gaeil will rise to the occasion.
There is not a home in Ireland but should have the
image of Eibhlín hanging in it as she was a girl who
was completely loyal to her country, and were it not
for death she would surely have made a wonderful
contribution to Ireland, and she shows by her noble
actions that she had wonderful potential in her to
give her life for a fellow creature. Never before has
the nation been so devastated by the death of anyone.
It is as if they knew her value. Gone from us is a gentle girl, a fine scholar, a developed mind, a fine disposition, a generous spirit and a girl who was
completely loyal to her nation.

May God grant eternal rest to her soul and to the
soul of poor Domhnall without guile.

Seán Mac M. Caomhánach

Copies of the photograph continued to be sold

throughout the winter of 1909–10, with an occasional reminder in *An Claidheamh Soluis* that such a project was in progress and that there were a small number of the pictures still available. The project concluded in July 1910, and by that time there were about 300 pictures sold and distributed around the country, hanging in homes and halls, on walls and over mantelpieces. They realised £21. 8s. 3d. Fíonán Mac Coluim, who was present on the island quay the day of the tragedy, was nominated to present the money on behalf of Conán Maol and Stiofán Bairéad, the organisers of the project.[2]

On 20 July, Donnchadh Ó Loingsigh and Fíonán went into the island. They were given a hearty welcome, especially by the family of the deceased lad, Domhnall Ó Criomhthain, and by the *Rí* (King) and his family, particularly Cáit *an Rí*, or "an Princess" as she was known. The islanders old and young gathered round the two visitors, and Irish in all its Blasket richness was heard on all sides. "We learn with satisfaction that he [Tomás] has been a consistent friend of An Ghaedhilge and an enemy of An Galldachas for many years and that he was the first of the islanders to learn to read his native tongue."[3]

Tomás had by now begun to recover from the tragic events of the previous year, though the effect of Domhnall's death remained with him always. Seán later said, "With the passing of time the memory of the Tráigh Bhán began to fade from his memory, and when Cáit, his daughter, married a man of the Malones in Dún Chaoin, it gave him great satisfaction."[4]

Tomás himself sent a letter of thanks to those who had bought the picture. It appeared in *An Claidheamh Soluis* on 30 July 1910 – translated here – and it seems to be the first time Tomás wrote in Irish for publication.

> An Blascaod Mór,
>> Today the 20th July.
>> To Stiophán Bairéad.
>> A Chara,

This is to say that I received from the hands of Fíonán Mac Coluim twenty-one pounds, eight and half a sixpence as a gift from the Irish-speaking people. I would like to thank them seven thousand times and to say that I will remember for ever what they have done for me. All my dead son did was to do the same as would befit any Gael, the same as every single man in this island would do.

I hope to God that you will succeed in the great work you are undertaking and I promise you that both I and the people of the island will do our bit to keep the Irish alive and well in our midst here.

I with affection to you,
Tomás Ó Criomhthain

It is about this time that Tomás began to take an active interest in Irish and begins to write through that medium, the first of the islanders to do so. In the 1901 census, Tomás entered his own name and that of all his family in English, i.e. Crohan. But in the 1911 census he filled in his name and those of his family in English, but signs his name as the head of the family at the bottom of the form in Irish, "Tomás Ó Criomhthain", the only head of family on the island to do so. It was the form of his name that he was to use afterwards in his books. By 1910 he was writing frequently to Robin Flower in Irish. From then on his output in Irish was wondrous. Each day as soon as evening set in, he sat in his kitchen writing by lamplight to escape from the loneliness of the long nights.

Regarding the photograph of Eibhlín, Máire Ní Ghuithín had this to say: "For a long time the picture of Eibhlín Nic Niocaill hung over the bed in the room in which she stayed in the King's house. I well remember seeing that picture myself."[5]

There was another copy of the picture in the house of the Kavanaghs (Seán Óg and Kruger) in Baile na Rátha. Kruger seemed to think that it was Eibhlín herself gave it to them. It remained in the old home until it was finally closed when the family moved up to Badger's Hill in Kildare in the 1930s. It was then taken to Kruger's new home, which later became a pub. Kruger took great care of the picture, even when people had forgotten whose picture it was, and had it hanging by the window. One Christmas it almost met its end when the curtains took fire from a Christmas candle lighting in the window. Fortunately it was rescued in time. It is from this that the copy was made that hangs in Krugers to the present day. It was from this also that the picture of Eibhlín appearing in these pages was taken. According to Kruger again, his family and the Nicolls continued on in friendship for many years afterwards: "I often visited the Nicolls in their home in Rathgar."[6]

Such a pity that he did not leave us any further accounts of the family.

In addition to the picture fund, another committee was formed in the Mansion House, Dublin, on 8 September 1909, to make a permanent commemoration to Eibhlín and Domhnall. The lord mayor himself took the chair before a large attendance.Various speeches in praise of Eibhlín and Domhnall were made, a committee was then formed. *Sinn Féin,* reporting on the meeting on 9 September, used Colum's verse:

> Behold the perfect life
> Hath its own perfect close

as the logo for the scheme. The appeal began: "It is fitting that we should cherish the memory of her heroism in the way most suitable . . ."[7]

On that night alone £49. 2s. 6d. was collected for the purpose. It was agreed, firstly, that a scholarship be established to send a girl to the Gaeltacht to study the language and, secondly, that a plaque or statue be raised in their memory.[8]

This effort seems to have been even more successful than the former, as by March 1910 in excess of £100 had been collected. Handsome donations had been made in particular by Eibhlín's old Alma Mater, Loreto College, St Stephen's Green, which put up £7. 10s. 0d., and by Lord Mayor William Coffey, Cathal Brugha, Seán Mac Murchadha Caomhánach (Seán Óg), Eoin MacNéill and Thomas MacDonagh. Many of those would later play a prominent part in the 1916 Rising.

A full committee meeting was announced for Friday, 18 March, at 4.30 to allocate the funds and to determine the conditions under which the scholarships would be tenable.

Then, for some reason, the drive for funds suddenly stopped, and both myself and others have been unable to trace any further account of it. Neither plaque nor statue was ever raised, to my knowledge, nor did I succeed in finding any account of a girl being sent to the Gaeltacht on scholarship. It is likely that due to the outbreak of war in 1914 and the subsequent insurrection in 1916, followed by the War of Independence and, even more so, the Civil War that followed in 1922, matters such as erecting statues and awarding scholarships were given very low priority.

There was a surprising and happy sequel for Peats Tom Ó Cearnaigh: "The gallant fellow [who] had plunged partly undressed into the sea, and swam a considerable distance before saving Miss Crehan."[9]

We have it in his own words: "A master who lived in Baile an Fheirtéaraigh named Liam Ó Lúing saw on a paper that he was reading that a medal had been awarded to a man from the County Clare for saving someone, and he took the paper to the parish priest and told him that the man who had done the deed in his own parish should also get something."[10]

Liam Ó Lúing was a teacher in the school in Baile an Fheirtéaraigh and had a pub cum guest house. It seems likely now that the person who was saved from drowning was not from County Clare, but from St Finan's Bay, Ballinskelligs, in Kerry, a rescue which had taken place a few days before the Blasket drowning.

It is very likely that Liam Ó Lúing saw the report of this rescue in the *Kerry People* on 14 August 1909 and brought it to the attention of the parish priest, and between them they applied to the Humane Society for Peats Tom's act of bravery to be recognised. The case did not take long. It was heard and decided upon on 15 October, and shortly afterwards the medal was dispatched to the priest:

> So, one Sunday some time after that the parish priest called me one Sunday back in Dún Chaoin chapel after Mass and said, "It's like this," he said, "a medal has arrived for you for the brave deed you did when you saved the girl who was drowning back on the island Strand." He got the medal and took it out of his case.
>
> "Wear this on your clothes, and I'm only sorry that I haven't one for young Criomhthain who was drowned that day, but I can't help that now. May the will of God be done."[11]

The medal was of bronze and was presented to "Patrick Kearney" on 15 October 1909, together with a certificate signed by the King of England himself. He was one of about 130 various rescuers who were awarded the medal in 1909. Of him it was cited:

> Kearney, Patrick. Case 37021.
>
> On the 13th August 1909, two ladies were bathing in the sea at Great Blasket Island, County Kerry, and could not land owing to the strong backwash. Daniel Crohan swam out to their help, but lost his own life. Kearney then swam out and succeeded in saving one, the other being drowned.[12]

The citation adds another bit of vital information that has been forgotten, if indeed it was ever known. Domhnall did not get a medal, but he got a testimonial: "'In Memoriam' to relatives of Crohan."[13]

The "In Memoriam" testimonials on vellum had been

introduced in the 1890s and were awarded to the next-of-kin of rescuers who had died in a rescue attempt.

Peats Tom wore his medal with pride and distinction. When Deasún Mac Aindriú visited the island in 1937, he met him and his wife, Neilí Jerry Ní Shé. Before he left he asked if he could take a "snap" of them both. They were happy for him to do so, but no snap was taken until Peats Tom had pinned on his medal.

After his death the medal came into the possession of Pádraig Ó Cearnaigh, the grandson of Peats Tom, a garda in Killarney. It is now on display in the Blasket Heritage Centre in Dún Chaoin. The certificate that came with it is also on the wall of Kruger's pub, with another copy in the Heritage Centre alongside the medal.

And even that wasn't all:

> So, a while after the Dublin girl was drowned and it heading for Christmas or thereabouts, a sum of money arrived to us from the mother of the girl as a token of thanks to us for the hardship we got from it.
>
> The money was returned to her and we told her that we very much regretted what had happened to her and her girl, but that we were prepared to do that and a lot more besides if any good could come of it. We sent back the money and the cheque.
>
> We were managing along all right, from hand to mouth, as you might say, without great want, but still not going wild, with plenty of hardship and work from time to time both on sea and on dry land also, working on the turf and the potatoes and so on. You would have to be looking after the house, putting tar on the roof in case you might find a leak through carelessness. At the same time it's often we'd be idle enough, particularly during the winter.
>
> So! After we sending back the money, things rested so until the following Easter. Didn't she send the money again, with an extra thirty shillings added to it, and she said to us . . . she asked us to accept is as

an Easter Present for Easter, and we accepted it this time, because we could not refuse her again.[14]

Eibhlín's mother was also very good to Tomás, Domhnall's father, and she sent £1 according to certain people, a guinea according to others, to him weekly as long as he lived. Tomás himself doesn't deny it: "The young lady's people did well to me for years afterwards."[15]

The years passed. Sometime after Archibald J. had retired, he and Mary sold the house in 3 Kenilworth Road and moved to a smaller home at 112 Mountain View Road in Ranelagh. The family had scattered and Kenilworth had become too big for them. Archibald lived on until 30 May 1924. He continued to be involved in his work for the Temperance Movement, as well as being a good chess player and, as the *Irish Independent* on the day after his death describes, "a man of considerable literary taste". In his obituary notice no mention is made of Eibhlín or any other member of the family except George, TD for Galway since 1921, to whom sympathy is extended. It was noted that the home in 112 Mountain View Road had been frequently raided during the turbulent years of the Black and Tan regime, when Seoirse (as George was now called) was either in prison or on the run. Archibald's career as a higher government official in the employment of Dublin Castle didn't seem to give them any protection. The "Terrible Beauty" had turned the old world upside down.

Eibhlín's mother lived till 1938 when she died aged ninety-three. She spent her last days at 112 Mountain View Road. They must have been lonely times. There are no memories of her there, even from the oldest resident. She was buried in Glasnevin with Eibhlín and Archibald.

As regards Seoirse, Eibhlín's brother: after his early education in the Dominican College, Newbridge in County Kildare, he became involved in Sinn Féin as early as 1907, and from his youth was a staunch member of the Gaelic League and the Volunteers. He took his BA degree in University College, Dublin, in 1908 and followed it with a degree in law in 1909. He moved to Galway and set up practice shortly before Eibhlín's death. He must have been very like Eibhlín, with ability and a kindly generous manner, and soon had a large practice. The losing of his only sister at such a young age must have affected him greatly.

Seoirse was captured in Galway even before the Rising got started. He was shipped to Reading Jail, where he spent some time before being transferred to join the other 1916 prisoners at Frongoch prison camp in Wales, which had just been specially established for the Irish rebels. He, too, must have been fairly proficient at Irish as he was appointed Irish teacher by his fellow prisoners in the camp. He was released on Christmas Eve 1916 with the other prisoners. He was re-arrested in the roundup of 1917 and sent to prison again in England where he remained until 1919.

Back in Galway, he put his name forward as a republican candidate for the Galway County Council elections in 1920. The republicans got an overwhelming majority on the council, and George was elected chairman, a position which he held until 1925. The first meeting was held almost entirely in Irish. His first action was to propose the rescinding of the resolution passed by the very same Galway County Council in the aftermath of the 1916 Rising condemning it. George's new proposal was passed unanimously. George, as chairman, formally crossed out the 1916 resolution in red ink, and marked it "Rescinded, but preserved as a document of historical importance."

George was arrested once more in September 1920 and lodged in Kilmainham Jail. While still in jail he was nominated as a Sinn Féin TD for Galway in 1921 and returned unopposed.

With the signing of the Treaty he was released again and voted in Dáil Éireann in favour of the Treaty at the meeting of the Dáil on 7 January 1922. He also voted for Arthur Griffith in the election for president. He became assistant minister for home affairs from 1922 to 1923 and afterwards was for a period parliamentary assistant to the minister for defence. He must have been very upset by the split caused by the Treaty as he refused to take part in discussion the Galway County Council held on the matter. These were turbulent years in the council, trying to get the county up and running after the destruction to the roads and bridges and other infrastructure resulting both from the War of Independence and, even more so, the Civil War that followed, as well as trying to overcome the difficulties in the change-over from British rule in the local government. A photograph of George from those times shows him to be rather tense and tired looking.

He was appointed chairman and commissioner of the Saorstát Military Pension, which position he held until 1928 when he was appointed county registrar. This position he held until 1941 when he retired. He did not stand for election in 1927, and with the Fianna Fáil government taking over in 1932 he seems to disappear from politics. He still took an active part in the social life of the city and county, he was a keen GAA follower and was, like his sister before him, a member of the Executive Committee (*Coiste Gnó*) of the Gaelic League. He organised numerous feiseanna all around the county. He founded the Galway Pipers' Band and purchased the instruments out of his own pocket.

He married Margaret McHugh of Kilconly, who died before him in March 1939.

He died on 13 May 1942, only fifty-six years of age, after being ill for some time. He had been through tough times, and they had obviously taken their toll. He was buried in the New Cemetery outside Galway. In his obituary in the *Connacht Tribune* of 16 May 1942, there is no mention of any children. Neither is there any mention of either of his other brothers, though it does state that his only sister was drowned in the Blasket Islands some years previously, "while endeavouring to rescue one of the islanders".[16]

Cáit an Rí mentioned a brother of Eibhlín's in her account to Séamus Ware in 1970 whom she mistakenly called Henry. Like Seán an Chóta, she said, he began to wear the "*filleadh beag*", or kilt, especially to Irish language gatherings such as the Oireachtas. He spent two weeks on the island in 1913, having stayed in the Kavanagh home in Dún Chaoin for some time before plucking up the courage to visit the island. He became friendly with the members of the Kavanagh family, particularly with Seán an Chóta.[17]

The publication of *An tOileánach* in 1928, almost twenty years after the tragedy of Eibhlín and Domhnall, brought it to public notice again. It seems that Mrs Nicolls and Seoirse disagreed strongly with the account of the tragedy as presented by Tomás. Canon Jack McKenna, then a young curate in Ballyferriter, recalls the parish priest, An tAthair Tomás Ó Muircheartaigh, better known to all as Father Tom, receiving a letter from her brother expressing his unhappiness with the account as presented by Tomás, i.e., that Domhnall had drowned in the attempt to save Eibhlín, without adding that it was Eibhlín who had drowned in the attempt to save Cáit. Canon McKenna remembers that the letter concluded by saying that if the story was to be perpetuated it was only fair that it should be told truthfully. He asked, furthermore, that the account be corrected in any further editions which were sure to follow. Walter McGrath, who has always taken an interest in the history of the Blaskets, stated:

> Eileen Nicholls was the expert swimmer of the three, and it was she who was the foremost rescuer. Domhnall's bravery was, of course, above reproach but in later years his father's account of the tragedy and its constant repetition caused no little resentment among family and friends of Miss Nicholls. Printing after printing of the great Blasket classic (which first appeared in 1928) gave the incorrect slant of Domhnall's giving his life to save Eileen, where as the

emphasis should have been on Eileen's giving her life
in helping to save Tomás' daughter.

McGrath furthermore concluded: "Tomás Ó Criomhthain was a wonderful storyteller and peerless chronicler of
island life. But neither he nor Peig Sayers nor Muiris Ó
Súilleabháin was a factual recorder of details of events. Nor
were they accurate historians. In Blasket literature there is
need of a chronological recording of the history of the island
families."[18]

Needless to say, neither Eibhlín's brother, nor her mother, had been present at the drowning, nor for that matter
had Tomás. The islanders did think it strange that Tomás
did not mention Peats Tom Ó Cearnaigh in his book and
give him the credit due to him. He had done a wonderfully
brave deed when he saved Cáit. Tomás, rather sparingly,
said, "Another man took in Cáit, and she barely alive."[19]

Suffice it to be said that both Domhnall and Eibhlín had
no shortage of courage when they gave up their lives in an
effort to save others. And let's not forget Peats Tom Ó
Cearnaigh, who showed the same courage in an attempt to
cheat death of its victims.

Peats Tom and Neilí Jerry went to live with their daughter, Siobhán, who was married to Muiris Ó Sé and lived in
Na Gorta Dubha, a few miles away in the parish of
Ferriter. The Ó Sé family moved to Arklow, County
Wicklow, in the 1950s. The last of the Cearnaigh family to
live on the island, Seán Pheats Tom, with his wife and family left their home in 1953 and set up their new home in
Baile na Rátha, Dún Chaoin, from where they could see
the island. Peats Tom and his wife Neilí Jerry then moved
back to live with their son in Baile na Rátha, Dún Chaoin.

Peats Tom is still remembered in Dún Chaoin, walking
along the roads, stopping to gaze in at the island. He
would stop if he met a group of youngsters on the road and
explain in anxious tones: "Let ye all get home quick before
the drop of soup gets cold."[20]

Both Peats Tom and Neilí Jerry died in 1964.[21]

CHAPTER 10

# Over the Hills and Far Away

AND SO THOSE whom fate had brought together for a short while on that dark day in the Blaskets, 13 August 1909, on the strand and by the quay: they parted and all went their separate ways in life, conscious that they had shared something that would stay with them for ever.

### Cáit Ní Chríomhthain

Cáit, thankfully, made a full recovery from the accident. A few years later, when she married Tomás Ó Maoileoin, or Tomás an Dúna, so called from the place he lived, An Dún Mór, she left the island to live in Com Dhíneol. She didn't live to be old but died in childbirth early in the twenties. She had by that time six children, one being the well-known Irish writer Pádraig Ua Maoileoin, born in 1913, who, along with other eminent works, edited the 1973 edition of his grandfather's *An tOileánach*. Due to the early death of his mother, he frequently visited his grandfather and uncles on the island, often spending the long months of the summer there. He does not remember "the Day of the White Strand", as it was by then known, ever being recalled in his family. As I write these words (20 October 2002), I have just returned from Pádraig's wake (RIP) in Dónal O'Connor's funeral home in Dingle, once the station of the Dingle Railway where Eibhlín stepped down from the train in July 1909. Tomorrow he will be brought to Dublin, and on Wednesday he will be buried in Sutton,

Dublin, not far from the girl who shared the tragedy with his mother and uncle.

Cáit's father remembered:

> The young girl of a daughter that I had, she it was who lived after the day of the White Strand, she had a woman relative in the Dún Mór and they wished to have her close to them. She left and married in the Dún Mór and had a fine place there.
>
> Her going left me in great need. I was now without anyone to put any sort of shape on me, but we tried to carry on in life as best we could. I was dark and lonely when the daughter parted from me.
>
> A dozen years she lived in the Dún Mór after this. She left six children. As bad as things were her death was the worst of all.[1]

## Cáit Ní Chatháin

Cáit Ní Chatháin, Cáit an Rí, or the Princess as she was also known, lived on happily on the island. She was a very good housekeeper, and it was in her home that many of the famous visitors later stayed. She married Seán Ó Cathasaigh from Baile an Teampaill, Dún Chaoin, and went to live in the house in Dún Chaoin opposite the church. She had all the attributes of a princess, being handsome, tough and strong. It was said that on more than one occasion she rowed single-handed from the island to Dún Chaoin and brought back a bag of flour, carrying it on her back down to the quay. When she set up home in Dún Chaoin, many visitors who had previously stayed on the island came to stay with her. Her niece, Máire Ní Ghuithín, her sister's daughter, came out to live with her, and between them they ran a very fine guest house. Máire herself was the author of two books, *An tOileán a Bhí* and *Bean an Oileáin*, which add much to our knowledge of the island, particularly from the woman's point of view. She married Labhrás Ó Cíobháin (Laurence Larry) from Baile na Rátha in the same parish and had two fine daughters, Máirín and Caitlín. Cáit herself died in 1974 and is buried in Reilig Chaitlíona, Ventry.

## Máire Ní Chatháin

Máire was the young girl who accompanied Eibhlín and the other girls down to the strand on that tragic day. She did not go swimming, but rather remained paddling by the edge. She was also known as Mary Cooney, and that family were called the Cooneys from an ancestor named Counihan who had come to the island from the Anascaul area. Máire went to America when still a young girl, and there we lose her as there seems to be no other word of her as she fades into the American masses. Mícheál Ó Gaoithín, Maidhc File, Peig's son, who said he was on the beach the day of the tragedy, gave an account to Séamus Ware in 1966 and mentioned that she was still living in America at that time.[2] Her brother was Pádraig Ó Catháin, who had the nickname "Ceaist" because of his prowess in throwing the "cast", a large rock, a favourite game in the island at one period. His son, Seán Ó Catháin, or Seán Cheaist, a well-known fiddler, was the last to marry on the island. He left the island in the early 1950s and settled in Baile na hAbha in Dún Chaoin, where his daughter, Áine, herself an accomplished musician, still lives.

## Méiní Uí Dhuinnshléibhe

Mrs Méiní Dunleavy, or Méiní Céitinn as she was better known, was Méiní Shea from An Muileann, Dún Chaoin. She married Seán Eoghain Dunleavy from the island and moved in there. She was called Méiní Céitinn (Keating) from her grandfather or Méiní Jacko from her father. The Keatings had come from the next peninsula, Baile an Sceilg, Uíbh Ráthach, during the famine. They had been evicted from their holding and went wandering until they finally settled in the Gleann Mór in Dún Chaoin. Tobar Chéitinn, a well in the Gleann, still bears their name, and a field there is called Páirc Chéitinn. From there they moved to Baile Ícín and lived beside the old chapel in that village. Méiní was best known as the Blasket nurse and midwife. Her grandmother was an Emperor, a family of Spanish descent, which seems to have come to Corca Dhuibhne in the ill-fated Spanish expedition that sailed into Smerwick Harbour in 1580.

Méiní and her family moved out of the island in the early thirties to be with her mother on the cliff top in Dún Chaoin. Her mother died in 1934, but Méiní remained on there. It was the first port of call for the island people when they came out to the mainland, and she was the first that was called upon in case of illness or of childbirth.

She gave her life story and many other accounts, including that of the drowning of Eibhlín and Domhnall, to Peig Sayers' son Maidhc, and her collection can be still seen in the Folklore Commission in UCD in Dublin. *Blasket Island Nurse*, an excellent book by Leslie Matson, appeared in 1992. She and Leslie became great friends back in the sixties when he first visited Dún Chaoin.

Méiní died in 1967 in her eighties.[3]

### James and Gretta Cousins

And what became of these two interesting people who had played such a central part in the whole tragedy on the Tráigh Bhán? They left Ventry and returned to their home in 35 Strand Road, Sandymount, beside Dublin Bay, a much larger house than the Bungalow, which they had sold in 1906. James was on the committee formed to honour the memory of Eibhlín and Domhnall, the apparently never realised scheme known as Duais Dhomhnaill Criomhthain, or the Donal Crohan Prize, to send a girl to the Gaeltacht and to raise a monument to the two.

They continued to be involved in the social issues of the day. They were both very devoted to good causes, and both had good hearts. Gretta continued in the struggle for women's rights, ably assisted by James. They toured the countryside on their bikes, Jim with the tent on the back of his, stopping to set up camp for the night, brewing tea on the primus stove and sharing out sweets to the curious bare-footed children that gathered round them, and receiving, in turn, presents of potatoes and milk from their parents.

They were always observing the people and writing about them, leaving us valuable pen-pictures of the poor people of a bygone age: "A comely young woman was carding wool for stockings and clothes for home use. A flaxen haired shy little girl, her daughter, was at her knee. A collie, with three and a half legs limped tragically to meet us."[4] They listened to gossip in Irish and in local English, not understanding either.

On 28 November 1911, James entertained an audience in the Molesworth Hall, off Dawson Street, with his lec-ture, "The Celt at Home". The lecture was illustrated by magic lantern slides presented by the photographer Mr T. H. Mason, who had visited Ventry and stayed both in Sea View and on the Blaskets. The notice announcing the lec-ture said that James had spent several long periods among the peasantry of Donegal, Connemara and Kerry, and would deal with the native scenery, history and antiquity and the life of the people in the "Celtic Fringe". Admission was a shilling.

The lecture was an unqualified success. It included numerous little episodes and sayings which aroused hearty laughter among the audience and was, according to the reporter for the *Irish Cyclist*, one of the most interesting lectures he had ever listened to.

James became involved in the setting up of a credit union which never achieved any degree of success. This and other matters seem to have led to financial difficulties, and he and Gretta even became bankrupt, or near enough to it. Poets do not often make good business people, and Gretta can't have been great either. This seems to have been the main reason they decided to leave.

James and Gretta finally bade farewell to Ireland in

1913 and emigrated, first to Liverpool and, in 1915, to India. James had been been appointed sub-editor of the *New India,* a journal published by the theosophical movement. From that time on, both he and Gretta became deeply involved in the movement and remained so for the rest of their lives. They had become disillusioned with the way life was shaping up in Ireland. Certainly the lack of appreciation from both Yeats and Joyce didn't help. However, before his departure the Irish National Theatre organised a special theatre night in his honour, and the proceeds of the night were presented to him, and Yeats wrote a letter of thanks and good luck containing a £5 note.

They were missed. Pádraic Colum commented on their leaving: "There would be less good will in our midst."[5]

They were not around in 1918 to celebrate the victory of the suffragist movement. In that year the Representation of the People Act extended the vote to women over the age of thirty, while a separate act permitted women to become members of parliament. It was the crowning breakthrough that women activists had been working towards for forty years. To add to the victory, Countess Markievicz was elected as Sinn Féin member for the St Patrick's division of South Dublin, the first women ever to be elected to the British parliament, though she never took her seat.[6]

When independence was achieved, the 1922 Constitution of the Irish Free State granted the vote to women on the same terms as men, i.e. votes for all over twenty-one years of age, both men and women. In this they were more successful than their British and Northern Irish sisters who did not achieve the full vote until 1928.

James continued writing in India and was regarded with a great deal more appreciation than in Dublin. They both travelled extensively, not alone in their new home but around the world. He succeeded in getting a post as a literary journalist, as well as being appointed principal of Mandanaplee College of Theosophy. He founded the first national art gallery in Travancore, and when India became independent, he was appointed vice-president of the International Academy of the Arts.

Gretta took up teaching. She was the type of woman who couldn't be put down either. She was the first non-Indian woman to attend the Indian University for Women in Poona. She was later appointed the principal mistress of the university. She never ceased to agitate against what she considered injustice. In 1917, she helped found the Indian Women's Association, which was instrumental in achieving the vote for women in India four years later. She was appointed the first woman magistrate in India in 1923. In 1926 she was co-founder of the All-India Women's Conference, a women's right movement which has 200,000 members today and is active in social and political life. In 1932 she was sentenced to a year in prison for protesting at unjust laws. She was very highly regarded by all, including Pandit Nehru, the prime minister, who used to send her gifts. She wrote many articles, books and pamphlets on education, theosophy, philosophy and education. A stroke left her paralysed in 1943 at the age of sixty-five, and she remained so until her death on 11 March 1954, in Adyar, Tamil Nadu.

James continued on writing, and an amazing number of books appeared under his name, including many books of poetry and other works such as *The Bases of Theosophy*, 1913; *The Garland of Life,* 1917; *The Renaissance in India,* 1918; and *We Two Together,* co-written with Gretta, 1950. Financial problems continued, and they were poverty stricken and depending on their friends in their latter days. James was shabbily treated by the then Indian government at the end of his career, having been dismissed six months retrospectively from his position, meaning that he did not get paid for the last six months of his work. Again he showed no bitterness in his writings, but remained brave and cheerful as always. Towards the end of their lives, they paid a short visit home to Ireland where they were received by President Éamon de Valera, Taoiseach John A. Costello and Seán MacBride, TD. Seán MacBride was very pleased to meet them, as they had both been friendly with his mother, Maud Gonne MacBride. She had dabbled with the idea of theosophy for a while, but had given up on it, thinking it to be too close to the Freemasons, with secret rituals, costumes and the likes.

James died on the 20 February 1956. He and Gretta were both cremated and their ashes scattered in India.

Alan Denson, who wrote the biography of James and Gretta in 1967, says of James: "The unflattering and offensive jibes levelled at him by W.B. Yeats and James Joyce deserved to be weighed against one important fact. Neither Yeats nor Joyce appears to have had any knowledge of Cousins' books written after 1915. Whilst they lived out their lives in service of their own self-centred ideas, James Cousins devoted his best energies and his subtlest intellectual powers to the education of the young and the welfare of the poor and oppressed."[7]

### Fr Tom Jones

Tom Jones was born in No. 13, Rock Street, Tralee, on 19 December 1868. His people had a pub there, and the premises is still a pub, now named the Old Oak. His mother was a Stack. He grew up a strong and sturdy youth. From his earliest days he excelled at any sport he set himself to: running, weight throwing, hurling, but above all, handball.

When first I came to this parish some thirty years ago, stories and accounts of Fr Jones and his exploits abounded. He achieved notoriety in 1916, when he succeeded – along with Paddy na Jimeanna O'Connor, Pats an Lord O'Connor from Baile Reo, and Pats Lynch from Baile na bPoc – in going down to the bottom of the 200ft high cliffs at Cuas na Ceannainne at Baile na bPoc and bringing to safety eight sailors and the captain of the crew of a Norwegian ship, the *Carmanian* of Stavanger, which had been torpedoed by a German submarine some fifty miles from the coast of Kerry on 26 April 1916 (the same week as the Easter Rising). The crew were set adrift in lifeboats. One reached land safely, but the other drifted on the sea for over fifty hours until she reached the sheer and sloping cliffs at Cuas na Ceannainne. They first had to haul to the top two of the men who had collapsed from exposure. Fr Jones and Pats Lynch succeeded in slowly bringing the two unconscious men to safety on the cliff top. They then returned to the bottom, and with the aid of rope and a human chain formed by the rescuers clinging to the rope, they eventually all reached the top. The rescue was a complete success and was described as a feat of bravery that was rarely surpassed in the annals of sea rescues.

After Ballyferriter he moved to Killorglin and back west again to Dingle from 1921 to 1928. He is remembered in Dingle also for his skill at handball, particularly at hardball.

He died on 19 September 1950.

### Seán Ó Caomhánaigh (Seán Óg, Seán an Chóta)

The fame of Seán Ó Caomhánaigh lives on in Ireland in general and in Corca Dhuibhne in particular. He was born in 1885, the same year as Eibhlín, in Cloichear in the parish of Ferriter. His mother had returned home to have her first child, though she was living in Baile na Rátha, Dún Chaoin.

When Eibhlín came to Corca Dhuibhne, Seán was already a *timire* (organiser) of the Gaelic League in Dún Chaoin, where a branch had been formed in the last years of the previous century. The Caomhánach family were well known in Corca Dhuibhne and besides being famed for their generosity, were also well known for their fluency in Irish and for their wit and turn of phrase, none more so than Seán. He is remembered as the first to have introduced the bicycle to Corca Dhuibhne, and not alone that, but in later years as a scholar he named it *"rothar"*, a word which is still used. Before this it was called "*an capall maide*" or the wooden horse.

Seán, like all the Caomhánach family, was also known for his adventurous spirit and originality.

In the year 1915, Seán set off for the States and did not return till 1922. Because of that he was absent in those heady years 1916–21, which was later a source of great disappointment to him, particularly as he had been involved in the plans leading up to the Rising. He was training the local members in the Volunteers, and that in Irish.

It is not clear what work he did when in the States, but his novel *Fánaí*, published in 1928, suggests that he was working as a cowboy in a ranch in the Red River Valley in North Dakota. It is thought that Seán himself was the hero, Seán Ó Lonargáin, and that the novel is in part, if not entirely, autobiographical.

He returned in time for the Civil War, in which he took an active part on the side of the Republicans and was commander of the Dingle area. He was captured in Lispole and sentenced to imprisonment in the Curragh, in what was known as Baile an Stáin, or Tintown, where he spent his time teaching Irish.

Again he returned to Dún Chaoin when he was released and published his novel *Fánaí* in 1928 to great acclamation. It was to be short-lived, however, because a certain cleric objected to certain passages, which caused the book to be withdrawn from the shelves. It was republished in 1928 with the offending passages omitted, something with which Seán Óg wasn't happy, but what could be done? Sixty years later, in 1989, the book was republished by An Sagart, Maynooth, this time in its full form.

Seán Óg spent from 1928 to 1937 teaching Irish in St Andrew's College and the Masonic Boys' School, both in Dublin. He achieved notable success as a teacher, though his methods were rather unorthodox, something which won favour with his pupils. Any boy who studied under him fell under his influence, and many went on to achieve great success, an example being Daithí Ó hUaithne, whose parents were Quakers and who ended up as professor of Irish in Trinity College.

By this time he had a small cabin in Dún Chaoin at An Tobar on the way up the Clasach, where Muintir Lúing had formerly lived. He came there whenever he had a break from school and particularly during the long summer holidays. Often he brought two or three of his pupils to spend a while in the Gaeltacht and hear the language from the lips of the people. This also proved successful in that, as well as familiarising themselves with the language, they got to know the people and had a healthy outdoor holiday by the sea, on the hills and helping the farmers cut the turf and save the hay.

He had by this time become well-known as an Irish scholar. This led to his getting a special assignment from the Department of Education, the compiling of a dictionary of Kerry Irish. He left teaching to concentrate on this task, and the result is *Croidhe Cainnte Chiarraí*, all twenty-nine volumes of it now in the National Library. Those volumes contain above two million words, with a precise account of each word and examples of their use in ordinary language. There was no corner of Kerry that he did not travel to in his donkey's cart in search of unusual words or forms. Tales are still told of his escapades in the collecting of the words, and of questions put to the Dáil by James Dillon regarding the same dictionary. It is a great pity that the dictionary has never been published, though there have been various moves in that direction.

He was nicknamed "Seán an Chóta", or "An Cóta" by the locals when he took to wearing the kilt. The kilt, he held, was the proper garment for the Gael, just as it had been long ago, and it was only right for the people to return to wearing it. It became a fashion for a short while, but fortunately, most might say, died out again. The name held, however, and he liked it himself, often signing his name that way.

His name lives on as, like his mother and other members of his family, he had a generous heart. He used to enter a pub, flush with his latest money from his word gathering, and call for "Drinks from door to door." Both he and his equally famous brother Muiris, or Kruger, did much to put Dún Chaoin on the map.

He lived for some time also at the strand of Béal Bán in a small house belonging to Paddy an Chró beside the famous lodging house of Eibhlín Feiritéar.

Though he was always very attractive to women, he never married.

He used to write regular articles for *The Irish Press* and various magazines, and wherever he wrote he never ceased to praise the Blaskets, Dún Chaoin and Corca Dhuibhne. "Dubh Dorcha" was the *nom de plume* he usually used, and a collection of his articles were published, again by An Sagart, Maynooth, in 1990, edited by Tadhg Ó Dubhshláine, under the title *Éist le Dubh Dorcha*.

Seán eventually returned to Dublin and began to work on de Bhaldraithe's dictionary in 1945, but his health was rapidly failing. He died at his lodgings, Kennedy's on St Stephen's Green, just at the entrance to the old Wesley College, on 16 January 1947. His remains were brought back to Dún Chaoin, and he is buried in the old cemetery in Baile an Teampaill. A commemorative plaque was raised over his grave in 1987 on the centenary of his birth. Another plaque was raised to his memory on the same occasion on the wall of his old home in Baile na Rátha, now owned by Colette Delaney. Jesús Modia, a Spaniard living in Connemara, who has now also passed on, executed the work which was unveiled by the then Taoiseach, Charles J. Haughey. An *éigse* was held in his memory at that time. Many of his old friends and neighbours still living gathered to exchange stories of his exploits, and it is remembered as a joyous occasion.

A booklet, *Seán an Chóta,* by Seán Ó Lúing, which was first published as an article in *The Kerry Archaeological and Historical Journal* and re-published by Coiscéim, was launched.

## Fíonán Mac Coluim

Fíonán Mac Coluim was born in County Antrim in 1875. His mother was from Sponcán in Uíbh Ráthach in County Kerry, a woman of the McCarthys. A schoolmistress, she went to Antrim to teach, where she met and married a local man. Fíonán was only four when they left Antrim, went to Kilkenny, and from there to Cork. His mother died soon after, still a very young woman, and Fíonán was sent to his grandparents in Kilmakeran close to Caherciveen. He went to school there to his own uncle, Fíonán Ó Loingsigh. A son of this Fíonán took part in the 1916 Rebellion in King's Street in Dublin. When Fíonán finished school he went to Cork where he got a job as a customs officer. Shortly after this he was transferred to London, where he joined the Irish Republican Brotherhood, something which drew the attention of the British police on him.

Fíonán had a great interest in Irish, inherited from his mother and her people, and understood quickly that there were vast possibilities in the teeming crowds of Irish in London. In 1896 the O'Curry Branch of the Gaelic League was set up there, three years after the founding of the League in Dublin. Fíonán was elected the secretary. From then on he was deeply involved in the language movement, teaching classes, organising concerts, writing and pushing the language forward at every opportunity. He used to return to Ireland frequently as the League representative at the Ard-Fheis, and he was present at the first Oireachtas in 1897. He was also present at the Ard-Fheis of 1898 which passed a motion to appoint travelling teachers and organisers in the Gaeltacht counties, known as *timirí*. In September 1902, Fíonán himself was appointed the *timire* for Munster. He left London and returned to Ireland.

His great loss to the Gael and the language movement there was mentioned in the "London Notes" in *An*

# A Dark Day on the Blaskets

*Claidheamh Soluis* on 27 September 1902: "Before these notes are in print Fíonán Mac Coluim will have left London for Ireland, as organiser in Munster. Fíonán's interest as a personality we all know, yet one always thinks of him as a part and parcel of a cause; picture him apart from the movement, pursuing the even tenor of his ways, interested only in his personal fortunes is impossible."[8]

He left the crowded streets of London to travel the length of the narrow crooked roads of Munster in the rain and winds on a pushbike. And he brought his fame with him, for it is said that wherever he went that the police in Tralee were not far behind keeping a close eye on him.

He settled into his new work well, cycling from place to place, organising language events, plays, *céilithe*, classes and meetings. He paid a visit to the States with Thomas Ashe in 1912 in a fund-raising expedition for the Gaelic League.

He is mentioned as having visited the Blaskets as far back as 1905, was very impressed with the island and the culture and language there, and advised the members of the League to go there to improve their fluency and immerse themselves in the culture. According to Seán Ó Criomhthain, the Islandman's son, it was he who persuaded Tomás to write, and he was the first to recognise Tomás' writing ability and potential. Certainly the islanders had a great affection for Fíonán down through the years. For many years he returned, and An File, Mícheál Ó Gaoithín, mentions in his diary that Fíonán paid them a visit in the summer of 1923. He hadn't been there for a good many years, and the first place he visited after landing was Tomás' house. Tomás was delighted to see him, as he always regarded him as a great friend and often mentioned him in his letters. Even when finishing his book, *An tOileánach*, he sent the following note to the Seabhac: "'Tis long since I had any letter from my old friend, Fíonán Mac Coluim. I hope you are taking good care of him."[9]

Again Tomás declared: "He is a very nice man and a

178

fine speaker. He speaks to the child as well as to the old person."[10]

Fíonán, who had a special interest in folklore, was one of the founders of the Irish Folklore Society, along with An Seabhac, Douglas Hyde and Séamus Ó Duillearga, in 1926. He was very involved in this movement as he was in the following Irish Folklore Commission, founded in 1935.

When the State was founded, Fíonán got a position as a music inspector for schools, but because of his age, it was not a permanent position and had no pension rights. He married very late in life, in 1939, to a woman named McGrath from Cork. They had one child, a son, also Fíonán, who became a noted artist in the Slade Gallery in London, but died young.

Fíonán himself lived on till 1966, penniless and lonely, depending on small payments from the Department of Education. That's as much as he got for his efforts on behalf of the language and the culture of the nation. He had separated from his wife, she going to London and he left alone struggling with old age.

He is buried in Dean's Grange in Dublin awaiting the Resurrection.

# The Commemoration of Domhnall Ó Criomhthain and Eibhlín Nic Niocaill

## *13ú Lúnasa 1989*

A N EVENT TO commemorate Domhnall Ó Criomhthain and Eibhlín Nic Niocaill was held in Dún Chaoin on 13 August 1989, eighty years to the day that Eibhlín and Domhnall were drowned. It was organised by the people of Dún Chaoin with the support of the Gaelic League in Dublin, and in particular with the support of the ardrúnaí, Seán Mac Mathúna.

The day's proceedings were opened with mass in Dún Chaoin church at nine o'clock in the morning, celebrated by An tAthair Mícheál de Liostún, offered for Domhnall and Eibhlín and for all drowned on the coasts of Corca Dhuibhne, and for Tomás Ó Catháin who was drowned while going in to the Blasket thirteen years before that day. Tomás' wife, Eibhlín, read one of the lessons, as did Niamh Uí Laoithe, Niamh Ní Chriomhthain before marriage, daughter of Seán Ó Criomhthain, son of the Islandman and brother to Domhnall.

After mass a small plaque was unveiled in memory of Domhnall in the old churchyard. The plaque was created by An tAthair Mícheál Ó Nuadháin. It has been incorporated into the side wall of the old Norman church by the side of the grave of the Islandman himself, marked by the fine monument executed by Séamus Murphy. It is not known where Domhnall's grave is, and in its absence the site chosen is suitable. There is a representation of an angel and the name Domhnall Ó Criomhthain and the date of his drowning "13/8/1909".

There was a fine crowd present, between local people, islanders and visitors.

I, as teacher in Scoil Dhún Chaoin, welcomed everyone, and explained why they were gathered there.

Pádraig Ua Maoileoin, the son of Cáit Ní Chriomhthain, who was rescued that day in 1909, was present and delivered his newly composed poem in memory of his uncle and Eibhlín Nic Niocaill.

The next speaker was Seán Pheats Tom Ó Cearnaigh, son of Peats Tom, who had saved Cáit eighty years before and who recalled the tragedy as described by his father and the old people down through the years:

> This day, as it happened, there was a full tide, and the sea was breaking hard on the strand, and that is not very safe. And she and Cáit went out and they were swimming away as well as they could, and it was said they had little bags, little air bags for to help them swim. Anyhow the two got caught up in each other. She had a brother, Domhnall, and he was in at home that day, very close to his own home, with no thought of what the night held in store, the poor fellow. Himself and the woman of the house were chatting together. After a while he rose, and the last word he said to the woman was that Eibhlín was his own woman, dead or alive. He had no idea of what was ahead at the time, but when he came out he ran to his own house and took a basket to dig a share of potatoes for the dinner. But when he went to the bottom of the field, it was then he heard the noise, the screaming and calling. And he looked up and saw them. He knew at once that his sister and Eibhlín Nic Niocaill were in trouble . . . Now there were three of them out in the sea, and none of them were coming in, but they screaming and screeching. And my father was

returning from drawing lobster pots . . . and on their way home they heard the noise and screaming on the strand. And they thought something was wrong. And then, sure, they said, that was the way women carry on always, fooling and screaming. But that was not how it was. He made for the strand as quick as he could, and when he came to the place they were, he was on the strand and they were outside, and he made an attempt to break the laces of his boots, big nail boots he was wearing, but there was some woman there on the strand who said he had no time to do that. He did nothing then but to remove his gansey and make his way out. He went out as far as the struggle. He could see nothing but hair, locks of hair coming to the surface. He caught one of the locks of hair, in any case and turned it on his left hand, but she was very upset and he had to hit her to quieten her . . . And he saw Domhnall's boots.

The two bodies were on the quay now. It was then that Domhnall's father and his brother were coming in from Beginish where they had been drawing lobster pots. There were people looking after the Lady and my father and a relative of his, Peats Shéamuis were looking after Domhnall. But when the father came in, wasn't it a strange thing that he recognised the boots, and he let out a scream that could be heard on the two sides of the village. And to be sure, that was no wonder. . .

Seán Pheats Tom then unveiled the plaque, and it was blessed by An tAthair de Liostún as follows:

O God of Glory, who created the sea, rock, ground and strand, bless this plaque and as your Son Jesus gave his life to save us, remember Domhnall who gave his life to save the life of another. And with the help of the Holy Spirit may this plaque be of spiritual guidance to us today.

*Ag Críost an mhuir, ag Críost an t-iasc,*
*I líontaibh Dé go gcastar sinn.*

Everyone who had helped to make this event possible was then thanked, and in particular Mícheál Mistéal who erected the plaque, Kerry County Council who had tidied up the graveyard and cut the grass and briars, An tAthair Mícheál Ó Nuadháin, who sculpted the plaque, and also Pádraig Ua Maoileoin.

Though the morning had been fine, rain and wind set in for the rest of the day and a planned trip to the island by a number of local *naomhóga* to commemorate the event of eighty years before had to be called off. Nevertheless, that night about eight o'clock the company gathered in Tigh Kruger to hang a photo of Eibhlín on the wall. The ardrúnaí of the Gaelic League, Seán Mac Mathúna spoke of Eibhlín and her love for the Irish language.

> Many years have passed since that tragedy occurred, and it is good and wonderful that we should be gathered here to commemorate what happened. It shows that the Blasket people and the Dún Chaoin people have not forgotten the tragedy. It is with great pleasure and is a great privilege that I as representative of the Gaelic League come to beautiful Dún Chaoin, where the Irish language lives, as live as it was in Eibhlín's and Domhnall's time, with a view into the Tráigh Bhán, where the two were drowned, and to hang this picture of Eibhlín. It's a pity we have no picture of Domhnall, but we must be satisfied with the thought. Thanks to you all and to everyone who organised this occasion.

Then Seán hung the picture, that will be seen, let us hope, for many a year.

Pádraig Ó Néill, nephew of Seán Óg and of Kruger, then spoke. He was then the proprietor of Tigh Kruger. He welcomed everyone, and thanked Seán for coming, for speaking and for hanging the picture, and presented him with a copy of the publication *Oidhreacht an Bhlascaoid*.

Also present on behalf of the Executive Committee (Coiste Gnó) of the Gaelic League was Séamus Ruiséal from Cork.

The night continued with music, song and dance from the local people, the type of night that would have greatly pleased Eibhlín Nic Niocaill and Domhnall Ó Criomhthain had they been present, and who is to say that they weren't.

Driving home in the twilight by Casadh na Gráige, I decided that it was time that the story of Domhnall and Eibhlín should be put on paper.

# Epilogue
## *Clabhsúr*

THE TIDE EBBS and fills on the Tráigh Bhán as it has done since the beginning of time. Small waves break on the golden sand. A black-backed gull skims in from the sea, and an inquisitive seal raises his head and looks around and gives a sneeze. A person would think it was always so. The Gráig poet, Tomás Ó Cinnéide, wrote:

> Weakness of body, and weakness of mind,
> And another weakness to be bound by the sea,
> The sea is wild, and it's she that is angry,
> And she cares not who dresses her bed.[1]

A while before he died, Tomás Ó Criomhthain was able to write in his *Dinnsheanchas na mBlascaodaí*:

> An Tráigh Mhór Bhán: There is no time of day but that you would see a person, or people, as long as you had the light of day, on this strand. Small wonder, for it is many the thing that's to be seen on this strand. There are the waves to be seen, continually pressing on each other up and down; there is the young seal, and the old one back and forth there; there is the otter there with her pack of pups, and their mother teaching them how to live; the gannet down from the skies dives down below the water, catching a fish this time, and seven times left without one; and the great motor boats in quest of the fish, from early morning till the sun sinks in the sea, they take very much fish from the sea, now and again.[2]

185

And again he wrote in 1926:

> There was never a stranger, a beggar man, a profes-
> sor nor a scholar who ever came to this island but
> that paid three daily visits to this strand. It is the
> place they prefer to spend most of the days.
>
> There are sights for them to see on this strand
> every time they look, the unending breaking of the
> waves up and down, the seal on his way with a fine
> fish across his mouth, the otter close by and he with
> a fish as well, the cormorants among them up and
> down in the water trying to find a fish for themselves,
> sometimes with a fish, a dozen times with none.[3]

And concerning Cúltráigh an Fhíona, or Cúltráigh an
Líonadh, where his son was drowned: "At the end closest
to the Tráigh Bhán, near the houses, is the part of the
strand that is given this name, because a great pipe of wine
once came in and it full to the top and that is why it is
named so."[4]

The island is now forsaken, and the little houses have
fallen in on each other. Where the King's Palace stood and
even Tomás' house are nothing but empty ruins. All you
find there now are rabbits and seabirds and ghosts. You
will feel them around you if ever you go there. And you
will feel ghosts also if you walk the Tráigh Bhán. You
might see the girls full of happiness and merriment as they
race down the slope and into the water with nothing in
mind but having a while of sport. And look and see that
woman, Cáit Bhán, sitting there above the strand watching
them and she knitting a stocking. Look at her face as she
happily watches them giggling and splashing, and then see
as her face changes suddenly from pleasure to horror as the
strand echoes to screams. And look at the youth, fine and
strong as he races down the sandy slope, leaping and jump-
ing, "every leap as long as the day", as he plunges into the
water. . .

And the old island people told for years afterwards the

stories they heard from their people when they were young, of the beautiful young girl who came over the waves, who was full of respect and love for them, and that they too were full of love and respect for her. They would say that Eibhlín, too, did her part to place the Blaskets on the map, not only of Ireland, but of the world. 'Tis an ill wind that blows nobody good, and 'tis true.

It might even be said that Eibhlín started the tourist industry on the island.

After a number of years the King's Palace stopped taking visitors when Cáit an Rí married and went across the Bealach to live opposite the church in Baile an Teampaill, Dún Chaoin. By this time other families like the Guithíns, the Cathánaigh, the Kearneys, the Dunleavys and the Sullivans were also keeping visitors. The Blaskets had become famous as a holiday retreat. Some came for the scenery, but most came for fun, music, dancing, sport and, of course, the Irish language and culture. Those were halcyon days in the Blaskets, remembered all their lives by those who visited them.

The Great Blasket was in full bloom, a bloom that left the world in awe, an awe whose echo continues to the present day. Such a pity that it was a celebration of death, because shortly after the withering began.

Seán an Chóta wrote on 13 August 1946, a short few months before his death:

> Eibhlín was a great loss to her people and to the nation. All over the country people raised their voices in sorrow. She was a great loss to the language. Often and often I think to myself that her death has not been in vain. Her death drew crowds of people to the place, people who did Trojan work and who encouraged and guided other people to work also. Would we have *The Islandman*, *Peig*, *Twenty Years a-Growing* and *An Old Woman's Reflections*, were it not for the misfortune that Eibhlín Nic Niocaill was drowned here? I don't think so. It was I who accompanied her to the

island alive and it was I who accompanied her from the island dead.[5]

The Dingle train changed, too. What was meant to bring in visitors to enjoy the beauty and culture of the area, though it did do that, became better known for bringing emigrants away from their native place to foreign parts, most of them never to return. Among these emigrants who took the train for the last time were many young men and women from the Blaskets. It seems that the women and girls were the first to realise that the days of the island were numbered. Very many of them emigrated to America. Others, like Cáit an Rí herself, married on the mainland. Those who did marry on the island were never easy until they had left and established themselves on the mainland. In 1925 the island lost its principal teacher, Thomas Savage. He was not an islandman, but came there from the vicinity of Abbeydorney on the Kerry-Limerick border. An tOileánach writes at the end of May, 1925: "The school-teacher has gone away from the island. From Abbeydorney he came to us the first day. I doubt if there was ever a teacher here as good as him. He had fluent Irish. I think he must have spent about twenty years of his life here. He's gone to a school in his own native area. Nobody knows where we will get the next teacher. I don't think the last man was unhappy amongst us, himself and the islanders got on well together and we'll miss him."[6]

He was appointed principal teacher in Knocklough National School where he became known as "Oul Master Savage", particularly after his son, Christy, who was born on the Blasket, qualified as a teacher and began to teach in the same school.

Thady and Máire Kevane's home, shop and their guest house, Sea View, continued to thrive for another season. Then tragedy struck when Máire died suddenly and unexpectedly in 1911. It was a cruel blow to Thady and his dreams and hopes. He struggled on as best he could, helped out by two local girls, "the Misses Devanes".

Visitors were still generous in their praise, but there was no further mention of Máire. It was clear that she was the heart of the project, and slowly the visitors began to drift further west to Dún Chaoin, Baile an Fheirtéaraigh and the Blaskets as the Irish around Ventry began to fade and English began to take over. Thady continued on in the shop and did a good trade, especially on days when the old people from the surrounding villages collected their pension. The kitchen adjoined the shop and most people called in to sit by the fire and chat with Thady. He always had a pack of cards handy and needed but the smallest excuse to pass them around for a game of forty-one. Older people remember his shop as being the first to have the luxury of dates, a rare delicacy. They came pressed together in a box, and for a few pennies Thady would cut a big hunk from the block.

Thady died on 17 December 1943.

The Dingle train experienced financial difficulties from the very start and was the subject of continual neglect until, with the improvements in the road and the introduction of the CIÉ bus, it ceased carrying passengers in 1939 and was used only as a cattle train on monthly fair days until its final closure in 1953, the same year as the island was evacuated. Even then it brought the odd traveller in the guard's van, unofficially, of course, like students returning home for the school holidays from St Brendan's College, Killarney.

Today the station itself is a funeral parlour. The platform behind is covered in rubbish and the site of the turntable a parking site for buses and porter barrels. All that is recognisable as belonging to a train station is the water tower where the engine was watered before setting out.

> Now often in my dreams I see,
> Tralee, the sea, the sky,
> And a small train struggle bravely on

Across the mountains high,
A memory of the days that were,
A ghost from out the years,
Climbing the heights of Gleann na nGealt,
Like an old man full of tears.[7]

Did Eibhlín achieve anything, in life or in death? She brought the country people and the city people together, and she brought the native Irish speaker and the Gaeilgeoir, or the non-native Irish speaker, together. One further achievement of hers was to break down the class barriers that were so strong at that time. She understood that it were better that people of all classes and back-grounds unite, not alone in human terms but in an effort to promote the Irish language. There would be nothing as bad as to create a split. "A wedge of oak splits itself" was an old Irish saying. Eibhlín understood this. Although from the city, she had a great affection for the country peo-ple, their culture, customs and everything that pertained to them. She was happy to sit by a fire listening patiently until she had picked up the language herself. Such a pity that more did not do likewise, especially in later years when so many from outside settled down in the Gaeltacht, who instead of sitting and listening, spread English among the little villages of Corca Dhuibhne.

The country people never forgot her. Her memory remained fresh and green in the Blaskets and Dún Chaoin and in Fionntrá, fresher and greener than it did in her own native Rathgar or Kenilworth Road.

The memory of Domhnall Ó Criomhthain and Eibhlín Nic Niocaill will remain fresh as long as the Irish language lives in Corca Dhuibhne, and stories will be told and accounts will be read and people will discuss Eibhlín, "the noble young woman from Ireland's principal city".

# Some Thoughts About the Future of Irish Literature

(A Paper read before Cumann Náisiúnta
na Mac Léinn)

*Eibhlín Nic Niocaill*
(As published in An Claidheamh Soluis,
12 June 1909)

THERE HAS BEEN nothing more amazing in the recent past in Ireland than the growth of the Language Movement. Fifteen years ago, the people that would not grant that the national language was doomed, were counted by units; today there are thousands, even hundred of thousands, who are determined that it shall not die. Yet it must not be supposed that the attitude of these numbers towards the language is identical; as might be expected the appeal of the movement to different minds varies considerably. Broadly speaking, its adherents may be divided into two classes: there are some who do not look beyond the *effort* to save the language; their hope is to see all Ireland united in this work, but they do not go on to ask themselves, "What then?" There are others to whom the present struggle is but a passing phase, the sooner over the better, all their thoughts are centred on the goal, an Irish-speaking Ireland, holding her due place among the nations. To all but these, the idea of a future Irish Literature is an absurdity; to them there is no subject of more absorbing interest.

Whether or not there will be an Irish literature in the future depends on the extent of the success of the language movement. If English remains, as it is at present, the medium of thought of the great majority of this country, then Irish literature will never be more than a forced growth. Work of genuine value may be produced here and there, but much cannot be expected from authors, writing in a language that is not the natural one for them for a public that will read their works mainly as a duty. With this thought, many dismiss the subject as one that does not concern us of today; but others, recognising that the future is, to a large extent, in our hands, and proceeding rather by faith than by knowledge, have already set themselves to lay the foundations of the literature that they believe is to be.

There is a growing demand for Irish books, and these writers today are creating a supply. It may be that little of what they produce will live; but they are doing necessary work, and that under hard conditions. For the present, he who writes in Irish must be content with a small circle of readers – a thing which is not easy for one who is conscious of literary ability. To such, the temptation to make use of a widely known language, of which he has command, in one which only a strong purpose can overcome. Moreover, Irish is an imperfect instrument – not in itself, for it is a most expressive language, but in our imperfect knowledge of it, and in the fact that it has yet to be adapted to modern ideas. There are, as we have all probably experienced, times when even the learner is astonished at the facility with which he can express himself in Irish; indeed the Gaelic phrase seems to come to mind sooner than the English, and to convey his meaning better. But on the other hand, there are realms of thought where Irish fails us, or where we must wrestle with it, in order to bend it to our will. Every language is moulded by the people that use it to suit their needs. In general this process is gradual, but the growth of our language was interrupted so that we have now to strive consciously to adapt it for the expression of our thought. There is therefore much weary journey-work to be done in the field of Irish writing; it augurs well for the future that men and women are willing to undertake this work.

Till now, the full wealth of the Irish language has been at the disposal of a few. There is, as everyone knows, an extensive literature in Middle Irish, but it can be reached only by those who are competent to cope with its linguistic difficulties. For many years this literature has attracted the attention of philologists and translations have been made from it into several foreign tongues. This country produced some few scholars worthy to take their place among the Celtologists of Europe, but by most of these Modern Irish was utterly neglected. With the language revival, however, a new interest in this older literature has sprung up, and many are now devoting themselves to the study of Old and Middle Irish, whose zeal is not purely philological. This fact is full of promise for the future. What with poetry, religious and secular, the heroic stories, the lives of the saints, the homilies, the range of Middle Irish literature was wide and its vocabulary very copious. Much may be expected from a generation of writers, who, with a knowledge of modern Irish works and of the spoken language of the various provinces, add an acquaintance with any considerable portion of this older literature.

It is not only with a view to developing the language that these studies are important. We Irish of to-day are more in touch with the past of other nations than of our own; if we wish to preserve our national characteristics, we stand to gain much by making ourselves familiar with the way of thinking of our forefathers. For this reason, it is desirable that our older literature should be brought within the reach of all, who have the future progress of our race at heart. This can best be done by means of modernised versions – for these would be read eagerly by all who know the modern language. A little had already been done in this direction; but it is the general practice even for the modern scholars, who work on the old MSS, to translate them into English. The loss to the language revival through this is manifold. In the first place, these English translations fail entirely to recommend themselves to many, who would delight in reading Irish versions of old texts. Moreover, the actual work of modernising the Old and Middle writings would be of great service towards the widening and perfecting of the language. This, then, is one of the ways in which those, who are willing to work for the future, can prepare the way for the rise of the new literature. It demands, perhaps, more self-sacrifice than any other; for while those who produce original work may hope that their name will live, he who labours over the writings of another can have little expectation of winning fame by such work.

One of the outstanding facts with regard to the Irish literature of the past is the failure of our race in poetry. It is generally admitted that the bards, with their complicated metrical schemes, sacrifice sense to sound. Some hold that the revolution in poetical form in the 17th century heralded a new era, and that the poetry of the 18th century is all that could be desired. This is a matter of taste and the humblest is free to have an opinion: for my own part, I would gladly exchange all that I have ever read of Irish poetry for many a single short lyric in the English and German languages! This failure in the past does not prove that we can accomplish nothing in the future, for the causes are plain enough and can be avoided now. But there is no use in our trying to force the growth of poetry. This is a mistake into which those who cherish hopes of the future literature might easily be led; they may hold that it will not be complete if it can boast of no great poems, and that they may set themselves deliberately to produce these. This cannot be done and we can only trust, that if there is to be a new poetry, it will come without our taking thought. Above all, it must be spontaneous, and free from the artificiality that marred our poetry up to this.

Appendices

With all the diffidence that ought to characterise the men on the fence, I venture to express my opinion, that even already a false start has been made in this branch of literature. It is customary to regard the metrical systems of the 18th century poets as the only possible ones for us; and a really beautiful poem might easily be condemned unread, if it was seen at a glance not to be in any of these recognised metres. Yet another Mary McLeod may arise, who will break with this system, as she did with that of the bards. It has not been proved that the assonance is more suitable than rhyme for Irish poetry. Assonance had its day in other languages, and was discarded for rhyme; it may be that this will never happen in Irish, but it would be unwise to determine now that it is not to happen. With the rest of our past literature, the poets, earlier and later, should be studied. If their metres suit us, when the impulse to write poetry arises, we shall adopt them; but it would be fatal to set ourselves against the dictates of our taste, to imitate them slavishly.

In the region of prose, too, the Irish writer of to-day is needlessly hampered. We are moderns, steeped in the modern literature of other nations; we cannot be satisfied with the literary forms that were in vogue centuries ago. The story, the novel, the drama of modern life, these are what we demand, and what are our authors ambition to produce. Little has yet been accomplished in this direction, and progress will be slow under the present conditions. The whole Irish Renaissance is a new movement; it has not yet cast aside all the absurdities of youthful zeal. Hardly less openly avowed than the principle, that we ought to support Irish manufacture, is the prejudice that compels him who writes in Irish to deal with Irish subjects and personages. This is no slight limitation; for it confines the author, in so far as he deals with modern life in story or drama, to one call of the people of this country. It is strange, to how small an extent Irish has yet made its way into our social life. I suppose this is due to the fact that every gathering has its sprinkling of those who do not know it, so that politeness perhaps overstrained in this case, makes English the language of intercourse. Then, too, families are divided in the matter; where the younger generation can speak Irish, their parents often know none; where the husband knows it, the wife may not, so that there are very few homes outside the native-speaking districts, where Irish has got a firm footing. The result is, that peasant life forms the whole theme of modern Irish fiction and drama. We are too conscious still of the Irish language, to be able to accept the fact that the people, who would not be speaking it in real life, are doing so in a story or on the stage; our train of thought would be continually interrupted by the improbability of the thing. Of course, the past offers a rich field to the dramatist and the novelist, and one that is beginning to be worked; but the appeal of the historical play or novel is never very wide, and work of this kind will not satisfy the growing demand of popular Irish literature. It may sound paradoxical, but to my mind, little progress will be made, till our writers break with the convention that binds them to the choice of Irish subjects. Consider for a moment such a play as *Arms and the Man*: in it most of the personages are Bulgarians; they talk English throughout, yet we are not troubled by the fact; it is covered by the "suspension of judgement", in virtue of which, alone, Coleridge says, drama is possible. Similarly, we might have plays and stories in Irish dealing with English, French, American, *any* life; but try to represent middle-class life in this country, and at once the language question arises and spoils the effect.

There are people, who are very hostile to any innovation on a large scale in Irish literature; they maintain that we must let things take their course, and not overtax the capabilities of the language. We shall never achieve much, if we measure our work to suit the language, instead of making it serve us. No language would ever have grown, if men had not forced it to express new ideas as they arose.

Dante did not leave Italian as he found it nor Chaucer English; while German was poor enough, till the writers of the 18th century had pressed it into their service. The best that they can do in literature – that must be the standard for Irish writers. If the best cannot be given in Irish, it would be better to let the language die. But, indeed, it is just because they believe that Irish will prove a better medium for us than another language could, that so many look forward to the rise of an Irish literature. Mazzini held that each nation stood for an idea, and that a nationality was worth preserving only so long as it could contribute something to the world's thought. We believe that we have something to contribute. The English language is already formed, and not by our nation; in Irish we have an instrument that we can mould for ourselves. To most, it is probable, those who look for an Irish literature in the future are dreamers – but there have been prophetic dreams.

# Nationality in Irish Education

## Eibhlín Nic Niocaill

*(Irisleabhar na Gaedhilge, Meitheamh 1909)*

IT HAS BEEN remarked that never before had the nature of Nationality been made so frequent a subject of philosophical speculation as in the 19th century. In the views expressed on the matter by such men as Fichte, Mazzini, Thomas Davis, Edgar Quinet, one idea stands out clearly: they all agree in defining a nation as a people bound together by a common development in the past, and by the consciousness of a common destiny in the future. Fichte finds the basis of patriotism in the desire that is in man for, as it were, an eternity even on earth; this desire is realised in his relation to the past and to the future of his nation. Mazzini regards the nations as the citizens of humanity, each with a special work to do for the cause of human progress, and a special aptitude, developed through a long process of growth, fitting it to that work. An educationalist, still amongst us, has said: "The nation is the sum of the individuals now existing within it. But it is more. It is the heir of all the ages, and it is the resultant of all the generations that have lived and worked since the nation began to be. A common tradition, a common history, a common language, a common literature, common institutions, common sorrows and common joys, common hopes and common aspirations – these things make up a nation, these things shape its destiny, these things determine its place in civilisation."

Nationality being then, as it were, the permanent identity of a people, what constitutes the past, the present, and the future generations into a historical unity, the all-importance of education, as a factor in the preservation of this continuity is clear. It is the function of education to transmit to the children, who are to be the men and women of the future, the heritage of the past, and to develop in them those faculties that will enable them to take their part in the march of progress, and to hand on a richer and nobler tradition to their descendants. Where national life is vigorous, the function of education is certain to be discharged. The legends of their country are the first that the children hear, her songs the first that they sing; as they grow older, they become familiar with her history and literature; later they are introduced to the history and literature of other lands; but to the end they are taught to regard everything from the point of view of their own nation. By degrees a pride in the past and a sense of responsibility for the future of their country grows up in the mind of the children, to bear fruit in after years. All this happens as of course and imperceptibility. It is as natural that the child's knowledge of man as a social being, and of the history of civilisation, should take its country and the achievements of its race as starting-point, as that its acquaintance with individual human beings should begin in its own home. It would probably seem inconceivable to a German, a Frenchman, an American, that there should be any land where this is not so. Unfortunately, that anomaly exists; for in Ireland we have systems of education, unstable in many respects, consistent in the effort to keep from Irish children all knowledge of the past of their nation, and, consequently, all possibility of forming adequate ideals for her future.

This state of things, has its root in penal times. One of the provisions of the Penal Laws debarred Catholics, and consequently the great mass of the Irish people, from education. Attempts were made to evade the law, and the "hedge schools" at least kept alive the desire for learning, that was so ancient a characteristic of the Irish race. Towards the end of the 18th century most of the Penal Laws were repealed; and in the beginning of the 19th several religious teaching orders were founded. Owing to the poverty of the Catholic community, the powers of these Orders, unaided by the State, was very limited; so that little was done for the education of the masses till the Act of 1831, which established the National system of education in Ireland, was passed. At that time the country was much more definitely divided on questions of religion than on political or national matters; grave attempts at proselytism had been made by means of endowed schools; so that, at the outset, the people for whom the National system was intended looked on it with suspicion; once assured, however, that the interests of their religion were safeguarded, they hesitated no longer to avail themselves of the National Schools. Yet the whole system was designed for the crushing of Irish nationality: the curriculum was based entirely on English ideas, and was inspired by the aim admitted by Dr. Whately, one of the first Commissioners, of making every Irish pupil, "a happy English child."

One might expect to find a different spirit in secondary education; for our secondary schools have been always free from State control, and are the creations of the Irish people themselves. Yet they are quite as un-national as the primary schools. It is customary to blame the Intermediate Board largely in this matter; but we must remember that that Board came into being only in 1878, while this state of things is very much older. It, too, is a survival from the penal times. Education had been long the prerogative of the enemies of nationality in this country; it was natural enough that they continued to give the tone in educated circles, even when those conditions had passed away. Yet it is strange to find victims of the Penal Laws, endeavouring, hardly less consistently than did English legislators, to divorce Irish nationality and education. Their efforts have been crowned with success; till to-day, Irish education is a colourless, un-national thing, from which every element has been eliminated that might serve as a link between the future and the past, or help to make his country dear to the child.

So thoroughly, indeed, has the denationalisation of education in this country been carried on, that it is not only in the school that everything Irish is tacitly ignored, but even at the earliest stage of education, in the home. When in other countries children are feasting their imagination on the legends of their native land, and being sung to sleep by her songs, Irish children are already cut off from the tradition of their race. Taught in their own school-days that everything distinctively Irish was to be despised, the mothers of a few generations ago took care not to impart to their children what of Irish tradition had come down to themselves; and so those children, and the generations that came after them, were deprived of the wealth of fairy lore and heroic story, that was their birth-right. For the poorer classes, who could not procure books, nothing has supplied this deficiency; and it is instructive to-day to compare the intellectual and imaginative poverty of such people, throughout the greater part of Ireland, with the wealth of peasantry in the Irish-speaking districts. For there, with the language, the folk-lore and the heroic sagas of the race have lived on; and still, the people, gathered round the turf fire of a winter's evening, grow angry over the old tale of Fionn's treachery to Diarmuid on Ben Bulben, or wander in imagination with Oisin to the land of the Ever-young; while the children of the west coast still look into the sunset clouds, hoping to catch a glimpse of the floating "Isle of the Blest." For other children, books have taken the place of oral tradition: Greek legends, German fairy-tales, the Arabian nights – these reign supreme in our nurseries. We would not exclude these: but why must the child, who plays at Achilles, never hear of Cuchulainn or of Fionn? Why should the sprites of the Black Forest, or the genii of the East usurp the place of the sidhe, the embodiments of the imagination of our own race? As they grow older, and are no longer content with palpable myth, Irish children are given the tales of Robin Hood, of William Tell: they delight in the anecdotes of Alfred and the burnt cakes, of Canute bidding the waves retire, of Robert Bruce and the spider; but with the consistency worthy of a better cause, every heroic figure from Ireland's history or literature is kept from their ken.

When the school-days begin, the education of the Irish child continues on the same un-national lines. The history, the language, the literature of Ireland – these subjects are either omitted from the curriculum, or they occupy a very inferior position in it. History is a subject which receives little attention in our primary schools, but for the teacher's examination a certain amount is prescribed. A glance at the programme for monitors bears eloquent testimony to the importance of the history of Ireland in the eyes of those who control the National system of education. Lest the monitor should be led to imagine that Irish history is a subject that deserves to studied for its own sake, it is thrown in with the history of Great Britain and his courses are marked off by dates that have absolutely no significance in the history of this country, whatever may be their importance in that of the neighbouring island.

In our secondary schools, Irish history is, and long has been, nominally taught: from my own recollections I will say this, of all the subjects in the curriculum there is hardly one more tedious. Roman history, which seems remote enough from an Irish child, is thrilling in comparison. In itself this seems strange; for if there be a subject that one could count on to fire the imagination and stir the sympathies of children, it is the history of past triumphs and suffering of their race. But remember the way in which Irish history is taught; from start to finish it is treated as a mere appendage to English history; there is no such thing as an effort to view it as a whole, or to give an insight into the spirit of the nation as manifested in it. Take the struggle maintained for so many hundred years against the invasion:

the hopes that sustained it, the moments of despair when all seemed lost, the indomitable courage that rose against every failure – surely, these are the things it is important for us to realise. In our schools, that portion of our history is measured out by the reign of English kings, sub divided by the periods of office of English lords deputy; the activity of the champions of Irish liberty is given in terms of the amount of inconvenience that they caused to English governors; all through, England is the central point; Ireland seems to have no existence except in relation to her. This is the history of Ireland as it might be taught to English children, to supplement the history of their own country – small wonder it leaves us cold.

So it comes to pass that, in general, amongst the historical heroes that the Irish children enshrine in their hearts, none of their race finds a place. Yet it is not that our history could not afford them fitting objects for the admiration that children lavish so generously on the brave. There is no other nation in the world where such a tale as that of the youth of Hugh Roe O'Donnell would not be an inspiration to boyhood: our boys can tell the date of his escape from Dublin Castle; they probably can tell who was Lord Deputy at the time, and how that event affected him; but the joy in Tirconnell when young Hugh returned in safety from captivity, having made his way alone through the midst of his enemies, the high hopes that were raised all over the country when it became known that he was free, these things are " mere details", for which there is no room in the crowded curriculum.

As they grow older, a proportion of Irish youth, in spite of their educators, realise that they have a country, whose history should be treasured by them. They then add to their list of heroes some of the great names of Ireland's past; they recognise that Art Mac Murrough Kavanagh, Hugh O'Donnell, Owen Roe O'Neill, and the men that died for Ireland in later times, have a claim to their imagination far beyond that of the Coeur de Lions and the

Black Princes, to whom they paid the tribute of their earliest hero-worship. 'Tis well that this is so; but such deliberate admiration is possible only at an age when opinions are already formed; and is, therefore, a less potent factor in the moulding of character than the spontaneous, unreasoning devotion of children to their first heroes.

Those responsible for education in this country may well lay to heart the words of Thomas Davis, addressed to the College Historical Society of Dublin University; "I shall not now reprove", he says, "your neglect of Irish history; I shall say nothing of it but this, that I never heard of any famous nation which did not honour the names of its departed great, study the facts and the misfortunes – the annals of the land, and cherish the associations of its history and theirs. The national mind should be filled to overflowing with such thoughts. They are more enriching than mines of gold, or ten thousand fields of corn, or the cattle of a thousand hills, more ennobling than palaced cities stored with the triumphs of war or art, more supporting in danger's hour than colonies, or fleets, or armies. The history of a nation is the birth-right of her sons – who strips them of that "takes that which not enriches him, but makes them very poor indeed." '

During the last few years the Irish language, long utterly neglected, has made its way, not without encountering much opposition, into our schools. Irish is now taught in the greater number of Catholic schools, and it would be hard to over rate its effect at present as a stimulant to national consciousness. There are some to whom the cause of Irish nationality is dear, who desire nothing more than that all the schools of the country should fall into line in this matter. Little would be gained by that; for the value of Irish, as taught at present in our schools, is accidental rather than intrinsic, and springs mainly from the opposition which it yet encounters. The taking up of the study of the language by each individual pupil involves a profession of faith in Irish nationality, either on the part of his parents

204

Appendices

or on his own; and the child studies Irish with the feeling that by that act it is doing a special service to its country. Moreover, while many amongst its school-fellows and even among its teachers, despise the Irish language, and do not hesitate to give expression to their contempt, the fighting instincts of the child are aroused, and it is ever on the defensive for the honour of the national language. At best, this state of things is artificial, and it would cease if Irish came to form a necessary part of the curriculum. Yet who, that recognises the importance of the language revival, but looks forward to the day, and hopes too that it will soon come, when Irish will be an essential subject in the curriculum of every educational institution in the country – only it must be taught in a manner altogether different from what it is at present.

For, in our schools, the same treatment is meted out to Irish as to any foreign language. The attention of the pupils is restricted to the programme for whatever examination lies ahead. Those who have been brought face to face with the fact cannot but feel shocked at the utter ignorance of all that concerns the literature and traditions of this country displayed at times by boys and girls, who have learned Irish at school, and succeeded at every examination. Yet we do not expect our school-children to possess comprehensive views of French of German; we recognise the fact that what French or German child learns at school is the merest ground-work, on which some few will raise a superstructure of knowledge in after years. But we cherish the delusion that it is otherwise with the Irish language; we have a sub-conscious idea that it ought to be taught differently from other languages, and we don't all realise that this is not so. But the fact remains; and yearly boys and girls go forth from the schools, both primary and secondary, having had, as regards Irish, all the advantages afforded in these institutions, yet whose knowledge of Irish literature does not go beyond the few text-books that they studied for their successive examinations; of that literature as a whole, of the great cycles of story so dear still to the Irish-speaking peasantry, of the books regarded as almost their most precious treasures by many continental libraries, they know nothing. Taught in this manner, it is clear that the Irish language cannot play the part it should in education, transmitting to the present and the future generations of our race the heritage that comes to them from their forefathers.

It is not only the history, the language, and the literature of Ireland that embody the tradition of our race. Here in Dublin we have visible proofs of the high degree of civilisation to which our ancestors had attained, long before the coming of the Normans. From their infancy Irish children are accustomed to hear vaguely of this early splendour; the phrase "Island of Saints and Scholars" is familiar to them; but nothing is done to substantiate Ireland's former claim to that high-sounding title. As they grow older, and more sceptical, our boys and girls begin to doubt that any such claim existed. They hear of Pope Adrian's Bull, of the accounts of the savagery of the Irish given by the Elizabethan conquerors; these things are well attested, for the rest they have only hearsay; and hence comes the attitude of many of the Irish towards the past of their own nation – the air of good-humoured contempt with which they receive references to its greatness, as who would say, "By all means let us glorify ourselves; it costs us nothing."

If such treasures as those in the National Museum, Trinity College Library, the Royal Irish Academy, were in a city of any other country, it would be impossible that children should be educated at the very doors of these institutions in ignorance of the national relics they contain. One visit to Trinity College Library, with a discourse on the Book of Kells, would be of more value than a daily assertion that Ireland was once called the "Island of Saints and Scholars;" yet neither their parents nor their teachers trouble to procure that advantage for our children. In other countries it is the custom to make use of all the historical monuments within reach for educational purposes; a whole day is considered well spent, if sacrificed from actual school work, to take a class to see anything that will bring the children into touch with the past, and especially with the past of their own nation. In this city the educational value of visits to museums has not so far been recognised – probably because we have so little of the treasures of other lands to show the children. But might not an occasional half-day be spent in showing a class the Irish metal ornaments, the chalices and the crosses stored in the Museum, or the ancient books in the Royal Irish Academy and Trinity College. Even children would recognise that the workers who wrought that metal, the scribes who copied and illuminated the manuscripts, had not the volatile disposition, incapable of sustained effort, that we are accustomed to associate with the Celtic temperament, and accordingly to condone in ourselves.

And so, all through the Irish education, from its beginning in the home, nationality is utterly disregarded. This policy is hardly less reprehensible from an educational point of view than from a national; for no true educationalist will deliberately set aside any legitimate means of awakening the interest and developing the imagination of children. It stands to reason that the legends and the songs of their race will appeal more forcibly to them than those of strangers. The history that was enacted on the scenes that they look upon, in which their ancestors were the agents, of which the conditions of their own lives are the outcome, must possess an interest for them far beyond that of other histories, which have no special relation to themselves. Where education runs a natural course, the historical sense is awakened in children through their interest in the past of their own race; and they are led on by degrees to study the history of mankind as a whole. Only in Ireland is this natural sequence neglected; the system has resemblances to that, now universally condemned, of endeavouring to teach children through the medium of a language that they do not understand.

Moreover, education should aim at making the world in which they are to live beautiful for men and women. For generations the educators of this country have set aside the means to this end that lay ready to their hand. When the language, the literature, the history of Ireland were banished from our schools, the very land itself was shorn of half its beauty; for the legendary and historical associations that had been for thousands of years gathering round our hills, our valleys, our rivers, and our plains, were lost to our children. Those who have made the Rhine tour know the value of such compared with other places in Europe. It is due to the fact that every crag along its banks is rich in story, that, on the Rhine steamers, one meets people from the ends of the earth. We Irish go, too, to visit the Rhine; we are stirred by the memories that cling around it – few of us know what treasures in that kind we have left behind us in our own country.

In fine, the educator who would train up the men and women of the future without reference to their heritage from the past, is at variance with the best traditions of his profession. Here the uncompromising terms in which a great English educationalist condemns such a system.

J.J. Findlay, in his "Principles of Class Teaching", writes:

*There abides a steadying force of conservatism, which, in the sphere of education, pleads for the child as the Inheritor of Tradition. This motive finds its roots in ancient use, and can be traced from the dawn of the teacher's art. This instruction of the young among all great nations has been a transmission – of literature, of story, of song, of pious exercises from the days of old, kept in memory by many visible signs and memorials. To deny the force, the eternal value of this principle, is to deny our kinship with mankind; and to deny its worth as a guide to the teacher is to send the child back to be suckled by the wolf.*

But, after all, it may be urged, we live at so high pressure nowadays that education must be utilitarian; neither for the sake of the individual, nor for that of the nation, can time be wasted on a matter so unproductive as the fostering of nationality. What is its commercial value? This insistence on measuring everything by a material standard is one of the evidence of decadence in the Ireland of today. The German and the American recognise the value of national pride, as making for greatness and success in every department of life – but we would be less sentimental, more practical than they. Let us hope that results will justify us! But, indeed, have we not given the present system a fair trial? Three generations of Irishmen and women have been already been cut off from the tradition of their race: could Ireland be in a more wretched condition, commercially and intellectually, than she is? Let us now rather take a lesson from American educators, who, so convinced are they of the necessity of binding their citizens together by a strong sense of nationality, endeavour to make up by direct teaching of patriotism in their schools what they lack in historical associations.

Others would urge against any change in our educational system that the breach with our past is so wide now that it is useless trying to bridge it. They would advise us to give up the struggle to maintain our national identity, seeing how few of the elements of nationhood we still retain. But the Irish are still held together by one bond – that of common wrongs in the past. The average Irishman still maintains that he belongs to a nation apart; he does not ask himself what he means by the assertion. If he did, he would probably find that the chief element in his sense of nationality is a grudge against the people that caused the past suffering of his race. This is not an ennobling sentiment; but it is enough to prevent the Irish from becoming merged in another nation. It is the outcome of the unnational character of education in this country that nationality has sunk so low. Perhaps it will be the glory of the educators of the future on this unpromising foundation to build up the nation again.

# Irish Women's Franchise League

## *Public Meeting at Dingle*

### *The Kerry People,* Saturday, 28 August 1909

O N SUNDAY LAST a public meeting was held under the auspices of the above League, the speaker being Mrs. J. Cousins, member of the Committee, Dublin, opposite the Irish College, Dingle.

The object of the meeting having been explained by Mr. T. Galvin, M.C.C., in the vernacular.

Mrs. Cousins said that she had been very slow to address a meeting at Dingle; many of you must think a woman very brazen-faced to address a public meeting. (Cries of, "You're welcome.") They found that they have certain grievances. She remembered when travelling through the country during the past fine weather, she told a farmer that he had now no grievances, but he replied that he had not always the fine weather. She now said not only men but women have their grievances, and she wanted to tell them what these grievances were. There was a great agitation going on in the towns and cities, and she thought the city women were not more important than the women of the country. She thought it right to catch it in every field of labour and every public board; she was a member of the Committee of the Irish Women's Franchise League; the Ventry women have as good a right to be aware of the objects of this League as the Dublin women, as the Dingle women have just the same right to be treated as citizens. What the women are saying they may ask her, and she would leave it to them to say whether they are right. They are saying that about two millions who are paying equally with men have no person to represent them. Now these women did not ask for any foreign or strange rights; they paid taxes, they had to manage their own business, and got nothing in exchange for the taxes they pay; they had to pay and get nothing in exchange. A woman should not be denied citizenship because she is a woman; think of a widow who has to carry on her business the same as a man, and yet she has none to represent her. Women are only asking for a vote the same as men who qualify. A woman will not deny she is 21 if she is entitled to any property. What else should be the qualifications. She has then gained an interest in that place. She knew men who were not able to read or write who had votes; all they had to do was to put on a cross; while women who could qualify were denied the right, the law was there and the women were misrepresented. Is it fair to exclude them? No, they have asked now for their rights, so do not be led astray, do not misrepresent them. It is a question of women who have no husbands. There is always something peculiar about the laws; these women say they are just as responsible as men; the laws are made as if the men were only responsible; it is all one-sided, the men made laws, but the women got no direct benefit; they pay rates and taxes and should get equal recognition. Whatever would apply to England and Scotland should apply to Ireland. There is a Bill to be passed, and that Bill will be passed for England and Scotland. Ireland will be excluded. The Irish members are saying nothing in the matter; the English and Scotch people tell us we have no interest in our country, and that we will be left out. But she was going to ask them will Ireland be excluded from the Bill. We deserve it if we do not come out boldly; we do not like to come out talking, but what will our neighbours say if we neglect the interests of the people. They wanted to create a public opinion so that Irish members of Parliament would not say that Irish women do not care about votes. Ireland did not want to be excluded. These women have votes for County Councillors and District Councillors, and why have they not a vote for an MP. Imperial taxes may be passed; do you think do these effect the women, even the taxes of the last Boer War which the majority of Irishmen were against, though not properly opposed for want of proper representation do affect the women. The men may say we will do them justice. She wanted that every woman should have a vote. Ireland is always talking of being overtaxed; the women are taxed and have no representation. If you consider this you will immediately say that they are right; all sensible Irishmen will admit it. Some of you have to go to America to labour in the workshops, to the same work both of them have to learn their business thoroughly, but when it comes to the money she is cut down, they simply say she is a woman. The women come along and say the men are underselling them. She goes out with a stigma upon her. Leagues are created in the towns and in the cities, and a woman's work must be put on the same foundation as a man's work. The only thing they are asking is equality with the men, and it takes away this stigma; they are asking only for common justice. The women who are asking for votes are right; the women who are working are the women who want to get justice. My intimate friend, Miss Nicolls had seen this, and has ever any man taken a deeper interest in her country than she? She was to speak here in Irish today; because she was a worker for the Gaelic League; she found that women were working under a disadvantage; she was a member of this League; do you think was she qualified? Would you deprive that noble lady of a vote? (A voice: We are all very sorry for her loss.) Do you think she (speaker) should not have a vote; supposing she had to manage her own business, she could work, pay taxes, move along, but would be left out in the line of representation. Now, if this bill came up in the House of Commons our MPs would have heard nothing; therefore they should win the MPs to their side, so when the bill is brought along they will not say that England and Scotland want the bill, they will have the franchise, but not Ireland. Are we going to be left out? They should get every MP in Ireland. Mr. O'Donnell may say the people in Dingle know nothing about it. It is no matter whether Ireland is excluded the Irish women take no interest in the subject. If the people here raise their voice the MPs will support them and Ireland will be included. Women can vote for District Councillors and County Councillors, and these gentlemen have an interest in them and they will do their duty. They can see if Mr. O'Donnell vote for it. They were working for the people, and it was their business to see that Ireland was included. They were going to go through the country; they were going to do their best; they had 14 years in a quiet way (the English ladies) worked for this; they had heard that there was no taxation without representation, but they found that they would be left out of the list unless they started on agitation. Irish people know what agitation is and they know they can only get certain things by agitation. They were going to have a touch of this, but their agitation was public education. They had no claim in Parliament! They had no direct representation. They were sent to Parliament by the men and were only responsible to men. But now with this League of fourteen million women they had a real agitation to meet. They were not going to quarrel with them, but they wanted equality; this was composed of women who were combined together and they had to meet something than a mere individual. Now, they had women in all associations; in all leagues, and she simply put her case before them. Women are different from men; if a woman has a good thing she will divide it; laws were made by men for their own interests; it is for the men to say we share with the women. But they cry, "Oh, if the women get the votes." They were only asking for the vote for equal rights. They were only asking for a measure of equality. They were only ordinary human beings; they were liable to mistake, but their object was to help them. She would be glad if there was anyone in the meeting who disagreed with her; in other places they had very interesting discussions. (A voice: "There is no one against it.") She was delighted that Irishmen and women could see common sense when laid before them. She would long remember the meeting she had here today. She was going to appeal to the Irish members of Parliament, and hoped that the Kerry members would be favourable; they could say to their member, Mr. O'Donnell, that the suffrage had come to Dingle. The women are looking after the interests of the people and looking after them in the best possible way. They were working for women but not against men, and she hoped that their little League would be successful; that they would have a good number to fall back on; their centre was in Dublin and they were trying to get as many members as they could. The women were not asking to go into Parliament, and even if they did there would be seven men against every woman, and they would be left out. The first step was to take away the disqualification. The first is to get qualified; if they get the vote there is no law at present to keep them out of Parliament; they may then pass a law to exclude them from Parliament, but all they ask is the vote. She had met the Kerry people and she found it a compliment to meet Irish people as she had met here; all of the same class, not the different sects as you meet in large cities and towns; therefore she had all the confidence that she could convince them of anything honest. It was that nerved her to speak, and she had to return her sincerest thanks for the patient hearing they gave her (applause.)

# Sea View, Ventry

## *Some comments from the visitors' book at Sea View, 1902–1909*

Ventry is a very bracing and pretty place, with sea, mountain and romantic scenery. Mr. Kavanagh's house is a good one facing the sea and both he and Mrs. Kavanagh are most obliging and anxious to please.

The peasantry are very interesting and original.

M. Kennedy, 5 August 1902.

After 8 weeks we are sorry we are not coming instead of going.

H. Williams, 23 September 1904.

The country is excellent for those who enjoy cycling or walking.

Margaret K. Dixon, Dublin, 26 April, 1905.

This is quite an ideal place for studying the sweet Irish language and the Kerry reels and dances. Every success and blessings may attend the efforts of Mr. and Mrs. Kevane in furthering the revival of the old tongue.

Adelle Cockburn, September 1903.

At Ventry. September 1903.

Of Ventry's lively little Bay
I have a souvenir
To keep with me for many a day,
And hold for many a year.

# A Dark Day on the Blaskets

There I beheld the mighty sea,
Or calm, or restless tossed,
It brought back childish days to me,
Those memories never lost.

The days, when with my brother
Played on Killiney's Beach,
Ah! happy, happy days gone by,
Would backwards we might reach.

And clasp once more our little hands
In innocent child's play,
Or build our castles on the sand,
Till they are washed away.

Alas! for us it may not be
Far off that merry shore,
We only in our minds can see
Those castles built of yore.

Though still in fancy's realm we build
High castles in the air,
With every longed for wish fulfill'd,
And all things good and fair.

Till life's wild torrent bears away
Each structure grand and tall,
We waken to the coming day,
To find them vanished all . . .

As once our castles made of sand
Were levelled by the tide,
Then higher up upon the strand,
Our art the waves defied.

Now when they fall, what hope have we
To raise the pile again?
Life's torrent sweeps them off to sea,
And we sigh forth–Amen.

In Ventry's quiet little Bay,
One need not seek for peace,
From busy turmoil far away
Here rush and bustle cease.

No noise of train or traffic's din
Disturb the tranquil scene,
Where nature's stillness reigns within,
An undisputed Queen.

Save when some carts come rustling down
And homewards with them bring
From off the beach the seaweed brown
That storm waves on it fling.

Or from the town there comes a car
That wheels a merry load,
Their mirth resounding from afar
Upon the echoing road.

A Bay, it is surrounded by
The mountains' dizzy height,
While sands of gold beneath them lie,
In shadow or in light.

They sparkle on the sunny shore,
When days are bright and fine,
Or in the wind's and sea's uproar,
Make one vast sullen line.

Great rocks and mountains, sea and sky,
How much the soul they move,
With tow'ring peaks and mounts on high,
And more, God's gift to love.

The people simple and sincere
Their Irish folklore tell,
And ancient Irish songs sing here,
And speak its accents well.

To those who learn and would defend
The soft sweet Irish tongue,
To Ventry's shore their steps must wend,
To hear it spoke or sung.

The morn I left, the sun's bright face
Shone smiling o'er the Bay,
Last souvenir of that dear place,
I with me bore away.
  Mary. F. Quin, from Temple Mungret, Limerick.

*Fionntrágha na nár dtréan dtreo,*
*Bhreágh an áit í, dom' ard mheas,*
*Sliabh an Iolair na n-aill mór,*
*Aoibh a chlos ann guth bhinn–smól.*

*Cruach Mhárthan thuaidh, maol an beann,*
*Air leaba Laoich Mic Dhaibheann*
*Gaisgíoch, fear faire Fionn,*
*Codail ar theacht don cham-dhroing.*
           Maolmhuire Mac Carthaigh, July 1904

Vast, the mighty mountains! lovely changeful sea:
Enchanted land, where giants fought of old,
Nor deemed it less that they should die for thee,
Thy hues, thy glories long shall haunt my dreams
Rendering life sweet amid the city's din
Your wintry sky be brighter for thy gleams.
           K. A. Gifford, Dublin, July 1905

APPENDIX FIVE

# "Fionn and The Spanish Giant"

*This was Thady's favourite story, and he told it to everyone shortly after their arrival in Sea View. It was published in* Sinn Féin, *23 August, 1909.*

Fionn Mac Cumhaill was out walking on the broad beach of Fionntrá one fine May morning with his two fine hounds, Bran and Sceolaing, and kicking around a football at the same time. He walked as far as Cé na Cathrach and then turned back again. As he was walking below Teampall Chaitlíona he noticed way out to sea a huge man wading in towards land. The man was a very giant. He was striding through the sea and the water was scarce up to his oxters.

When he finally reached the shore he stepped out of the water and shook himself like a dog.

"I am from Spain," says he. "Could you tell me the where-abouts of the man they call Fionn Mac Cumhaill?" he asked in a voice like thunder.

Fionn thought it as well to play for time, so he answered. "And what business would a big man like you have with Fionn?"

"It be no business of yours," shouted the giant, "but since you ask, I'll tell you. It is not I who want him but my master has a need of him back in the eastern world, and he sent me to fetch him."

"Small chance have you of getting Fionn to go with you. There is no chance he would leave home, and he with a small child in the cradle and all."

"'Tis not to ask him I came, but to tell him. And if he refuses I will grab him and put him under my oxter and away back to the far eastern world with the two of us. But enough! Tell me where Fionn lives?"

"He lives in the fine castle of Rath Conáin," said Fionn.

"And how will I get there?"

Fionn directed him to Rath Conáin, which could be seen from where they stood, but instead of sending him the direct route he sent him a roundabout way by the Clasach.

The giant started out in his strides out by the Poll Gorm and turned up the Clasach.

In the meantime Fionn started out for Rath Conáin, but he went the direct way, which wasn't long at all.

Of course he got there before the giant.

"The likes of this," says he to the wife as soon as he crossed the threshold, "there is a fierce giant on his way to carry me away with him. It is a time for brains rather than brawn, if you understand me."

With that he wrapped a blanket around himself and jumped into the child's cradle beside the fire. He pulled a bonnet on his head and stuck a bottle in his mouth. He was just in time, for shortly were heard the footsteps of the giant as he approached the door. He bent and came into the kitchen without as much as a by your leave.

"'Tis Fionn Mac Cumhaill I'm after," says he. "This is his house, I take it. Is he around anywhere?"

"He's not then," said the wife. "Unfortunately he has gone to the bottom of Ireland hunting. But he should be back later on this evening, if you care to wait."

"I will, then," says the giant, "sure, there's no rush." He sat himself down to wait.

Just then the baby in the cradle cooed.

"That's a fine baby there, God bless him," says the giant. "I suppose that's your own?"

"My own and Fionn's," answered the wife.

"What age might he be then?" asked the giant.

"Not a year yet," she answered.

"I suppose he must be getting the teeth so?"

"He is too."

"How many has he got?"

"About that I'm not sure, I didn't look into his mouth lately. But if you put your finger in his mouth you should find out for yourself."

The giant put his forefinger into the baby's mouth. Well, he got such a bite that he gave a roar that could be heard back at the beach.

"Well, if a baby can bite like that and he less than a year old, what will he be like when he's grown up? He nearly took the finger clean off me!"

"Oh, Fionn himself has good teeth," replied the wife.

He sat down for a while and was quizzing her up about Fionn, trying to get as much information as he could.

"What sort of pastime does Fionn have when he is at home?"

"Indeed, he has many. But there is one thing he likes particularly to do," answered the wife, "and he often does it just to pass away a while. At the gable end above there is a big rock. He lifts up that rock, and tosses it over the roof. Then he runs and is before the rock on the other side and catches it before it hits the ground. He then flings it across the roof again and meets it the other side. He keeps this up for a couple of hours and gets great enjoyment out of it."

The giant then went outside to see the rock. He studied it for a while wondering how anyone could throw it over the roof. He was beginning to think that Fionn MacCumhaill must be no joke.

He took up the rock with great difficulty and with a huge heave hurled it over the roof. Then he tore around as fast as he could and was there to catch it as it fell. The rock was so big and heavy that it slipped from his hands and tore a sliver of skin from his leg from the hip to the ankle.

He gave another great roar of pain.

"Enough!" shouts he. "'Tis much better that I leave Fionn Mac Cumhaill be. His baby nearly took off my finger, and Fionn's pastime nearly destroyed my leg."

He started away limping towards the beach.

The last seen of him was going out Pointe na Báirce with the water up to his neck.

Fionn jumped out of the cradle and did a little dance of joy around the kitchen with the wife.

"There's no doubt about it," says Fionn, "but the old saying is true, *An té ná fuil láidir, ní foláir dó bheith glic.*" (He who has not the power needs to be crafty.)

## Appendix Six

## Letter to Walter McGrath, editor,
## *Cork Holly Bough*

St. Joseph's,
Berkley Road,
Dublin 7.
May 18th 1986.

Dear Mr. McGrath,

I hope I am not intruding on you ungraciously with this letter. If so, I ask your pardon. Your days are full of letters and other literary activities, I know, but perhaps you can spare a few minutes to answer my queries. If that is not possible, I understand, and you must not worry.

May I introduce myself as a missionary priest of the Carmelite Order, currently stationed in Israel and due to return there shortly. For the past several months, I have been convalescing and resting at the above address.

Being a Corkman (from Carrigtwohill) with something of a bent for history, I have always read with interest your articles in the *Cork Examiner*, *Evening Echo* and the *Holly Bough*, i.e. whenever I could get them. Last Christmas I was struck by your article "James Cousins and a Blasket Tragedy." It brought me back to my student days, when I first read *An tOileánach*, and heard an tAth. Benedict Langton O.C.D., speak of things Gaelic, and the people who made up the Gaelic League in its early days. One name that came up frequently was Eibhlín Ní Niocaill. The story of her glorious but tragic death impressed me. Your article in the *Holly Bough* impressed me too and brought back clear memories after an interval of almost 50 years.

As I say, I have been convalescing here, but as soon as weather and health permitted, I decided to visit the grave of Eibhlín Ní Niocaill; Glasnevin is only a mile away from where I am staying. I had no difficulty in locating the grave, thanks to the direction given me at the cemetery office. I found the headstone, a Celtic cross, in good condition, but the grave itself seems rather neglected. Eibhlín's name is given as Eveleen Constance; her age was 24. Her father Archibald was also buried here in 1924. The last recorded burial is that of Mary Nicholls, presumably her mother, who died in 1938, at the age of 93. This means that she survived Eibhlín by almost 30 years. What a lonely life she must have had!

I am wondering if you possess any other details about Eibhlín or her family. I was out of the country in August 1984, when you wrote the articles on the tragedy of An Tráigh Bhán, and so I have not seen them. In my spare time I have been searching whatever sources are at hand, but beyond what you wrote in the *Holly Bough*. I have found nothing.

Can you tell me what was her address in Dublin; what school did she attend; what did she specialise in for M.A., or anything else that would be of interest.

The day I visited the grave, I had the feeling that I was the first to come there for a long time. We should not overlook our unsung heroes or heroines thus. It is they who kept our country afloat, in dark and evil days.

Sincerely yours,
Fr Gabriel Barry. O.C.D.

# DARK DAY FOOTNOTES

**Preface**
1. Tomás Ó Criomhthain, Seán Ó Coileáin, eag., *An tOileánach* (Baile Átha Cliath: Cló Talbóid, 1929), p. 216. Mícheál Ó Dubhshláine, trans.

**Chapter 1: *Fáilte Anoir***
1. Tom O'Donnell, "Lament for The Dingle Train", copy in Dingle Library.
2. *Thro' Rare West Kerry* (Tralee: Tralee and Dingle Railway Company, reprint 1911), p. 20.
3. Máire de Buitléir (1873–1920) was thirty-six at the time. She was born in England of the upper-class Butlers of County Clare. Her mother was a Ryan of County Tipperary stock who had settled in Australia after the famine and had become prosperous due to the discovery of copper on their land. Marianne Ryan, a Catholic, married Peter Lambert Butler, whose mother was Ellen Lambert of Protestant Cromwellian stock and an aunt of Edward Carson, who was, in fact, Dublin born and had a Dublin accent. Máire's father, Peter, contacted TB in Australia and the family decided to return to County Clare. From there they moved to Dublin. Peter died in 1880 and is buried in the O'Connell tomb in Glasnevin. Máire and her sister, Belinda, were educated in Alexandra College, Dublin. Though they were happy there, there was no effort made to teach anything to do with the Irish language or culture. It was through reading John Mitchell's *Jail Journal* that she became interested in things Irish.

    See Máiréad Ní Chinnéide, *Máire de Buitléir: Bean Athbheochana* (Baile Átha Cliath: Comhar, 1993), pp. 11–30. Also, information from Cáit an Rí as given to Imelda Hallahan, "The Girl Who Was Loved by Pearse", *Irish Independent*, 21 May 1974.
4. There is a Simon Nicolls MD in the parish of Templemichael in Main Street, Longford, included in

*Griffith's Valuation c.* 1852. In the 1901 census there remains but two with the surname "Nicolls" in the County of Longford, both women, Elizabeth of Edgeworthstown and Brigid of Kiltycreevagh.

5. *An Lóchrann*, Deireadh Fómhair 1910.

6. *Thro' Rare West Kerry*, p. 12. Fourteen students attended the college, held in Mr John O'Donnell's licensed premises, Bridge Street. The professors were Patrick Corkery and Michael O'Flynn.

7. Donnchdh Ó Súilleabháin, *Na Timirí, 1893–1927* (Baile Átha Cliath: Conradh na Gaeilge, 1990), p.40.

8. Thomas O'Sullivan, *Romantic Hidden Kerry* (Tralee: The Kerryman, 1931), p. 317, from report of letter from "Gaedhal Ogue" in the *Kerry People*.

9. Jack McKenna, *Dingle: Some of Its Story* (Tralee: Kenno, n.d.), p. 21.

10. Inscription on Mullins' tomb, St James' Churchyard, Dingle. See also Mícheál Ó Dubhshláine, in "Na Ventrys", Pádraig Ó Fiannachta, eag, *An Clabhsúr* (An Daingean: An Sagart, 2002).

11. Seosamh Laoide, *Tonn Tóime*, story taken down from Máire Curran, Thady Kevane's wife.

12. Mrs D.P.A. Thompson, *A Brief Account of the Rise and Progress of the Change in Religious Opinions now Taking Place in Dingle, and the West of the County of Kerry* (London: Seely, Burnside and Seely, 1847), p. 49.

13. *Ceann Trá a hAon*, lch 24.

14. Diarmaid Trínseach, *The Irish Year Book*, Gaelic League, 1908, p. 180.

15 C.P. Crane, *Memories of a Resident Magistrate 1880–1920* (Edinburgh: University Press, 1938), p. 184.

16. John Millington Synge, *Plays, Poems and Prose* (London: Everyman Classics, 1958), p.107.
    J. M. Synge's signature does not appear on the visitor's book in Sea View, but that of his brother R. Anthony Synge does in the year 1905. Below it in different handwriting is the following verse and message:
    Ye crags and peaks I'm with you once again,
    I hold to you the hands I once beheld,
    To show they are still free,

> And I have loved the ocean,
> For I was, as it were, a child of thee.

I leave Ventry after an all too brief sojourn among its wonderful scenery, bringing away with me pleasant memories of most kindly entertainment in Mr. Kevane's hostel and of the fellow tourists I first met therein. Nowhere may a pleasanter few days be spent by the tourist.

A Pilgrim from the Leinster Hills.

17. These comments and poems are from the visitors' book, Sea View, courtesy Noel Ó Ciobháin.
18. *The United Irishman*, 20 September 1902.
19. Thomas MacDonagh, *Through the Ivory Gate*, presentation copy to Eibhlín in the Pearse Museum, Rathfarnham.
20. *The Irish Year Book*, 1907, pp. 209–16.
21. Margaret Ó hÓgartaigh, "Women in University Education in Ireland: The Historical Background" in UCD Women's Graduate Association, *Newman to New Woman, UCD Women Remember* (Dublin: New Island, 2001), pp. iii–xi.
22. Seoirse Ó Múnáin, "Eveleen Nicolls as a Worker", *An Claidheamh Soluis*, 21 August 1909.
23. Eibhlín Ní Niocaill, *"An Bhan-Ghaodhal"*, in *Bean na hÉireann*, February 1909. Contributors included Constance Markievicz, Roger Casement, George Russell (AE), Katherine Tynan, James Stephens, Séamus O'Sullivan and Maud Gonne MacBride.
24. *An Claidheamh Soluis*, 8 May 1909.

**Chapter 2: The Bell-Branch**

1. *Sinn Féin*, 23 August 1909.
2. James H. and Margaret E. Cousins, *We Two Together* (Madras: Ganesh, 1950), p.146.

   > Sea Side Resort, Ventry,
   > Four miles from Dingle
   > Comfortable lodgings at reasonable terms
   > Apply Timothy Kevane
   > Sea-View House, Ventry

   Thady Kevane's business card and in possession of Noel Ó Ciobháin
3. *Ibid.*, p.147.

4. *Ibid.*, p. 50.
5. James H. Cousins, "The Sleep of the King", in *The Quest* (Dublin: Maunsel, 1906).
6. Cousins, *We Two Together*, p. 89.
7. *Ibid.*, p. 108.
8. *Irish Homestead*, 22 May 1908. The *Irish Homestead*, one of the most important journals at the beginning of the last century, was the organ of the co-operative movement and was edited by George Russell (AE) from 1905–23.
9. James Joyce, *Gas from a Burner*, 1912. See also at http://members.ozemail.com.au/Joyce/Dubliners/gas_poem .htm. Other of the Cousins' friends to be mentioned in the broadside include "Patrick-what-do-you-Column" and "the great John Millington Synge / Who soars above on an angel's wing." This satire written by Joyce in 1912 attacks the publisher Maunsel for failing to publish "Dubliners" while publishing others like Cousins, Colum and Synge. Maunsel was afraid to publish Joyce's book for legal reasons.

## Chapter 3: Fragments of a Dream

1. James H. and Margaret E. Cousins, *We Two Together* (Madras: Ganesh, 1950).
2. *Sinn Féin*, 11 September 1909.
3. James Cousins, "Mount Brandon", *The Irish Cyclist*, 22 May 1911, p. 66.
4  *Thro' Rare West Kerry* (Tralee: Tralee and Dingle Railway Company, reprint 1911), p. 22.
5. James H. Cousins, "At a Holy Well", in *A Bardic Pilgrimage* (New York: Roerich Museum Press, 1934), p. 53. Templemanaghan, County Kerry.
6. *Ibid.*, "A Donegal Sketch", p. 54.
7  Cousins, *We Two Together*, p. 147.
8. Earnán de Blaghd, *Trasna na Bóinne* (Baile Átha Cliath: Sáirseál agus Dill, 1957), p. 146. Mícheál Ó Dubhshláine, trans.
9. Cousins, *We Two Together*, p. 148.
10. *Ibid.*, p. 148.
11. John M. Synge, *Plays, Poems and Prose* (London: Everyman Classics, 1958), p. 107.

12. Cousins, *We Two Together*, p. 148.
13. *Sinn Féin*, 27 August 1909.
14. *Ibid.*
15. Cousins, *We Two Together*, p. 147.
16. "Seán an Chóta", "*Báthadh Eibhlín Nic Niocaill*", *Irish Press*, 13 August 1946. Mícheál Ó Dubhshláine, trans.
17. Cousins, *We Two Together*, p. 147.
18. *Ibid.*

**Chapter 4: Not the Same to Go to the King's House as to Leave**
1. *Thro' Rare West Kerry* (Tralee: Tralee and Dingle Railway Company, reprint 1911), p. 27.
2. "Donn Mac Mílidh", "*Beachtchuntas ar na Blascaodaí*", i Breandán Ó Conaire, *Tomás an Bhlascaoid* (An Ghaillimh: Cló Iar-Chonnachta, 1992), vol. 1, pp. 120–21.
3. Walter McGrath, "To Kerry for Folklore and Mythology (2)", *Evening Echo*, 9 August 1983.
4. John M. Synge, *In West Kerry* (Cork: Mercier, 1979), p. 38.
5. Imelda Hallahan, "The Girl Who Was Loved by Pearse", *Irish Independent*, 21 May 1974.
6. Pádraig Tyers, *Leoithne Aniar* (Baile an Fheirtéaraigh: Cló Dhuibhne, 1982), speaking to Seán Ó Criomhthain, p. 69. Mícheál Ó Dubhshláine, trans.
7. Mícheál Ó Gaoithín collected from Méiní Bean Uí Dhuinnshléibhe, CBÉ. Ms. 1602, p.458.
8. Thomas H. Mason, *The Islands of Ireland* (Cork: Mercier, 1978), pp 12, 13, 14. Mason and his wife had also stayed in Sea View, and may have moved into Eibhlín's room a week after her departure to the Island. He wrote in the visitors' book on 1 August 1909:

> My wife and I spent a most enjoyable ten days in this hospitable home. We found Mr. and Mrs. Kevane, indeed everybody with whom we came in contact most kind and courteous.
> We look forward with greatest pleasure to another holiday here.
> Thomas H. Mason.
> Meta E. Mason.

9. Tomás Ó Criomhthain, Pádraig Ua Maoileoin ed., *Allagar*

*II* (Baile Átha Cliath: Coiscéim, 1999), p. 110. Mícheál Ó Dubhshláine, trans.

10. Máire Ní Ghaoithín, *Bean an Oileáin* (Baile Átha Cliath: Coiscéim, 1986), pp. 7–8. Mícheál Ó Dubhshláine, trans.

11. Tomás Ó Criomhthain, Breandán Ó Conaire eag., *"Fáinne an Lae"*, *Bloghanna* (Baile Átha Cliath: Coiscéim, 1997), 19 October 1918, p. 26. Mícheál Ó Dubhshláine, trans.

12. Hallahan, "The Girl Who Was Loved by Pearse".

13. James H. and Margaret E. Cousins, *We Two Together* (Madras: Ganesh, 1950), p. 148.

14. Pádraig Tyers speaking to Seán Ó Criomhthain, *Leoithne Aniar* (Baile an Fheirtéaraigh: Cló Dhuibhne, 1982), p. 75.

15. Donnchadh Ó Súilleabháin, *Na Timirí, 1893–1927* (Baile Átha Cliath: Conradh na Gaeilge, 1990), p. 40.

16. Risteárd Ó Glaisne, *"Mar a Bádh Searcóg an Phiarsaigh"*, *Inniu*, 27 Samhain 1964. Mícheál Ó Dubhshláine, trans.

17. Eibhlín Nic Niocaill, *"Bean na hÉireann"*, *An Bhan-Ghaodhal*, February 1909.

18. *An Claidheamh Soluis*, 14 August 1909.

**Chapter 5: The Gift of Patience**

1. Seán Ó Criomhthain, *"Tomás Ó Criomhthain mar is Cuimhin lena Mhac Seán É"*, *Feasta*, January 1957. From a talk given on Radio Éireann. Mícheál Ó Dubhshláine, trans.

2. Mícheál Ó Gaoithín collected from Méiní Bean Uí Dhuinnshléibhe, CBÉ Ms. 1602, p. 459.

3. Seán Ó Criomhthain, *"Tomás Ó Criomhthain mar is Cuimhin lena Mhac Seán É"*; and Breandán Ó Conaire, *Tomás an Bhlascaoid* (An Ghaillimh: Cló Iar-Chonnachta, 1992), p. 146.

4. Seán Ó Criomhthain, *"Tomás Ó Criomhthain mar is Cuimhin lena Mhac Seán É"*.

5. *An Claidheamh Soluis*, 28 August 1909.

6. "Seán an Chóta", *Báthadh Eibhlín Nic Niocaill"*, *Irish Press*, 13 August 1946.

7. Imelda Hallahan, "The Girl Who Was Loved by Pearse", *Irish Independent*, 21 May 1974.

8. Seán Ó Criomhthain, *"Tomás Ó Criomhthain mar is Cuimhin lena Mhac Seán É"*.

9. Mícheál Ó Gaoithín collected from Méiní Bean Uí Dhuinnshléibhe.
10. *An Claidheamh Soluis*, 21 August 1909.
11. Risteárd Ó Glaisne, "*Mar a Bádh Searcóg an Phiarsaigh*", *Inniu*, 27 November 1964.
12. *An Claidheamh Soluis*, 21 August 1909.
13. Ó Glaisne, "*Mar a Bádh Searcóg an Phiarsaigh*".
14. Mícheál Ó Gaoithín collected from Méiní Bean Uí Dhuinnshléibhe, p. 462.
15. Seán Ó Criomhthain, "*Tomás Ó Criomhthain mar is Cuimhin lena Mhac Seán É*".
16. Mícheál Ó Gaoithín collected from Méiní Bean Uí Dhuinnshléibhe, p. 463.
17 *An Claidheamg Soluis*, 21 August 1909.
18. Seán Ó Dubhda collected from Peats Tom Ó Cearnaigh, CBÉ Ms. 1477.
19. *Ibid.*
20. Imelda Hallahan, "The Girl Who Was Loved by Pearse".
21. Seán Ó Dubhda collected from Peats Tom Ó Cearnaigh.
22. *Sinn Féin*, 25 August 1909.
23. *Ibid.*
24 "Seán an Chóta", "*Báthadh Eibhlín Nic Niocaill*", *Irish Press*, 13 August 1946.
25. Mícheál Ó Gaoithín collected from Méiní Bean Uí Dhuinnshléibhe, p. 464.
26. Seán Ó Criomhthain, "*Tomás Ó Criomhthain mar is Cuimhin lena Mhac Seán É*".

**Chapter 6: And There Were Present**
1. "Seán an Chóta", "*Báthadh Eibhlín Nic Niocaill*", *Irish Press*, 13 August 1946. "I think he blames himself unnecessarily for the tragedy that befell Eibhlín." Seán Ó Lúing in letter to Walter McGrath.
2. Seán Ó Dubhda collected from Peats Tom Ó Cearnaigh, CBÉ Ms. 1477.
3. As told to Leslie Matson by Méiní Bean Uí Dhuinnshléibhe.
4. *Ibid.*
5. *Ibid.*
6. *Ibid.* See also Leslie Matson, *Méiní the Blasket Nurse*

(Cork: Mercier, 1967), p. 102, in which Méiní attributes
the statements to Peig Sayers and Máire Mhuiris, the wife
of Tom Kearney.

7. *Sinn Féin*, 28 August 1909.

Up to August 1909 *Sinn Féin* was a weekly, but became a
daily on August 1909, just in time to report on Eibhlín and
Domhnall's drowning. The newspaper was founded originally as the *United Irishman* by Arthur Griffith, but had to
cease publication because of lack of finances following a
court case. It was followed by the *Sinn Féin* weekly.

Michael O'Rahilly (later The O'Rahilly) became
involved in the publication. However, it was not a success
as a daily, in spite of O Rahilly and William Bulfin's trip to
America seeking funding. The *Sinn Féin Daily* ceased publication in January 1910 suffering also from repression
from the British authorities. *Bean na hÉireann* was started
by Maud Gonne MacBride in 1908 to aid the national
movement. Though aimed at women, it shortly became
known as the women's magazine that was read by men.

8. *Ibid.*
9. *Ibid.*
10. Seán Ó Dubhda collected from Peats Tom Ó Cearnaigh.
11. Máire Ní Ghaoithín, *An tOileán a Bhí* (Baile Átha Cliath:
An Clóchomhar, 1978), p. 71.
12. Tomás Ó Criomhthain, Seán Ó Coileáin, eag., *An
tOileánach* (Baile Átha Cliath: Cló Talbóid, 1929), p. 217.
Mícheál Ó Dubhshláine, trans.
13. Máire Ní Ghaoithín, *An tOileán a Bhí*, p. 71.
14. Seán Ó Dubhda collected from Peats Tom Ó Cearnaigh.
15. Mícheál Ó Gaoithín collected from Méiní Bean Uí
Dhuinnshléibhe, pp. 463–64.
16. Seán Ó Dubhda collected from Peats Tom Ó Cearnaigh.
17. *Cork Constitution*, 16 August 1909.
18. "Seán an Chóta", "*Báthadh Eibhlín Nic Niocaill*".
19. Mícheál Ó Gaoithín collected from Méiní Bean Uí
Dhuinnshléibhe, pp. 465–66.
20. Seán Ó Dubhda collected from Peats Tom Ó Cearnaigh.
21. *Ibid.*
22 *Sinn Féin*, 25 August 1909.
23 Seán Ó Dubhda collected from Peats Tom Ó Cearnaigh.

24. Tomás Ó Criomhthain, *An tOileánach*, p. 217. Tomás
    himself mentions the funeral of Siobhán Mhuiris Mhóir Uí
    Dhálaigh from Inis Mhic Uíleáin some years previous.
    Tomás was present at the funeral. Siobhán was an old
    sweetheart of his:
    "I had a long look. I don't think I ever before saw so many
    *naomhóga* together in one place. I started to count them,
    and found out that there were eighteen present. To the pre-
    sent day I have not seen as many boats attending a funeral
    on the sea. Sixteen and fourteen are the most I have seen
    since." p. 250. Mícheál Ó Dubhshláine, trans.
25. *Sinn Féin*, 25 August 1909.
26. Thomas H. Mason, *The Islands of Ireland* (Cork: Mercier,
    1996), p. 109.
27. Imelda Hallahan, "The Girl Who Was Loved by Pearse".
28. Seán Ó Dubhda collected from Peats Tom Ó Cearnaigh.
29. *Sinn Féin*, 25 August 1909.
30. Imelda Hallahan, "The Girl Who Was Loved by Pearse".
31. Seán Ó Dubhda collected from Peats Tom Ó Cearnaigh.
32. Tomás Ó Criomhthain, *An tOileánach*, p. 250.
33. *Sinn Féin*, 25 August 1909.
34. *Irish Weekly Independent*, 21 August 1909, et al.
35. *Sinn Féin*, 25 August 1909.
36. *Kerry Sentinel*, 18 August 1909.
37. *The Kerryman*, 21 August 1909.
    At 1pm on Wednesday 11th August the barometer regis-
    tered 102 degrees in the sun and 80 in the shade.
    At 1pm on Thursday 12th August the barometer registered
    102 degrees in the sun and 80 in the shade.
    At 1pm on Friday 13th August the barometer registered
    104 degrees in the sun and 78 in the shade.
    *Kerry People*, 14 August 1909.
38. *Irish Weekly Independent*, 21 August 1909 et al.
39. *Diary of Joseph Holloway*, National Library of Ireland, 16
    August 1909.
40. Louis N. Le Roux, Desmond Ryan trans. and adapt.,
    *Patrick H. Pearse* (Dublin: Talbot Press, 1932), p. 39. The
    account is clearly innacurate.
41. *Freeman's Journal*, 17August 1909.
42. Seán Ó Dubhda collected from Peats Tom Ó Cearnaigh.

43. Imelda Hallahan, "The Girl Who Was Loved by Pearse".
44. *Ibid.*
45. Risteárd Ó Glaisne, *"Mar a Bádh Searcóg an Phiarsaigh"*, *Inniu*, 27 November 1964.
46. *Ibid.*
47. Bernard Knight, *Legal Aspects of Medical Practice*, 5th ed. (Edinburgh; New York: Churchill Livingstone, 1992), p. 222.
48. Wolffe-Parkinson-White Syndrome. Information from Dr Conchúr Ó Brosnacháin, Dingle.

**Chapter 7: Beyond the Wash of Waves**
1. *An Claidheamh Soluis*, 21 August 1909.
2. *Ibid.*
3. *The Freeman's Journal*, 16 August 1909.
4. *An Claidheamh Soluis*, 21 August 1909.
5. Eamonn Ó Neill, schoolmaster at Coláiste Éanna, information on display at Pearse Museum (Scoil Éanna), Rathfarnham.
6. Imelda Hallahan, "The Girl Who Was Loved by Pearse", *Irish Independent*, 21 May 1974.
7. Risteárd Ó Glaisne, *"Mar a Bádh Searcóg an Phiarsaigh"*, *Inniu*, 27 November 1964.
8. Séamas Ó Buachalla, ed., *The Literary Writings of Patrick Pearse, The Singer* (Dublin and Cork: The Mercier Press, 1979), pp. 100–26. Text also available at http://website.lineone.net/~pearsebaby/index.html
9. *An Claidheamh Soluis*, 8 September 1909.
10. Seoirse Ó Múnáin, "Eveleen Nicolls as a Worker", *An Claidheamh Soluis*, 21 August 1909.
11. *An Claidheamh Soluis*, 11 September 1909.
12. *Ibid.*, 4 September 1909.
13. *Ibid.*
14. *Ibid.*, 28 August 1909.
15. *Ibid.*, 30 July 1910.
16. Mícheál Ó Gaoithín collected from Méiní Bean Uí Dhuinnshléibhe, CBÉ Ms. 1602, p. 465.
17. Visitors' Book, Sea View, Ventry.
18. *Ibid.*
19. James H. Cousins, "At Streamstown, Connemara" in *The Bell-Branch* (Dublin: Maunsel, 1908), p. 16.

**Chapter 8: Behold the Perfect Life**
1. Seán Ó Gaoithín (RIP) agus Muiris Ó Gaoithín, Baile na Rátha, Dún Chaoin, late of the Blaskets, nephews of Cáit an Rí and of Maidhc Pheats Mhicí.
2. Mícheál Ó Gaoithín collected from Méiní Bean Uí Dhuinnshléibhe, CBÉ. Ms. 1602, p. 466.
3. *Ibid.*
4. Tomás Ó Criomhthain, Seán Ó Coileáin, eag., *An tOileánach*, (Baile Átha Cliath: Cló Talbóid, 1929), p. 340. Mícheál Ó Dubhshláine, trans.
5. Long's Ledger, Dingle.
6. Tomás Ó Criomhthain, *An tOileánach*, p. 318.
7. James H. Cousins, "Death and Life", in *A Bardic Pilgrimage* (New York: Roerich Museum Press, 1934), p. 37, to the memory of Eveleen Nicolls.
8. Máire Ní Chinnéide, *Máire de Buitléir, Bean Athbheochana* (Baile Átha Cliath: Comhar, 1993), pp. 143–52. Máire de Buitléir's work also includes a book of short stories, *A Bundle of Rushes* (1899). Three of the short stories were translated into Irish by Tomás Ó Concheanainn and were published by the Gaelic League in 1901 under the title *Blátha Bealtaine*. Although an avid language enthusiast, Máire never had the confidence to write in Irish.
9. Mary Butler, *The Price, Irish Weekly Independent*, 9 October 1909–15 January 1910.

**Chapter 9: Her Fame Will Live**
1. *An Claidheamh Soluis*, 28 August 1909.
2. *Ibid.*, 16 July 1910 and 30 July 1910.
3. *Ibid.*, 30 July 1910.
4. *Feasta*, January 1957.
5. Máire Ní Ghaoithín, *An tOileán a Bhí* (Baile Átha Cliath: An Clóchomhar, 1978), p. 72.
6. Páipéirí Kruger, with the kind permission of Pádraig and Máiréad Ó Néill, Tigh Kruger, Dún Chaoin.
7. *An Claidheamh Soluis*, 26 March 1910. C. P. Curran (1880–1975), the secretary, had been in Thady and Máire Kevane's house, Sea View, around the time of the drowning. Cousins wrote in the visitors' book, though he did not

give the date: "Mr. C.P. Curran, M.A., of Dublin came to Ventry on a walking tour. He stayed from Monday evening till Thursday morning, having been captured by the natural beauty and the kindly life of the place. During his stay he and Mrs Curran succeeded in learning the four hand reel."

Curran had attended O'Connell Schools and UCD at the same time as James Joyce and was a lifelong friend of the author. His wife, Helen S. Laird, was one of the official founders of the Irish National Theatre Society, and created the role of Maurya in Synge's *Riders to the Sea* in the Molesworth Hall in 1904.

8. *An Claidheamh Soluis*, 18 September 1909.
9. *Sinn Féin*, 25 August 1909.
10. Seán Ó Dubhda collected from Peats Tom Ó Cearnaigh, CBÉ Ms. 1477.
11. *Ibid.*
12. Peter Helmore, Royal Humane Society Bronze Medals Citations taken from the Annual Report 1909.
13. *Ibid.*
14. Seán Ó Dubhda collected from Peats Tom Ó Cearnaigh.
15. Tomás Ó Criomhthain, Seán Ó Coileáin, eag., *An tOileánach* (Baile Átha Cliath: Cló Talbóid, 1929), p. 260. Mícheál Ó Dubhshláine, trans.
16. *Connacht Tribune*, 16 May 1942; also information from Ambrose de Róiste, 10 University Road, Galway.
17. Notes taken by Séamus Ware from Cáit an Rí, August 1970.
18. Walter McGrath, "Just 75 Years Ago–Double Tragedy Struck Blasket's White Strand", *Evening Echo*, 7 August 1984.
19. Tomás Ó Criomhthain, *An tOileánach*, p. 260.
20. Information from Bab Feiritéar, Dún Chaoin.
21. The headstone in Teampall Dhún Chaoin, erected by American relatives, reads:
> Blasket Islanders.
> In memory of
> Pats Tom Kearney
> Died 10th Dec. 1964
> Aged 84 yrs.

His wife Nelly Jerry Shea Kearney
Died 21st April 1964
Aged 82 yrs.
R.I.P.
Ó Cearna.

**Chapter 10: Over the Hills and Far Away**

1.  Tomás Ó Criomhthain, Seán Ó Coileáin, eag., *An tOileánach* (Baile Átha Cliath: Cló Talbóid, 1929), p. 318. Mícheál Ó Dubhshláine, trans.

2.  Notes taken by Séamus Ware from Mícheál Ó Gaoithín, Maidhc Pheig Sayers, in 1966.

3.  Leslie Matson, *Méiní the Blasket Nurse* (Cork: Mercier, 1996).

4.  James H. Cousins, "Irish Idles IV", *The Irish Cyclist*, 25 January 1911, p. 34.

5.  Alan Denson, *James H. Cousins and Margaret E. Cousins, a Biographical Survey, Family Reminiscences and Autobiographical Note* (Kendal: 1967), introduction by Padraic Colum.

6.  Eibhlín Ní Éireamhoin, *Two Great Irishwomen: Maud Gonne MacBride, Constance Markcievicz* (Dublin: C.J. Fallon, 1973), p. 67.

7.  Alan Denson, *James H. Cousins and Margaret E. Cousins, a Biographical Survey, Family Reminiscences and Autobiographical Note* (Kendal: 1967).

8.  *An Claidheamh Soluis*, 27 September 1902.

9.  Máiréad Nic Craith, *An tOileánach Léannta* (Baile Átha Cliath: An Clóchomhar, 1988), p. 54.

10. *Ibid.*, p. 55.

**Epilogue**

1.  Verse composed by Tomás Ó Cinnéide, An Ghráig (RIP).

2.  Tomás Ó Criomhthain, Caoilfhionn Nic Pháidín, eag., *Dinnsheanchas na mBlascaodaí* (Baile Átha Cliath: Cois Life, 1999; Céad eagrán 1935), p. 32. Mícheál Ó Dubhshláine, trans.

3.  Tomás Ó Criomhthain, *"Fáinne an Lae"*, 2 January 1926, *Bloghanna ón mBlascaod* (Baile Átha Cliath: Coiscéim, 1997), p. 216. Mícheál Ó Dubhshláine, trans.

4. *Dinnsheanchas na mBlascaodaí*, p. 32.
5. "Seán an Chóta", "*Báthadh Eibhlín Nic Niocaill*", *Irish Press*, 13 August 1946.
6. Tomás Ó Criomhthain, *Bloghanna*, p. 108, "*Fáinne an Lae*", 30 May 1925.
7. Tom O'Donnell, "Lament for The Dingle Train", copy in Dingle Library.

# Bibliography

Barklay, Craig. "An Introduction to the Medals of the Royal Humane Society".
http://www.lsars.eurobell.Countyuk/rhs.htm

Breathnach, Diarmuid agus Ní Mhurchú, Máire. *Beathaisnéis a Dó, 1882–1982*. Baile Átha Cliath: An Clóchomhar, 1990.

Cousins, James. H. *A Bardic Pilgrimage*. New York: Roerich Museum Press, 1934.

—. *The Bell-Branch*. Dublin: Maunsel, 1908.

—. *The Quest*. Dublin: Maunsel, 1906.

Cousins, James. H. and Margaret E. *We Two Together*. Madras: Ganesh, 1950.

Crane, C.P. *Memories of a Resident Magistrate 1880–1920*. Edinburgh: University Press, 1938.

De Blaghd, Earnán. *Trasna na Bóinne*. Baile Átha Cliath: Sáirséal agus Dill, 1957.

Denson, Alan. *James H. Cousins and Margaret E. Cousins, a Biographical Survey, Family Reminiscences and Autobiographical Note*. Kendal: 1967.

DeVillo, Stephen Paul. "This Month in Celtic History", http://www.celticleague.org/history_11-02.html

Dudley Edwards, Ruth. *The Triumph of Failure*, 2nd edition. Dublin: Poolbeg Press, 1990.

Fitzgerald, F. *The Memoirs of Desmond Fitzgerald*. London: Routledge and Kegan Paul, 1968.

Frances, Tom. "Fr Jones the Rescuer", in *Cork Holly Bough*, 1982.

Hallahan, Imelda. "The Girl Who Was Loved by Pearse", *Irish Independent*, 21 May 1974.

Helmore, Peter. "RHS Bronze 1909". Royal Humane Society Bronze Medals Citations taken from the Annual Report 1909.
http://www.users.globalnet.Countyuk/~tamarnet/bronz09s.htm

# Bibliography

Henchy, Deirdre. "Dublin 80 Years Ago", prize-winning essay, in *Dublin Historical Record*, December 1972.

Hogan, Robert, ed. *Dictionary of Irish Literature*. Dublin: Gill and MacMillan, 1979.

Iarsmalann an Phiarsaigh, The Pearse Museum, Grange Road, Rathfarnham, County Dublin.

Joyce, James. *Dubliners*. London: Jonathan Cape, 1956.

Laoide, Seosamh. *Tonn Tóime, Timargadh sean-phisreog, sean-rócán, sean-sgéal, sean-cheist, sean-naitheann, sean-fhocal agus sean-rádh ó Chiarraí Luachra*. Baile Átha Cliath: Connradh na Gaedhilge, 1915.

Le Roux, Louis N.; Ryan, Desmond, trans. and adapt. *Patrick H. Pearse*. Dublin: Talbot Press, 1932

MacCurtain, Margaret and Ó Corráin, Donncha, eds. *Women in Irish Society*. Dublin: Arlen House, The Women's Press, 1978.

McCormack, W.J. *Fool of the Family: A Life of J. M. Synge*. London: Weidenfield and Nicolson, 2000.

McElligott, T.J. "Unbeatable Fr. Tom Jones", *Cork Holly Bough*, 1982.

McGrath, Walter. "Just 75 Years ago – Double Tragedy Struck Blasket's White Strand", *Evening Echo*, 7 August 1984.

—. "To Kerry for Folklore and Mythology (2)", *Evening Echo*, 9 August 1983.

McKenna, Jack. *Dingle: Some of Its Story*. Tralee: Kenno, n.d.

"Mac Mílidh, Donn". *"Beachtchuntas ar na Blascaodaí"*. Ó Conaire, Breandán, eag. *Tomás an Bhlascaoid*. An Ghaillimh: Cló Iar-Chonnachta, 1992.

Mecredy R.J. and Percy, J.C. *The Irish Cyclist*, January 1911, May 1911, November 1911.

Mason, Thomas H. *The Islands of Ireland*. Cork: Mercier, 1967. First published 1937.

Matson, Leslie. *Méiní the Blasket Nurse*. Cork: Mercier, 1996.

Ní Chinnéide, Máiréad. *Máire de Buitléir: Bean Athbheochana*. Baile Átha Cliath: Comhar, 1993.

Nic Craith, Máiréad. *An tOileánach Léannta*. Baile Átha Cliath: An Clóchomhar, 1988.

Ní Éireamhoin, Eibhlín. *Two Great Irishwomen: Maud Gonne MacBride, Constance Markievicz*. Dublin: C.J. Fallon, 1971.

Ní Ghaoithín, Máire. *Bean an Oileáin*. Baile Átha Cliath: Coiscéim, 1986.

—. *An tOileán a Bhí*. Baile Átha Cliath: An Clóchomhar, 1978.

Ní Niocaill, Eibhlín. *"An Bhan-Ghaodhal"*, *Bean na hÉireann*, February 1909.

Ó Cearnaigh, Seán Pheats Tom. *Fiolar an Eireabaill Bháin*, Baile Átha Cliath: Coiscéim, 1992.

Ó Céirín, Kit and Cyril. *Women of Ireland, A Biographic Dictionary*. Kinvara, County Galway: Tír Eolas, 1996.

Ó Ciosáin, Mícheál, eag. *Céad Bliain 1871–1971*. Baile an Fheirtéaraigh: Muintir Phiarais, 1973.

O'Connor, Gabriel. *A History of Galway County Council*. Galway: Galway County Council, 1999.

Ó Criomhthain, Tomás; Ó Coileáin, Seán, eag. *An tOileánach*. Baile Átha Cliath: Cló Talbóid, 2002.

—. Nic Pháidín, Caoilfhionn, eag. *Dinnsheanchas na mBlascaodaí*. Baile Átha Cliath: Cois Life, 1999; céad eagrán 1935.

—. Ó Conaire, Breandán eag. *Bloghanna ón mBlascaod*. Baile Átha Cliath: Coiscéim, 1997.

—. Ua Maoileoin, Pádraig, eag. *Allagar II*. Baile Átha Cliath: Coiscéim, 1999.

Ó Criomhthain, Seán. *"Tomás Ó Criomhthain mar Is Cuimhin lena Mhac Seán É"*, *Feasta*, Eanáir 1957, from a talk given on Radio Éireann.

Ó Crohan, Tomás; Flower, Robin, trans. *The Islandman*. Talbot Press/Chatto and Windus, 1934; Oxford University Press 1951, etc.

Ó Dubhda, Seán, collected from Peats Tom Ó Ceárnaí [Cearnaigh]. CBÉ, Ms. 1477, September 1956.

Ó Dubhda, Seán. *Duanaire Duibhneach*. Baile Átha Cliath: Oifig Dhíolta Foilseachán Rialtais, 1933, reprinted 1973.

Ó Dubhshláine, Mícheál. *An Baol Dom Tú? Muintir Chorca Dhuibhne agus an Ghaeilge, 1860–1940*. Baile Átha Cliath: Conradh na Gaeilge, 2000.

Ó Dubhshláine Mícheál; Ó Fiannachta, Pádraig, eag. *An Clabhsúr, Na Ventrys*. An Daingean: An Sagart, 2002.

Ó Glaisne, Risteárd. *"Mar a Bádh Searcóg an Phiarsaigh"*, *Inniu*, 27 Samhain, 1964.

O'Guiheen, Mícheál; Enright, Tim, trans. *A Pity Youth Does Not Last*. Oxford: Oxford University Press, 1982.

# Bibliography

Ó Gaoithín, Mícheál, collected from Méiní Bean Uí Dhuinnshléibhe. CBÉ. Mss. 1602.

Ó Lubhaing, Bearnard. *Ceann Trá a hAon.* Baile Átha Cliath: Coiscéim, 1998.

Ó Lúing, Seán. *Seán an Chóta.* Baile Átha Cliath: Coiscéim, 1985. First published in *Journal of the Kerry Historical and Archaeological Society,* no. 11, 1978.

O'Mahony, Seán. *Frongoch, University of Revolution.* Dublin: FDR, 1987.

O'Neill, Marie. "The Dublin Women's Suffrage Association and Its Successors", *Dublin Historical Record,* September 1985.

O'Rahilly, Aodhogán. *Winding the Clock, O'Rahilly and the 1916 Rising.* Dublin: Lilliput Press, 1991.

Ó Súilleabháin, Donnchadh, *Na Timirí, 1893–1927.* Baile Átha Cliath: Conradh na Gaeilge, 1990.

O'Sullivan, Thomas F. *Romantic Hidden Kerry.* Tralee: The Kerryman, 1931.

Royal Humane Society. "London Ancestors". http://www.londonancestor.com

Sayers, Peig; Ní Mhainín, Máire agus Ó Murchú, Liam, eag. *Peig: A Scéal Féin.* An Daingean: An Sagart, 1998.

Stephen's Study Room, "Humane Society Medals", http://www.stephen-stratford.Countyuk/humane_medals. htm

Stephenson, Paul and Waters, Margie. "Bloomsday in the Bungalow", *The Irish Times,* 15 June 2002.

Synge, John, M. *In West Kerry.* Cork: The Mercier Press, 1979.

—. *Plays, Poems and Prose.* London: Everyman Classics, 1958.

Thompson, Mrs. D.P., *A Brief Account of the Rise and Progress of the Change in Religious Opinions now Taking Place in Dingle, and the West of the County of Kerry, Ireland.* London: Seely, Burnside and Seely, 1847.

*Thom's Directory,* 1880–1911.

*Thro' Rare West Kerry.* Tralee: Tralee and Dingle Railway Company: 1911. (reprint).

Tyers, Pádraig, eag. *Leoithne Aniar.* Baile an Fheirtéaraigh: Cló Dhuibhne, 1982.

Tynan, Katherine. "The Glorious Girl", *The Irish Monthly,* October 1909.

UCD Women Graduate's Association. *From Newman to New*

*Woman, UCD Women Remember*. Dublin: New Island, 2001.

Walker, Brian M., ed. *Parliamentary Results in Ireland, 1918–92*. Dublin: Royal Irish Academy, 1992.

Whitehouse, P.B., *Tralee and Dingle Railway*. n.d.

Wyse Jackson, John, and Costello, Peter. *John Stanislaus Joyce*. London: Fourth Estate, 1997.

*An Claidheamh Soluis*, 8 May 1909, 31 July 1909, 21 August 1909, 28 August, 1909, 4 September 1909, 16 July 1910,

*Kerry Evening Star*, Monday, 9 August 1909.

*Kerry People*, 14, 28 August, 1909.

*Kerryman*, Tralee, 14, 21, 28 August 1909.

*Sinn Féin Daily*, August–September 1909.

*United Irishman*, 20 September 1902.

# Glossary

*ainniseoir*: miserable, unfortunate person

*as Béarla*: in English

*as Gaeilge*: in Irish

*bairneach*: limpet

*bean uasal álainn*: beautiful lady

*cé*: quay

*céilí, céilithe* (pl): social evening; dance session

*cúpla focal*: couple of words

*éigse*: learned gathering

*máchail*: a physical impediment

*naomhóg, naomhóga* (pl): Kerry version of *currach*, the traditional tarred canvas boat

*seanchaí*: storyteller

*srathair fhada*: pannier-straddle

*timire, timirí* (pl): a travelling teacher employed by the Gaelic League to teach Irish

# Index

# Index

# Index

# Index

# Index

# Index

Fianna, 24, 68
Fianna Fáil, 162
Fionn Mac Cumhaill, 43, 68, 201, 218–221
Fionntrá (Ventry Strand and parish), 25, 190, 218
fishing industry, 27, 66
Five Provinces Branch (Gaelic League), 38
Flower, Robin, 69, 155
folklore, 66, 179
*The Freeman's Journal,* 38, 39, 117, 121
  tributes to Eibhlín Nic Niocaill, 127–130
Freemasons, 172
French Huguenots, 42
Frongoch prison camp (Wales), 161
funerals of Eibhlín and Domhnall (1909), 107–117

GAA (Gaelic Athletic Association), 35, 162
Gaelic League (Conradh na Gaeilge), 20–21, 28–29, 34, 38, 39, 43, 44, 54, 122, 160, 183, 184, 212, 222
  Ard Fheis (1898), 177
  Bolivia branch, 137
  Dún Chaoin, 173
  and Eibhlín Nic Niocaill, 79, 128–129
    memorial picture fund, 152–156
    motions of sympathy, 130–131
  Executive Committee (Coiste Gnó), 79, 162, 184
  Feis Committee, 128
  Five Provinces Branch, 38
  founding of, 36
  importance of, 79
  O'Curry Branch (London), 177
  Oireachtas and Ard Fheis, 79, 177
  Paris branch, 38
  *timirí,* 177, 178
Gaeltacht (Corca Dhuibhne), 21, 22, 26, 175, 190

  scholarship project, 156, 157, 168
  *timirí,* 177
Gallán an tSagairt, 50
Galvin, T., 210
Galway County Council, 161, 162
Galway Pipers' Band, 162
Geesala, 30
Geraldines, 24, 28, 50
Gillespie, Margaret E. *see* Cousins, Gretta
Glasnevin cemetery (Dublin), 116–117, 130, 160, 223
Gleann Mór, 75, 167
Gleann Fán, 50
Glenbeigh, 102
Goodman, Parson, 23
Goodman, Seamus, 23
Gort an Choirce, 137
Gorta Dubha, 93, 164
Great Blasket. *see* Blascaod Mór
Griffith, Arthur, 161
Grogan, Brigid, 19
Guithín family, 65, 85, 104, 187. *see also* Ní Ghuithín; Ó Guithín; Uí Ghuithín
Gwinn, Brian, 32

Hallahan, Imelda, 73, 84, 111, 125
Harcourt Street (Dublin), 47
Harold's Cross (Dublin), 17
Haslam, Anna A., 47
Haughey, Charles J., 176
Head, Revd P., 17, 117
Hedderman, B.V.,
  *Glimpses of My Life in Aran,* 133–134
Henrietta Street (Dublin), 17
Hickey, Rev. Dr, 132
High School (Dublin), 47, 149
historical monuments, 206–207
Holloway, Joseph, 116
*Holly Bough,* 222
Holy Stone (Dingle), 21
holy wells, 52
Humane Society, 158
Hyde, Douglas, 35–36, 44, 179

India, 170–171, 171

# Index

# Index

Kerry (county), *Croidhe Cainnte Chiarraí* (Ó Caomhánaigh), 175
Kerry County Council, 183
*Kerry People,* 21, 158
*Kerry Sentinel,* 59, 114
*The Kerryman,* 115
Kevane, Máire (née Curran), 30, 31, 32, 42, 49, 58, 59, 117, 138, 141. *see also* Sea View House
death of (1911), 188
Kevane, Thady, 25, 29–31, 42, 49, 55–56, 58, 59, 117, 138, 141, 188–189, 218. *see also* Sea View House
death of (1943), 189
Kilconly, 162
Kildorrihey (Cill Uru), 57
Kildrum, 52
Killarney, 45, 140, 159, 189
Killorglin, 173
Kilmainham Jail (Dublin), 161
Kilmakeran, 177
Kilronan (Co. Galway), 133
Kilvicadownaig (Cill Mhic an Domhnaigh), 57, 58
Kingsbridge Station (Dublin), 115
Knocklough National School, 188
Kruger. *see* Kavanagh, Muiris
Kruger's pub (Dún Chaoin), 159, 183

ladies' colleges, 37
"Lament for Owen Roe", 84
land agents, 70
Land League, 35
Langton, An tAthair Benedict, 222
Le Roux, Louis, 116
Lee's hotel (Dingle), 20
Limerick (county), 18
Lispole, 174
Liverpool (England), 53
Loan Fund of Ireland, 18
lobster fishing, 81–82, 90
*An Lóchrann,* 59
London (England), 43, 48, 62, 179
Gaelic League branch, 177–178
Long, John, 144
Long, Michael (Cooper Long), 26, 27, 63

Longford (county), 18, 147
Loreto College (St Stephen's Green, Dublin), 33, 37, 107, 157
Loreto Convent (Rathmines, Dublin), 33
Louis XVI, 22
Lúing, Muintir, 175
Lynch, Pats, 172, 173

Mac Aindriú, Deasún, 159
MacBride, Maud Gonne, 172
MacBride, Seán, 172
Mac Cárthaigh, Maolmhuire, 31–32, 218
McCarthys (Sponcán), 177
Mac Coluim, Fionán, 75, 81, 84, 95, 102, 117, 154, 155, 177–179
and Blasket Islands, 178
death of (1966), 179
folklore interests, 179
friendship with "An tOileánach", 178–179
and Irish language movement, 177
Mac Coluim, Pádraic. *see* Colum, Padraic
MacDonagh, Thomas, 157
*Through the Ivory Gate,* 33
McGrath, Walter, 163–164, 222
McHugh, Margaret, 162
McKenna, Canon Jack, 163
McLeod, Mary, 195
MacMahon, Marshal, 53
Mac Mathúna, Seán, 183
Mac Murchadh Caomhánach, Seán. *see* Ó Caomhánaigh, Seán
MacNéill, Eoin, 124, 157
Mac Oisín, Seamus. *see* Cousins, James
Mac Piarais, Pádraig. *see* Pearse, Pádraig
Mám an Óraigh, 49–50
Mám na Gaoithe, 114
Manchester (England), 47
Mandanaplee College of Theosophy (India), 170
Mangan, James Clarence, 95–96
Manning, Mary and Agnes, 99, 103

# Index

# Index

# Index

# Index

# Index

# Index

total abstinence associations, 127
tourism, 27–28, 32, 59, 187
Tráigh Bhán (Great Blasket), 71,
  72, 84, 85, 93, 94, 106, 137,
  144, 154, 183, 185–186, 223
  drowning tragedy (1909), 84–98
Tráigh Earraí (Great Blasket), 90
Tralee, 14, 16, 140
  Old Oak pub, 172
Trant's Leap, 23–24, 54
Travancore (India), 171
Treaty. *see* Anglo-Irish Treaty
  (1921)
Triantán na Marbh, 111
Trinity College, Dublin, 18, 23, 37,
  175
  College Historical Society, 204
  Library, 206, 207
Tynan, Katherine, "The Glorious
  Girl", 149–150
  "Sheep and Lambs", 149

Ua Maoileoin, Pádraig, 165, 181,
  183
Ua Séagha, Pádraig ("Conán
  Maol"), 153, 154
*Uaigh Bhacach na Seantórach*, 12
Uí Dhuinnshléibhe, Méiní. *see*
  Dunleavy, Méiní Bean
Uí Ghaoithín, Máire, 80, 85, 104
Uí Laoithe, Niamh, 180
Uíbh Ráthach, 27, 74, 75, 99, 157,
  167, 177
*Ulysses* (Joyce), 46
*The United Irishman*, 33
United Kingdom, 35
United States of America, 29, 70,
  142, 145, 167, 174, 178, 188

University College Dublin (UCD),
  125, 160
  Department of Folklore, 168
university education, women,
  36–37
University of Paris, 37

Valentia Island, 27, 66, 74, 75
Ventry, Lord, 14, 22–23, 23, 25,
  27, 53, 70
Ventry (Ceann Trá), 22, 24–28, 25,
  27–28, 41, 44, 48, 52, 53, 58,
  63, 74, 78, 81, 103, 114, 138,
  140, 169
  battle of Ventry, 24, 54
  guest houses, 28, 29. *see also*
    Sea View House
  Irish language, 57
  national school, 30
  parish, 25–26, 28
  Reilig Chaitlíona, 167
Ventry Harbour, 23, 41
Ventry Strand (*Fionntrá*), 24, 25,
  42, 54, 55
Victoria, Queen, 132
Volunteers, 160, 174

War of Independence (1919–21),
  157, 162
Ware, Seamus, 163, 167
Warren, Miss, 32
Wesley College (Dublin), 176
*Women's Advocate*, 47
women's movement, 47–48,
  76–77, 168–169, 211

Yeats, William Butler, 44, 46, 47,
  170, 172